~~KEY TEXT~~
REFERENCE

War and Genocide

Organized Killing in Modern Society

MARTIN SHAW

polity

First published in 2003 by Polity Press in association with Blackwell Publishing Ltd.

Reprinted 2008

Editorial office:
Polity Press
65 Bridge Street
Cambridge CB2 1UR, UK

Marketing and production:
Blackwell Publishing Ltd
108 Cowley Road
Oxford OX4 1JF, UK

Distributed in the USA by
Blackwell Publishing Inc.
350 Main Street
Malden, MA 02148, USA

A catalogue record for this book is available from the British Library.

Library of Congress Cataloging-in-Publication Data

Shaw, Martin.
War and genocide: organized killing in modern society/Martin Shaw.
  p. cm.
Includes bibliographical references and index.
ISBN 978-0-7456-1906-4 (hb)—ISBN 978-0-7456-1907-1 (pb)
1. War. 2. Genocide. 3. Military history, Modern–20th century.
I. Title.
U21.2.S523 2003
304.6′63–dc21
2002151767

Typeset in 10.5 on 12pt Palatino
by Kolam Information Services Pvt. Ltd, Pondicherry, India
Printed and bound in Great Britain by Biddles Ltd., King's Lynn, Norfolk

For further information on Polity, visit our website: www.polity.co.uk

Contents

Boxes

Tables

Acknowledgements

I gratefully acknowledge the financial support of the Leverhulme Trust, who granted me a Research Fellowship in 2000, in order to research and write this book, as well as of the University of Sussex, for a term's study leave in 1999–2000. At Polity, Tony Giddens pushed me to write this book in the first place, and the comments of my editor, Rachel Kerr, and three anonymous reviewers were both encouraging and helpful. I wish to express my gratitude to colleagues and students at Sussex with whom I have tested these ideas over the last few years. Many intellectual debts are, I hope, apparent in the pages that follow.

I broke a leg badly at a crucial stage in the preparation of the book, and I appreciated enormously the skill and care of National Health Service medical staff at the Royal Sussex County Hospital, Brighton, in helping me make a full recovery. This experience of accidental harm made me realize even more how terrible it is that people cause deliberate physical harm to others in war – and that so many victims lack the care that I received for my injury. I was enormously fortunate in having the loving support of my family throughout this difficult time, and during the writing of this book. What I owe to Annabel cannot be measured.

Martin Shaw, Brighton, 2002

Introduction

In the twentieth century, human beings killed each other on a horrendous scale. They did it most obviously in wars, including two 'world wars'. They also did it in politically motivated slaughter that came to be known (from mid-century on) as 'genocide'. This kind of killing was not new, of course, but it did have terrible new characteristics that made people think differently about it – and so led to this new label. This book is about the relationships between these two kinds of killing, war and genocide, and about how both are produced by and affect modern society.

At the dawn of the twenty-first century, many people in the Western world thought that they had left these kinds of slaughter behind. Others, aware that mass killing of civilians was still part of war in other regions of the world, hoped that international institutions would gradually develop ways of dealing with these problems. But few expected that mass killing would be brought home to the advanced West, as it was to New York and Washington, DC, on 11 September 2001. At the beginning of a new century, this shocking terrorist massacre reminded us that slaughter remains a fundamental problem for the entire world.

This book starts from the assumption that one of the most urgent problems of humankind is to prevent things like this being done to anyone, anywhere, by states as much as by terrorists. In order to prevent slaughter, however, we need to understand its roots in politics and society: to understand war and genocide historically and sociologically. To grasp the 'new' dangers in the emerging global world, we need to know where we have come from – to look again at the last century of extraordinary violence which some hoped we had escaped.

The history of mass slaughter and its threat

In the twentieth century, the age of 'mass' society and industrial technology, killing became doubly democratic. Huge sections of society became involved in fighting, and even more in supplying the killing machines. At the same time, many sections of society became targets and victims. Civilians constituted the majority among the tens of millions who died in the biggest killing episode of human history to date, the Second World War. Today we are in danger of forgetting that even this slaughter threatened to be just a curtain-raiser. For most of the second half of the century there was a threat of worldwide nuclear war, in which hundreds of millions of people could have been killed and the very survival of human society could have been threatened. Despite the end of the Cold War, this kind of war could still be fought in the twenty-first century, as many states – and possibly other organizations – possess nuclear and other weapons of mass destruction.

Not surprisingly, the danger of nuclear war reinforced the lesson of actual slaughter earlier in the century: that war was a supremely inhuman activity. Many people came to question what had been taken for granted in earlier periods – that war was a legitimate way of pursuing political goals. At the beginning of our new century, however, this ultimate threat of global destruction appears to have receded. Although more states have nuclear weapons, the end of the Cold War seems to have lessened the danger of conflagration. The world is groping once more towards the global order that was glimpsed briefly when the United Nations Organization was established in 1945. But because war no longer appears directly threatening – its dangers either long ago or far away – Western governments have been followed by many among their peoples in seeing more limited forms of war as increasingly necessary and viable.

Yet slaughter is still near the forefront of all those minds, even in Western societies, which engage with larger historical questions. The quintessential genocide of the twentieth century, the Nazis' extermination of the Jews, which became known as the Holocaust, preoccupies Western society more than ever before as the new century begins. And contemporary slaughter is not so distant: even before 11 September 2001, it erupted on the edges of Europe (across former Soviet and Yugoslav territories) as well as in many regions of Africa, Asia, Latin America and the Middle East. Wars of the new era frequently involve – albeit on a smaller scale than during the world wars – deliberate mass killings of civilians. Thanks to television, even the most distant wars can come straight into the living rooms of comfortable Westerners. Through mass media, new victims of slaughter demand the same justice that is sought retrospectively for the victims of earlier periods.

Attitudes to war

How then should we think and read about war? Colossal literatures commemorate – even celebrate – the immense struggles of the last century, down to the last detail of each battle (not to mention tank and aircraft design). Every bookshop's history section is weighed down with apparently popular hardback tomes which, while often conveying the enormity of events, generally legitimate the practice of war by the 'good' in modern history. Similar literatures also celebrate the more recent efforts of Western armed forces in places like the Persian Gulf, Kosovo and Afghanistan.

Paradoxically, even the commemoration of the Holocaust often encourages a relatively positive attitude to war. On the one hand, it isolates the slaughter of the Jews as something utterly different from the rest of Second World War killing. On the other, it makes the Nazis uniquely evil and so justifies (implicitly) even the most extreme actions the Allies took to defeat them. This way of looking at modern history gives us a simple paradigm of good war that skirts difficult issues. To depart from it does not mean denying the particular horrors of Nazism and its victimization of the Jews. To examine the general murderousness of modern war, including the uncomfortable overlap between the evils of Allied bombing and genocidal extermination, does not take all moral meaning from the struggle to defeat specific evils. It does, however, point us towards a discussion in which war as such is deeply problematic.

In many ways, this has been the common sense of the longer period since 1918. The slaughter of the trenches produced a profound disillusion with war in Western society. From this point of view, it was the *re*-legitimation of war in 1939–45 that was exceptional. In this light, we could argue that awareness of the dangers of nuclear war only reinstated the earlier anti-war common sense. In this sense also, the evils of localized slaughter since 1989 have given new force, and maybe new dimensions, to what had already become a dominant set of sceptical sentiments about warfare. But, at the same time, they have stimulated new ideas of possible 'good' wars – to halt genocide and punish the perpetrators of slaughter.

This chequered history suggests that a sceptical structure of feeling about war is never enough. Indeed, historically, moral sentiments of this kind have often been mobilized for new warlike ends once circumstances changed. Horror at the worst forms of war can easily lead to demands for action – that is, war – to stop it. It is fairly easy to get caught up in this kind of dynamic. We need to be aware of the inbuilt tensions in the ways we think about war, which can easily lead us to change our attitudes as the context of killing shifts. To get to the bottom of these tensions, we need to look at the complex roots of killing practices in our present world society.

The argument of this book

Thinking seriously about the sources of mass killing involves confronting realities that are deeply uncomfortable. Despite appearances in the more prosperous regions, the practice of slaughter is all too prevalent in today's world. Our 'peaceful' West is implicated, in many ways, in how killing comes about – and hence in demands to deal with it. Ways of organizing society and ways of thinking that we take for granted are parts of these processes. I shall try to explain in this book why, even though some areas of our world enjoy unprecedented 'peace', there is little room for complacency about many of our inherited ways of using violence.

The book has two aims: to *introduce* the study of war and genocide, and to make an *argument* about the connections between them. Readers should be aware that I am not simply conveying an established consensus, but reinterpreting war, genocide and the connections between them in a way that challenges dominant understandings. Conventionally, war and genocide are seen as being categorically distinct. War is a social practice that has possessed high legitimacy historically, however compromised this has become over the last hundred years. Genocide on the other hand, is killing that is, by definition, illegitimate – indeed criminal. Nevertheless, this book aims to show how what many regard as the deeply necessary, even noble, social institution of warfare has tended to produce its apparent opposite, genocide. Conversely, it aims to show how genocide utilizes the ideas as well as the machinery of war in distinctive ways. Hence I argue that genocide can be regarded as a particular form of modern warfare, and an extension of the more common form of *degenerate war*. The outlines of my argument are summarized in box 0.1.

Box 0.1 The core of the argument

In this book I make a distinctive case about war and genocide. Here I summarize the main points that are explored in subsequent chapters:

1 *War* is the clash of two organized armed forces that seek to destroy each other's power and especially their will to resist, principally by killing members of the opposing force. War has long been a legitimate practice within human societies, but as organized killing has always involved moral tensions with the general prohibitions on killing. Because of these tensions, legitimate killing is generally restricted to combatants, and even then is qualified by rules of war.

2 Real war has always tended, however, to surpass its legitimate limits, involving killing of non-combatants and of combatants beyond the scope of military necessity. In modern war, the tendency for war to involve slaughter of civilians – as well as of combatants in new ways and on an unprecedented scale – has been magnified. In particular, civilian populations have been systematically targeted as part of the enemy, leading to a rise of civilian mass death.

3 I call this form of war *degenerate war*, because it involves the deliberate and systematic extension of war against an organized armed enemy to war against a largely unarmed civilian population. Degenerate war can be seen both in the armed conquests and aerial bombing of great powers and in guerrilla and counter-insurgency wars. Degenerate war has brought to the fore the fundamentally problematic nature of war itself in late-modern and global society, leading to widespread questioning of its legitimacy.

4 *Genocide* is the destruction by an organized armed force of a largely unarmed civilian group (or groups) principally by killing members of the group(s). In genocide, therefore, civilian groups are enemies as such, or in themselves, and not merely through their relationship to an armed enemy, for the organized armed power that attacks them. Genocide can therefore be distinguished in principle from other forms of war.

5 However, in its definition of civilian groups as enemies to be destroyed, genocide utilizes the logic of war and can be seen as an extension of degenerate war. Historically, genocide has occurred mostly in the context of war, and in practice it is intertwined with other forms of war. Therefore the best way of making sense of genocide is to see it as *a distinctive form of war*.

6   War arises from the contradictions that surround state power, and is extensively produced within modern society, through state power, economic organization, military and general social ideologies and the mobilization and participation of whole populations. Genocide mobilizes these same forces, but the difference between the legitimacy of war and genocide has a marked bearing on how these social institutions are utilized.

7   Genocide exhibits the same tension between *discriminate* targeting and *indiscriminate* results that we find in war, especially degenerate war. Targeted attacks on specified groups lead to 'senseless' violence being experienced by victims. Thus the experience of the victims of war and genocide diverges radically from the aims of practitioners and perpetrators: this must also be seen as part of what war and genocide are.

8   Because the trends towards degeneracy in modern war are structural, the legitimacy of armed force remains fundamentally in question. The appropriate response to the prevalence of organized killing in modern society is a *historical pacifism* that recognizes the underlying trend towards the delegitimation of war as a social practice. There should therefore be a presumption against forcible responses, which can be justified only as exceptional, not normal, acts. Moreover, the general answer to the problems of war and genocide is not only peace but *justice*. Addressing the grievances of victims, of war and genocide as well as underlying political, social and economic inequalities, is the more profound answer to problems posed by organized killing. In the global era, there are important trends that give new hope for just peace.

9   Yet, because genocide is a form of war, usually in the context of wider war, the immediate means of halting or defeating genocide, once it is under way, are usually through the use of armed force. War is being renewed in new ways in the global era partly because it seems to answer such demands. However, many forms of war that are utilized against genocide may also be degenerate in their killing of civilians, so that it is not clear that war can be a general answer to genocide. A key issue is whether the new Western way of war in the twenty-first century, which I call *risk-transfer war*, really manages to escape the degeneracy of earlier modes of war. Is it part of a solution, or does it merely reproduce the problem of war?

This book has therefore two main concerns. My principal case is that organized mass killing, or slaughter, is a fundamental problem of modern society. I use these terms to indicate commonalities between war and genocide – and the thinness of the moral and explanatory lines generally drawn to separate them. I explain the reasoning behind this approach in chapters 1 and 2. Secondarily, however, I am concerned with whether, to what extent, and how such lines can still be drawn. Within a perspective on the problem of slaughter, I think it is still important to do two things: to examine the historical question – how the balance between legitimacy and illegitimacy of mass killing has come to change – and to address the contemporary dilemmas – how these issues are posed in practice in the relations of war and genocide today.

The organization of this book

This book examines the problem of slaughter from two main sides. It looks first at *how the organization of society produces mass killing*. Chapters 3–5 discuss the generation of slaughter in the relations of state, economic and ideological power. The book then looks at *how society is actually involved in war*. Chapters 6–8 deal with modern battlespaces, their combatants and victims. Finally, the book looks at *how society responds to war*. Chapters 9 and 10 discuss social movements relating to war, focusing especially on ideas of justice and peace and ways that people campaign for them.

These thematic discussions are necessarily quite abstract and general. The reader may legitimately wonder how far we can generalize about 'unique' historical events like wars and genocides. Generalization can appear to do violence – in the sense of inappropriate representation – to the particular characters of dramatic large-scale events, since these are not repeated in the way that smaller-scale, routine social actions appear to be. This issue is especially important in dealing with episodes of slaughter, which have huge emotional, moral and political significance. Yet we understand events through finding their common meaning. Uniqueness can be understood as the distinctive way in which generally intelligible features are combined in an individual case.

In this book I adopt two main devices to create interplay between generalization and particularity. I intersperse the main *thematic chapters* with short analytical summaries of the largest historical *episodes of slaughter*. These sections aim to suggest the specific dynamics of each set of events that involved large-scale killings. They thus show distinctive ways in which 'war' and 'genocide' have been linked historically. This method simultaneously defines the uniqueness of historical processes *and* enriches our understanding of the general connections that the book explores.

The other device that I adopt is the box. I use boxes flexibly to provide various kinds of detailed backing for the contentions of the thematic chapters. Some are ideas boxes, in which I expand on key concepts and thinkers. Other, history boxes deal with particular events that illustrate my arguments, as well as providing closer insight into the experiences of people caught up – as participants and victims – in large-scale historical processes (which are summarized still quite abstractly in the 'episodes' sections).

These devices are not unusual in books intended, as this is, for intelligent general readers as well as students. Nevertheless, they have a specific advantage for my argument. One of my prime concerns is to criticize the idea that the concepts and narratives of war-makers and genocidists are sufficient to define war and genocide. Their accounts define more or less what they do, but they don't define the whole phenomenon of slaughter. This is as much about the experiences and feelings of victims as it is about the intentions of perpetrators. In this book I develop a narrative of my own, strongly informed by victims' points of view but trying to understand the relationships with those of the perpetrators.

I hope that my narrative enlightens, but by breaking it up – even though 'episodes' and 'boxes' are still my accounts – I want to suggest some of the discontinuities. I do not propose a post-modern argument, according to which it is impossible to develop a grand narrative of war and genocide. I do want to draw attention, however, to the difficulty of encompassing killing, the arbitrary ending of life stories, in an untroubled story peopled by grand concepts and designs.

Sources and resources

This book is an entry point to studying the problem of organized killing. Boxes are often used to point the reader towards important areas of study and their intellectual sources. They often contain short citations that can be checked with full references at the end of the chapter, where I present 'Further reading'. In addition, because many sources of information are internet-based, I have developed a website linked to this book, www.martinshaw.org/warandgenocide. This site will lead you to many online study materials, including academic papers, and the websites of universities where you can study the issues raised in this book. This material will also be regularly updated on the website. You can help me to keep this information up to date by contacting me through this site. You may also write to me about the issues raised in the book. My contention is that these are questions for us all, and so I welcome your views.

Episode 0   The trenches

The Great War of 1914–18, as it was called until the outbreak of a second global conflict made it the *First World War*, was the war that, above all others, defined late-modern attitudes to war.

There had been long periods of catastrophic conflict across large parts of Europe before, notably the Thirty Years War (1618–48) and the French Revolutionary and Napoleonic Wars (1793–1815). These wars prefigured total war in their destructiveness, but they lacked the distinctively modern forms of military technology and mass mobilization that produced the events of 1914–18. The century from 1815 to 1914 had seen only more limited wars in Europe. Although the American Civil War (1861–5) had been a modern conflict of drastic proportions, this had receded into history by 4 August 1914. On that day the war broke out that marked the true beginning of the twentieth century – 'the age of extremes', as Eric Hobsbawm (1994) called it.

The effects of the war on Europe were all the more dramatic for occurring at the end of the long nineteenth-century period of economic expansion, during which most wars were in colonial locales. During the last decades before the war, internationalization of the world economy had accelerated, reaching levels not attained again until the 'globalization' of the late twentieth century. The United States had overtaken Europe in economic dynamism. The confidence of affluent Western elites has been reflected in subsequent images of these pre-war years: 'the Edwardian age' and 'la belle époque'. Although it was a time of desperate poverty for the metropolitan masses and frequent famine in the colonies, the catastrophe of the war enshrined it as an age of lost innocence for rich and poor alike. Generations that have not known large-scale war always experience it as epoch-making; but in this case it seemed truly disastrous.

The Great War was not a world war in the sense of the Second World War, which spanned Asia and the Pacific as much as Europe and the Atlantic. The First World War has been called a 'European civil war'. It was an all-out struggle for regional and world power between the empires of Great Britain, France, Italy, Russia and their allies (reinforced after 1917 by the United States) on the one hand, and Germany, Austria-Hungary, the Ottoman Turks and their allies on the other. Europe – from the Somme to the Dardanelles – was the main battleground, although episodes of the war were also fought out in the colonies.

The Great War was the culmination of imperial rivalries that had been growing throughout the previous hundred years. It was also, however, the outcome of the huge technical and social changes of the period. In 1815, horses and carts and sailing boats were still the prime means of military transport. In 1914–18 horses were widely used (my own grandfather, serving in the British army, rode one in France for the duration) – indeed, they were still used in 1939–45. But railways, steamships and motor vehicles had revolutionized military transport. Likewise with weaponry: the machine gun, a late nineteenth-century invention, had made mass killing so much easier. And three new developments during the war itself were to transform the face of warfare: tanks, chemical weapons and aeroplanes.

All of these technologies were applied, in part, to overcome the stalemate of the Western Front, where the contending armies became more or less stuck, for most of the war, in the positions that they had reached after the initial German advances in 1914. Although naval battle was also important to the war, and aerial warfare became more so towards the end, the centre of the gigantic struggle, with millions of men on each side, was the systems of trenches that the armies dug, facing each other, along a line stretching across north-western Europe. Here the war was reduced to the ability of the opposing forces to push each other back a few kilometres – or even a few hundred or tens of metres – at a time.

Although military forces in 1914 had new technologies in weaponry, transport and communications that had not been available a century before, their principle instruments were sheer masses of soldiers. Industrial and agricultural revolutions had caused population to soar, and had enabled states to create standing mass armies. Raised mostly by conscription – the standard Continental method that even Britain resorted to for the first time in 1915 – armies had almost limitless supplies of men, as they soaked up extra manpower not only from industry but from the swollen rural populations. Women were increasingly left to fill the industrial gaps that men left behind.

In the stalemated battlegrounds of the trenches, increasingly desperate generals squandered their human reserves with epoch-making callousness. Losses of tens of thousands in a single day were not uncommon in the Battle of the Somme in 1916. Even such enormous killing mostly failed, however, to make a strategic difference, and movement on the front was often negligible for long periods of time. The new resources that were thrown in often made little difference, except to increase the misery of the troops: tanks became bogged down in mud, mustard gas drifted back over the side that fired it, and aerial attacks were not developed enough to have a large effect.

The madness of the war was recognized in the more or less open conflicts that went on within armies. Some soldiers, desperate or traumatized, ran away from the front: when caught, they were generally shot. Others who remained in the trenches developed the 'live and let live system' to avoid killing each other (see chapter 9). There were even open rebellions, mainly in defeated armies, such as those that brought much of the Russian army into the revolutionary camp in 1917.

Eventually the Western Allies overcame the long stalemate and prevailed over Germany, not least because of the United States' entry into the war. However, the pattern of victory and defeat only sharpened, in the medium term, the conflicts within Europe that had produced the First World War. (It contributed directly to the outbreak of the Second World War only twenty years after the armistice that ended the first one on 11 November 1918.) With masses of disillusioned soldiers returning from defeated armies, many countries entered revolutionary phases. The successful Russian Revolution led through civil war and political struggle to Stalin's consolidation of power after 1924. Failed revolutions led to counter-revolutionary fascism, which triumphed in Italy in 1922 and, after the world slump, in Germany in 1933. These totalitarian developments polarized the continuing interstate conflicts, as Hitler focused on revising the post-war settlement dictated by the victors at Versailles in 1919 and defeating communism.

In the short term, however, the common legacy of 1914–18 was that of colossal mass death and harm. Even in victor states the war was widely recognized as an exercise in futility. In the first decade after the war, millions of wounded survivors, damaged by shell shock, gas and the trauma of the trenches, had to be reintegrated into society. The military illusions of 1914 seemed to give way to the recognition of the need for international order, as a means of avoiding repetition of the gigantic social disaster that the war had been. In the 1920s statesmen and populations alike believed that further wars had to be prevented at all costs. The League of Nations was founded with great hopes for a more peaceful world. It is this understanding of 1914–18 that has proved its enduring legacy: the trenches are the archetypal experience of the futility of war.

Historically, however, this lesson was partially eclipsed in a very short period of time. As often in the case of large-scale human suffering in war and genocide, the universal appropriation, whereby the trenches were grasped as a common experience of senseless slaughter, was overcome by particularistic interpretations. Both Italian Fascists and German National Socialists celebrated the camaraderie of the trenches as a formative national experience. For them, the lessons of the suffering were national rather than universal. Italians and Germans needed to expunge their nations' historic defeats, and military comradeship pointed in the direction of heroic new wars.

In the inter-war West, the pacifistic lessons of the trenches lingered on. They informed a Second World War struggle that was less naively nationalistic, and more informed by anti-fascism and the desire to defeat aggression. And there is no doubt that unheroic representations of the First

World War have persisted as powerful components of the peace consciousness that thrived throughout the Cold War. Nevertheless, the widespread recognition of the senselessness of slaughter in the trenches did *not* end war in its own time. This remains a salutary starting-point for understanding the problems of war and genocide today.

Further reading

Ashworth, T. (1981) *The Live and Let Live System*. London: Macmillan.
Gilbert, M. (1994) *First World War*. London: Weidenfeld and Nicolson.
Hobsbawm, E. (1994) *The Age of Extremes. 1914–89*. London: Joseph.
Keegan, J. (1998) *The First World War*. London: Hutchinson.
Strachan, H., ed. (1998) *The Oxford Illustrated History of the First World War*. Oxford: Oxford University Press.

— 1 —

War and Slaughter

Human beings are unique in the animal kingdom in the wide extent to which they kill their own kind. The ubiquity of human killing raises the question of whether it is built in to our individual make-up: thus some scientists search for biological or psychological roots of war (see box 1.1). Certainly killers' bodies, as well as minds, are often fully implicated in their activities. It is the argument of this book, however, that we will never find the key to understanding killing in such investigations. Killing is always and necessarily an extreme form of human social relation. When one person kills another, it is, on the one hand, an expression of their social relations and, on the other hand, their negation. One person destroys the life, meaning and story of the other by destroying their bodily existence. This is what the killing of humans by others means.

People kill each other within many different kinds of social relations. You may notice that I write relations, not relationships. Shockingly many relations in which people kill each other do not have the consistency to be dignified as relationships. A relationship involves some mutual, although not necessarily equal, understanding. The robber who shoots or the rapist who strangles often does not have a relationship with his victim. The social relation that he forces on his victim is one of transient exploitation, gratification or humiliation. A great deal of human killing is of this kind, casual and instrumental.

Other killing is the outcome of more developed social relationships. Notoriously, a small number of people regularly kill their wives, husbands and sexual partners – even their parents and children. Clearly such killing is the outcome of tensions within these relationships. But it cannot be understood only in terms of the relationship between killer and killed. Wider social relations, in which they are both involved, also contribute to the killing. A person may kill her spouse because he is having an affair with a third party, for insurance money because she is in debt to a bank, or even because her religious beliefs lead her to think of the victim as evil.

The contrast between opportunist killing and killing arising from relationship tells us something about how we can understand killing in general. Each killing comes out of larger sets of social relations that lead towards the result. These relations may include meaningful relationships between killer and killed, in which case we will want to trace the patterns, immediate and also remote, that lead to the final outcome. But even more in the absence of such relationships, we will want to trace the complex relationships of power which produce the need, greed, obsession or anger that leads one person to destroy another, in this case unknown, individual life.

Box 1.1   Natural versus social explanations of war

War is a near-universal feature of human societies. So it is not surprising that many think of it as something that people are programmed to engage in. In the twentieth century, arguments for understanding war as 'natural' centred on the idea that war expressed a universal 'instinct' for aggression (Lorenz 1966). There was even a feminist variant: that war expressed the aggressive instinct in men. At the beginning of the twenty-first century, it will not be surprising, given the widespread predilection for genetic explanations, if someone claims to find a 'gene for war'.

But, such naturalistic explanations of mass killing inevitably confuse relations between the natural and the social. They raise three insurmountable problems:

1   If anger and aggression may be considered universal human traits, so may love and co-operation. They all arise, however, through people's relations with each other. They cannot be separated from the social character of human life. Therefore we cannot explain aggressive behaviour except by examining the social circumstances in which people become aggressive.
2   Aggression may be universal, but we don't express it all the time, and certainly not usually through violence or killing. In our one-to-one social relations, anger and aggression are usually restrained by the norms that we live by. We express them mainly in socially designated ways. The ways in which we are aggressive are not universal, but are specific to our culture and social conditions. So we need to explain the specific circumstances and ways in which we express aggression. We particularly need to explain why we turn to violence and killing.

3   War and genocide are not simple outcomes of aggression. They are socially
defined forms of mass killing. These are complex collective activities,
undertaken by political authorities and other organized groups. They result
more from political calculation than from instinct or emotion. This is not to
deny that emotions enter into political leaders' decisions, nor that organizing killing fosters powerful emotions among armies and populations. Nevertheless, leaders keep a powerful grip on their own and their followers'
feelings, channel them in particular ways and have to overcome deep
instinctual revulsion to slaughter.

Arguments from the 'natural' character of warlike instincts are deeply
conservative. They diminish the areas of peace in human society and suggest
that we can only repeat behaviour that has brought catastrophic suffering to
previous generations. These ideas can have unfortunate political consequences.
For example, those feminists who believed that all men were naturally aggressive divided the 1980s peace movements by refusing to co-operate with men
who opposed nuclear weapons. Certainly, powerful emotions are involved in
political conflict. But there is no reason to believe that human beings as such
have to kill each other *en masse* in the pursuit of these rivalries. We can look
for other ways of expressing and overcoming them.

Mass killing

Killing is the ultimate violation of an individual human being by
another. Mass killing is merely the destruction of many individual
lives, either more or less simultaneously or in circumstances that
lead the killer, the killed or observers to see the killings as part of a
single process.

Individual human beings carry out mass killing, whether or
not these individuals are part of a group or an organization.
Thus mass killing can be the work of a lone mass murderer. Or
it may be the work of linked individuals, a group or an organization. When an individual kills repeatedly, we call him a serial
killer. The most prolific such killers have more victims than some
collective killers – the notorious late twentieth-century British
doctor, Harold Shipman, may have secretly killed as many as
250 people, more than some armed forces kill in some episodes of
war.

Where there is more than one killer, their killing too can be
limited to a single incident or be serial in character. What makes

it mass killing is simply that a number of people are killed. To be killed along with others often makes a difference to the experience leading to death, as well as to its meaning for people left alive. But the end, the annihilation of life, is the same for the victim whether she is alone or among millions. In this sense killing more than one person is not different in quality from killing a single individual, although the process of plural killing may normalize the act for killers. There is no intrinsic cut-off point at which plural killing becomes mass killing – this is simply a label that we use in the modern age. The term has something to do with our ambiguous attitudes to plural killing: both a shocking event outside our normal experience and something we know happens frequently across the world. Plural, even large-scale, killing has been common through-out recorded history, long before it was called mass killing. It is its forms, and the labels we give to it, that change.

The key question about any kind of killing, especially mass killing, is its legitimacy. Although killing is very common in human life, it is always the subject of intense moral discourse. The simple biblical injunction, 'You shall not kill', is shared within most cultures. It is almost always followed by 'except', but the extent of prohibitions on killings is generally wide. When a person kills another in pursuit of immoral ends, this is a singular aggrava-tion of his crime. In some societies individual killing in the pursuit of valid ends – for example, in revenge for the prior killing of a family member – may be accepted or even required. In most societies, however, the scope of such legitimate individual killing is narrow. Moreover, the ways in which killing is defined as justifi-able or not enter deeply into how people kill. The strength of the basic taboo, however much it is qualified or transgressed, means that killers are nearly always conscious of a problem of legitimacy. People kill either invoking law or moral right, or in the knowledge that they are violating it. The killing of one person by one other is never just an isolated act, but is connected in these ways to the patterns of social beliefs in which killers are involved.

Even when hunger and disease have made life cheap, deliberate life taking has always been problematic. But modernity has seen the introduction of deeper prohibitions. Law rigorously defines who can take life and when. The circumstances in which individuals can kill have increasingly been limited to (and in) self-defence. Pre-meditated killing is generally seen as an even more serious offence than killing in a spontaneous rage. Revenge is generally outlawed; righting of wrongs now belongs to states through formal systems of justice. Modern states have appropriated to themselves the definition of legitimate violence, and have delegitimized much individual killing. Until recently, however, they generally retained considerable rights for their own agents to kill, in law enforcement and through death penalties. But even these assertions of state power, almost universal a century ago, have been partially abandoned. Killing by the police is often subject to intense scrutiny, while many states have abolished the death penalty. They no longer claim special rights to kill their subjects through judicial process.

This narrowing of the scope of legitimate killing throws into even sharper relief those practices of mass killing, by states and state-like organizations, which continue to be regarded as legitimate. States that neither tolerate killing by their citizens, nor continue to practice the judicial killing of individual citizens, nevertheless still practice and legitimate certain kinds of mass killing. Not surprisingly, given our universal and growing sensitivity about ending others' lives, this requires complex justification.

Killing, mostly banned from one-to-one, interpersonal social relations, can only be made legitimate in mass forms through abstract sets of social relationships. In modern society, these centre on the connections of individuals to states, and depend on key interlinked sets of ideas. Some of these ideas, to which I return later in this book, are general notions about institutions that claim authority: state, nation, etc. Others are more specific and concern the particular place of violence in the relations of these authoritative institutions. Above all, they are about war as a set of practices in which it is legitimate not just to kill, but to kill on a large scale, in ways that would otherwise be utterly illegitimate.

War

As a type of social action, war can be defined simply as *an act of force by an organized social power to compel an enemy to submit to its will*. It involves the conscious organization of large numbers of people to inflict overwhelming force, to destroy the power of an enemy and its will to resist. The destruction of the enemy's power may be more or less total; it is usually its power in given contexts – that is, over certain issues or in particular territories – that is at stake, rather than its very existence (although it may often come to that). War is not only, of course, an act by one collective actor against another. It involves *the clash of conscious, intentional activity on the part of two or more organized groups*. In this sense, war is an organized conflict between two or more actors, distinguished from other kinds of social and political conflict by the aim of mutual destruction.

The destruction of power in war does not necessarily involve mass killing on each and every occasion, and does not usually entail killing all of the enemy. But the reason that war can be said to involve *destruction* – rather than the reduction of power or a change in the balance between the rival forces – is intimately connected with the violence that is used. Killing is central to war. Just as killing an individual is the ultimate coercion that can be used against him, *killing many individuals among a collective enemy is the ultimate means of forcing that enemy to submit*. The decisive moment of war is battle, in which slaughter is central. Indeed the German word, *Schlacht*, used by the classic theorist of war, Carl von Clausewitz (see box 1.2), to describe this decisive encounter, can be translated both as battle and as slaughter.

Box 1.2   *Clausewitz's theory of war*

Carl von Clausewitz (1780–1831) is the classic modern theorist of war. A Prussian army officer who fought in the Revolutionary and Napoleonic wars (1793–1815), he taught at the military academy, where he wrote the book published posthumously as *On War*. If social scientists fully recognized the centrality of war in modern society, this work of Clausewitz would figure in canons of social thought alongside those of near-contemporaries such as the philosophers Immanuel Kant and Georg Friedrich Wilhelm Hegel, the sociologist Auguste Comte and the revolutionary Karl Marx.

Clausewitz's book contained a number of seminal ideas:

- His most famous maxim is that 'war is the continuation of political intercourse [also translated as either policy or politics] by other means'. This is often interpreted as meaning that the course of war is determined by its political objectives. However, Clausewitz's real originality lay in his exploration of the 'otherness' of military means.
- He emphasized that war is 'an act of force' designed to compel an enemy to submit, and hence has 'no logical limit'. He concludes from this that *escalation* is a law of war, and that there is a general tendency for war to become *absolute*. Restricted political objectives can limit escalation, only partially, since the clash of arms is always likely to surpass pre-ordained political limits and so is intrinsically unpredictable.
- War was as likely to be contained by *friction*, i.e. the obstacles to escalation created by inhospitable climate and terrain together with the logistical difficulties of deploying armies over long distances.

- War can be compared as a social process to commerce. In this light, *battle* is the moment of realization – the end to which all activity is geared – in war in the same way as exchange in commerce.
- War is a *trinity* of policy (the province of governments), military craft (the business of generals) and raw violence (supplied by the people). Thus the involvement of the people (the nation in arms) is partly responsible for the peculiarly destructive character of modern war compared to earlier periods.

As with all great thinkers, Clausewitz's legacy has been understood in many different ways:

- For the German and other militaries in the era of world wars, 'absolute war' became a doctrine of the total annihilation of the enemy. This contributed to the development of total war.
- Since 'the enemy' was coming to include the civilian population, it was not long before the annihilation doctrine was applied – by the German military in colonial South-West Africa, the Ottoman military in the First World War, and then by the Nazis – to whole peoples, such as the Herero, Armenians and Jews.
- For Marx and Engels, Clausewitz's ideas lent themselves to a socio-historical explanation of war and to revolutionary military strategy. War was a continuation of politics, but politics itself was a reflection of economics. War could be understood as the clash of social forces, such as the slave-owning South and capitalist North in the American Civil War, or the democratic Poles against the Tsarist Empire.

Modern war is sometimes described as Clausewitzian. The main problem with this description is that industrial society gave war enormously more powerful means of destruction – not only weaponry, but military and political organization – than Clausewitz could foresee. Modern *total war* combined total social mobilization with absolute destructiveness. From the middle of the nineteenth century, this radically expanded the scope for slaughter beyond Clausewitzian conditions. The logical conclusion of this process was the truly total, simultaneous and mutual destruction threatened by nuclear war.

Strategic writers have responded to this change in various ways:

- Some late-modern strategists like Colin Gray (1998) still regard Clausewitz's approach as viable, indeed foundational, in the world of nuclear weapons.
- Others, like Michael Howard (1981), have acknowledged that nuclear weapons would abolish friction in war fighting, and have attempted to escape his destructive conclusions by finding more limited roles for force.

- Mary Kaldor (1982a, b) developed Clausewitz's ideas in a way that is more critical of war. She explained the 'baroque' character of much modern weaponry in terms of the infrequency of realization (battle) in today's war. I make a similar use of Clausewitz's ideas.

The moral theorist Michael Walzer tries to reinforce an old distinction of slaughter from war: 'Since slaughter is the killing of men as if they were animals – "it makes a massacre", wrote the poet Dryden, "what was a war" – it cannot often be called necessary' (Walzer 1992: 18). In this book I take the view that, while there is always an argument about the necessity of killing within war, the *general* rule of modern war is that it *does* involve slaughter, as Clausewitz's usage implies. Massacre may not be necessary by any acceptable moral standard, but it is the norm of war. It is war without massacre that is the exception, although there is certainly much variation in the scale and character of massacres.

Hence the general difficulty of legitimating war. To organize a force that can carry out slaughter requires extensive preparation. It takes organization and ideas for warriors to overcome pervasive taboos against killing. It takes discipline to make soldiers aggressive against people they don't know, to inflict force in a way that achieves intended results and to overcome powerful instincts of self-preservation and fear. If all human killing requires social relations and beliefs to make it possible, the kind of mass killing involved in war requires peculiarly developed, conscious social organization and justification.

War is thus a highly complex social institution. Taken as a whole, it is as far as can be imagined from spontaneous outbreaks of violence, even if it sometimes includes them. War is premeditated violence, precisely the kind that is most illegitimate in non-war social relations. War as a social practice is therefore highly institutionalized. States and state-like organizations maintain special bodies of armed men, trained and equipped for war, even when no war is in sight. Systems of rewards and prestige help maintain armed forces. The production of weaponry and equipment is organized on a huge scale, even if no immediate uses for them are envisaged. Military doctrines are developed, and in the belief systems of society, a special place is usually given to the ultimate necessity and value of war. In this way the possibility of mass killing, on a scale otherwise difficult to imagine, is maintained even during prolonged periods of peace.

Thus, while all killing is socially prepared, war preparation is a particular and very important social institution. Vast networks of social relationships, which interlock with all the other important social networks, are built around it. Many people live their whole lives within these networks, as civil servants, armament workers and even soldiers, without encountering the sharp end of war. But at the heart of these networks, the process of producing war is taking place. At its simplest, this process consists of three stages:

1   the raising of fighters, weaponry and equipment, to create and sustain armed forces that are prepared to fight;
2   the deployment of armed forces in war;
3   actual engagement in battle.

The relationship between these stages tends to be complex. It is one thing to mobilize armed forces. It is another to deploy them in war. It is another again to actually make them fight. In moving from one stage to another, there is always the possibility of what Clausewitz called 'friction'. Although a contest of force has (he argued) no intrinsic limit, the physical and social conditions in which war takes place, including the meshing of military with other social institutions, may hinder its practical implementation. Limits are determined not only by the goals of the contending parties, but also by their capacity to mobilize force to achieve them, which friction may also affect. Thus the extent of mass killing in war depends on the political goals of the contending actors, the scale of the human forces they mobilize and the manner of their deployment, the destructiveness of the means at their disposal and their strategies and methods of engagement.

The danger in this kind of abstract thinking is, of course, that it leaves out real people's actual experience of war's violence. War is the clash of conscious, intentional activity on the part of two or more organized groups. But that clash engages thousands and sometimes millions of individual human beings. Many of them are not actually involved in the physical violence of war. But in the moment of battle many individuals' lives are precariously balanced. The 'face of battle', as John Keegan (1976) classically called it, is cruel and unpredictable (see box 1.3). This remains true even though some modern battlespaces are remotely controlled, no longer requiring direct human interaction, as we shall see in chapter 5.

Battle is the moment of war in which armed combatants face each other in the final test of their collective and individual strengths. Keegan (1976: 297) writes that 'one would like to say that "a battle is something which happens between two armies leading to the moral and then physical disintegration of one or the other of them"'. But this definition fails to encompass the quintessentially *human* as well as *inhuman* reality of battle: 'the behaviour of men struggling to reconcile their instinct for self-preservation, their sense of honour and the achievement of some aim over which other men are ready to kill them'.

Battle is a brutally messy social clash – a mix of fear, courage, leadership, anxiety, uncertainty, misinformation, violence, cruelty, self-sacrifice and compassion. 'Above all', Keegan (1976: 298) argues, the study of battle 'is always a study of solidarity and usually also of disintegration – for it is towards the disintegration of human groups that battle is directed.' Moreover, this forced *disintegration* of enemy armed forces that is the end of battle proceeds through the physical and personal disintegration of individuals.

The soldier's view of war is always much more complicated than the commander's or the politician's. For the combatant, battle takes place in an unstable physical and emotional environment. For him, Keegan (1976: 48) argues, battle 'is a small-scale situation which will throw up its own leaders and will be fought by its own rules – alas, often by its own ethics'. The destruction of other human beings is also destructive, therefore, of those who do the destroying. For a mixture of reasons, including self-preservation, confusion and brutalization, the reality of battle constantly fudges the moral line between legitimate and illegitimate killing. 'Improper violence' is part and parcel of the meaning of battle. However noble the political intentions of governments, and however rational the strategies of generals, killing fields are never morally 'clean'. The most just war will be sullied by the harsh reality of battle.

Degenerate war

Although the general legitimacy of war has been accepted throughout human history, particular wars have still had to be justified – indeed, many have been widely regarded as unjustified. Moreover, the methods of each war have required justification: battle has always contained a tendency towards killing in ways that have been regarded as morally questionable. Moral theory has recognized this dilemma in the classic distinction between *ius ad bellum* (the justice of war, i.e. of its ends) and *ius in bello* (justice within war, i.e. of the means used). Unjustified aggression is the common source of the outbreak of war, so the first of the two remains important. However, in modern times the means of war have given even greater cause for concern. Even where the ends of war could be seen as just – for example, in defeating aggression – the means have often been increasingly questionable.

Although the basic structure of war remains as it has been throughout several millennia, the process of war has changed enormously. At the heart of the changes is the altered character of mass killing. This has two principal dimensions. First, it has become technically possible to kill on a vast *scale* with unprecedented rapidity. In pre-industrial times, great slaughter was committed in hand-to-hand fighting and other more or less proximate encounters. But with each modern advance in the technology of weapons, delivery and communications, mass killing has become ever easier to inflict, by more and more remote means. Thus, by the time of nuclear weapons and intercontinental missiles, it had become possible to kill, instantaneously, immense numbers of people over enormous distances. It has been suggested that in nuclear war, a whole war could be concentrated in a single, brief battle (i.e. an exchange of missiles). Friction would barely be part of actual war, but would be transferred back into war preparation – for example, bottlenecks of weapons production and political mobilization.

Second, it became increasingly seen as militarily necessary to define the *enemy* to include society as a whole within a given territory or space, rather than limiting it to the opposing armed forces. In the Second World War, even the Western democracies defined German and Japanese civilian populations as a major part of the enemy. Violating established prohibitions on the deliberate killing of civilians, they inflicted slaughter on a vast scale. This was a huge degeneration of war into killing that was illegitimate even by war's own historical standards. In the theory and planning of nuclear war, moreover, this was taken even further. The killing envisaged was not simply massive but virtually ubiquitous. If ever practised, it could have amounted – indeed, could still amount – to a catastrophic destruction of human society as a whole.

This extension of the logic of escalation was, in the end, a huge problem for the theory and practice of war. If war became simple, comprehensive slaughter – nothing but killing – any political meaning would be destroyed. In the twentieth century, therefore, war's chickens came home to roost. The attempt to treat mass killing as an extension of rational politics began to founder in the killing swamps of Flanders and burnt-out German cities, even before the nuclear age opened up in the irradiated ruins of Hiroshima. Warfare, on the grandest scale and in the hands of the most advanced, liberal states, repeatedly degenerated into little more than deliberate mass slaughter, first of soldiers and then of civilian populations. Strategy and politics wore very thin in the face of the enormities that their pursuit revealed.

These outcomes posed deep problems for the viability of war as a social practice. The reason lay in the fact that these outcomes were neither accidental, nor deviations from its inner logic. On the contrary, they were direct and, in a broad sense, inevitable results of a classic practice of war under modern conditions. Located within a competitive interstate system, fuelled by the technology, socio-economic organization and politics of mass industrial societies, slaughter on a huge scale was a predictable outcome of war. Supplied with unprecedented resources, destructive logic overrode all others, producing truly total war. Supplied with an ever wider range of human targets, warfare swallowed up (or threatened to swallow up) whole populations in a more or less indiscriminate fashion.

The dialectic between discriminating aims and indiscriminate results is the key to the meaning of *degeneration* in modern war. It involves simultaneously:

1   the extended definition of the enemy as civilian as well as military;
2   the deliberate targeting of elements of the civilian population as well as military forces;
3   intensified means of destruction which killed more people more speedily and efficiently;
4   but also increasingly indiscriminate slaughter which killed people across broader areas and with little precision as to their membership of any enemy group.

Thus, in the name of defeating each other's armies, First World War generals mowed down a generation of young men from across Europe. To destroy Chinese resistance, Japanese troops massacred civilian populations wholesale. To crush Soviet power, Nazi German forces slaughtered civilians and prisoners of war. To attack German industries in the Second World War, British leaders began to destroy whole cities. To crack German civilian morale, they obliterated tens of thousands, refugees and prisoners alongside citizens, soldiers and war-workers, in huge fire-storms. To defeat Imperial Japan, American leaders blew up two entire urban populations with atomic weapons. (All of these incidents are discussed further in the episode sections of this book.)

In the all-out use of massive force there was, therefore, by the middle of the last century, an overwhelming tendency for targeted violence to produce indiscriminate mass slaughter on a previously unimagined scale. In the last half of the twentieth century, both theorists and planners of war reluctantly recognized this as a danger to their practices. To avoid redundancy, politicians and generals devised more limited roles for, and means of, military force. On the one hand, they reinvented strategy as deterrence. This meant devising political uses, divorced as far as possible from their military realization, for nuclear and other weapons of mass destruction. On the other hand, they have sought new, limited ways of fighting wars, using a combination of computerized targeting and media manipulation, which has worked increasingly well in the limited campaigns that the West has fought since 1989 (see episode X).

To the extent that they have succeeded, the practice of war appears to have been rescued from its mid-twentieth-century dead end. But warfare remains fundamentally compromised by this degenerate tendency. It has led war, I shall argue, to produce what has come to be known as genocide.

Categories of violence

Most writing assumes that war and genocide, as categories of violence, can be clearly delineated – even if we might need to investigate the relationships between them. I argue, in contrast, that the distinctions are only partial, and have been all too easily blurred in historical practice. In this sense, the genocidal tendency in war is a manifestation of the internal linkages between these types of political violence. For war and genocide are not 'phenomena' in the sense that volcanic eruptions are natural events. They are, by contrast, general ways of representing different kinds of intentional actions by individual and collective social actors.

The nature of the linkages between war and genocide can be highlighted if we bring into the picture a third general type of political violence: *revolution*. All three concepts have a dual meaning, referring both to the courses of action of specific collective actors and to the clashes of the actions of opposing actors. However, the actors who make war, revolution and genocide, and the nature of their intentions, are generally supposed to differ sharply. The distinctions between the three concepts are well established:

- revolutions are social upheavals that aim to overturn the organization of political power;
- genocide is the destruction of a social group by organized political power;
- both of these clearly differ from war, in which two organized political forces aim to destroy each other's power.

However, the tendency to regard revolution, genocide and war as radically different types of social action rests on three fundamentally erroneous assumptions.

The first error is to regard the distinction between 'inside' and 'outside' the state as fundamental. From this point of view, states are established centres of power. It is assumed that contests between two or more states (or groups of states) are of a different kind from the contests that occur between states and social groups within them. However, states are merely centres of concentrated social power; they rest on complex supporting relations in society. On the other hand, social groups may produce state-like organizations, which form the basis of new state centres, as in revolutions. Hence the differences between the two types of conflict may not be so great in practice.

The corresponding second error is to regard revolution and genocide as state–society contests, but war as paradigmatically a state–state contest. In reality, even the most clearly interstate wars often involve tenser relations and violent clashes between state power and society; they frequently have a dimension of civil conflict. In total war, as we have seen, war is normally waged on the enemy society as well as the enemy state. Moreover, civil wars are not exceptions to the rule of war. The majority of wars throughout the modern period have been at least partially civil wars. Likewise, revolutions, at least in their most advanced stages, acquire the character of a conflict between two centres of state power. They often occur in contexts of war, and have taken increasingly militarized forms. Genocide is often assumed to involve states inflicting absolute violence on helpless populations. In fact, as we shall see in more detail later, it mostly occurs in the context of political and military struggle – revolution, counter-revolution and especially war – and is mostly ended by war.

The third error is to regard the asymmetrical character of power struggle in revolution and genocide as a definitive contrast with the symmetry of war. In fact, wars too, between state centres as well as between established states and insurgents, always involve asymmetries of power. The defining feature of war is not that the opposing forces have similar characters or comparable strengths, but that the two sides share the aim of destroying the enemy's power in a given context.

In this light, revolution and genocide not only involve elements of war and have clear affinities with it, but although both involve more than war, they are in the end *variants and often phases of war*, in which the nature and role of mass killing are posed in unique ways. Both revolution and genocide are contests that share two defining characteristics of war: the opposing sides aim to destroy each other's power, and they are prepared to engage in mass killing of the enemy in order to achieve their goals.

Revolution as war

Before we turn to genocide, let us look a little more closely at revolution. In revolutions, emergent centres of state power and social groups that support them aim to destroy the power of established state institutions. In counter-revolutions, established regimes and social groups that oppose change seek to destroy revolutionary power. But revolution was classically conceived, like war, as a process. The power necessary to overthrow established state institutions had to be mobilized, through social struggles and political organization. Only in this way would the basis for a new form of state emerge.

Insurrectionary war was therefore considered classically as the final stage of revolution, which occurred when the emergent revolutionary political centre acquired sufficient strength to openly challenge for power. Insurrection, the military phase, was the conclusion to the revolutionary process, and civil war was the probable outcome of the reaction to insurrection by the old power. The Russian revolutionary leader Leon Trotsky claimed in his famous history of the revolution (1934) that the revolutionary process itself was only minimally violent: the revolution seized power only when it had won over the military forces supporting the old regime. The extent of violence depended, he argued, principally on the extent of the resistance to change from counter-revolutionary forces. Certainly counter-revolution has often involved extensive slaughter.

However, in the mid- and late twentieth century, *revolution itself also increasingly took the form of war*, particularly guerrilla war (see box 1.4). Revolutionaries pursued armed struggle not as a conclusion to political struggle, but as a central means of that struggle from the outset. Likewise, established power has used force not merely to defeat open insurrection, but to stamp out revolutionary forces and terrorize their actual or potential social supporters. As revolution became armed struggle, counter-revolution became counter-insurgency. In this sense there has been a radical change in the character of many revolutionary processes.

Box 1.4   Guerrilla war

Guerrilla means 'small war'. Guerrilla wars are small in comparison with the greatest conflicts of states, but they may be carried out across larger areas with more combatants and casualties than many wars between armies. What distinguishes guerrilla warfare is chiefly that it is *unconventional* or *irregular*, distinguished from the direct confrontations of the conventional or regular armed forces of states – although it may take place in conjunction with these.

Guerrilla war, as Walter Lacqueur (1998: p. xviii) states, 'is as old as the hills and predates regular warfare'. Guerrilla war has lent itself to many kinds of politics, reactionary as well as progressive, right as well as left, and these can be found in all modern periods. So it is not true to say that guerrilla war was 'right-wing' in the nineteenth century and 'left-wing' in the twentieth. Nevertheless, the success of Mao Zedong's guerrilla war in China in the 1930s and 1940s popularized an idea of revolutionary armed struggle which overshadowed other concepts of both revolution and guerrilla warfare in the succeeding decades:

- Mao's turn to armed struggle followed the defeat of his movement in urban insurrection in the 1920s. He then reorganized his party as an armed movement and consolidated a liberated zone in a remote region of China, from which he fought a long war against the Nationalist regime of Chiang Kai-shek.
- Mao's struggle, in the world's most populous nation, developed in the context of the interstate war following Japan's invasion of China (1937) and the Second World War (1939–45) of which this became a part. It finally succeeded with the capture of China's coastal cities in 1949.
- The other major success of a Communist guerrilla movement, Josep Brod Tito's in Yugoslavia, occurred in 1941–5 under similar conditions.

- The difficulty of repeating these triumphs under different conditions did not prevent many lesser movements from trying over the succeeding decades. But the only major successes were those of the Cuban movement of Fidel Castro (not originally Communist) in 1958, and Ho Chi Minh's Vietnamese Communists after thirty years of war in 1975.
- By the end of the twentieth century, many notable guerrilla movements, such as the Afghan Muhajeddin and Angola's UNITA, were no longer of the left.

Because guerrilla war is irregular and often seeks to overcome the power advantages of orthodox states, its practice has long been accompanied by violence against (actual or putative) civilian supporters of the state. Likewise, established state armies often use widespread violence against civilian populations suspected of harbouring guerrillas. In modern times, large-scale guerrilla and counter-insurgency war has often systematically targeted civilian populations; so, for example:

- Chinese Communists probably killed several million civilians – actual or supposed Japanese collaborators, Nationalist supporters and 'rich peasants' – during their struggle for power.
- American forces killed hundreds of thousands of Vietnamese civilians in their attempt to defeat Communist guerrillas.

It is clear that guerrilla war, linked with modern political mobilization, has many characteristics of total war. It thrived under conditions of general total war and has had genocidal tendencies, with social and national groups systematically targeted for violence by both guerrilla and anti-guerrilla forces.

Thus, by the mid-twentieth century, most revolutions had come to clearly resemble wars. Moreover, the mass killing of civilians as well as combatants was often carried out on one side, or both. Like the mainstream military tradition of total interstate war, the struggle of revolution and counter-revolution became increasingly murderous of civilians – indeed (I shall argue) genocidal. Only in some largely peaceful democratic revolutions of the global era – for example, the 'velvet' revolution in Czechoslovakia in 1989 and the negotiated ending of South African apartheid in the early 1990s – have people begun to rescue the idea of revolution from its implication in war.

The connections of revolution to war show how categories of violence are not fixed, but fluid and overlapping, reflecting changes in the way that collective actors practice violence in pursuit of their political goals. In the next chapter, we shall see how the widespread practice of degenerate war has led to a new definition of a distinct type of organized violence against civilians: genocide.

Further reading

Bramson, L. and Goethals, G. W., eds (1978) *War: Studies from Psychology, Sociology and Anthropology*. New York: Basic Books.

Clausewitz, C. von (1976) *On War*, ed. M. Howard and P. Paret. Princeton: Princeton University Press.

Creveld, M. van (1991) *The Transformation of War*. London: Macmillan.

Earle, E. M., ed. (1971) *Makers of Modern Strategy*. Princeton: Princeton University Press.

Ehrenreich, B. (1997) *Blood Rites: Origins and History of the Passions of War*. London: Virago.

Freedman, L., ed. (1994) *War*. Oxford: Oxford University Press.

Gallie, W. B. (1978) *Philosophers of War and Peace*. Oxford: Oxford University Press.

Gray, C. (1998) *Modern Strategy*. Oxford: Oxford University Press.

Halliday, F. (1999) *Revolution in World Politics*. London: Macmillan.

Hanson, V. D. (2002) *Why the West Has Won*. London: Faber.

Howard, M. (1981) *Clausewitz*. Oxford: Oxford University Press.

Howard, M. (1985) *The Causes of Wars*. London: Allen & Unwin.

Kaldor, M. (1982a) *The Baroque Arsenal*. London: Deutsch.

Kaldor, M. (1982b) Warfare and capitalism. In New Left Review, ed., *Exterminism and Cold War*, London: Verso, 261–88.

Kaldor, M. (1999) *New and Old Wars*. Cambridge: Polity.

Keegan, J. (1976) *The Face of Battle*. London: Cape.

Lacqueur, W. (1998) *Guerrilla Warfare: A Historical and Critical Study*. New Brunswick, NJ: Transaction Publishers.

Lorenz, K. (1966) *On Aggression*. London: Methuen.

Shaw, M. (1988) *Dialectics of War: An Essay on the Social Theory of War and Peace*. London: Pluto.

Skocpol, T. (1979) *States and Social Revolutions*. Cambridge: Cambridge University Press.

Snyder, C. A., ed. (1999) *Contemporary Security and Strategy*. London: Macmillan.

Storr, A. (1991) *Human Destructiveness: The Roots of Genocide and Human Cruelty*. London: Routledge.

Trotsky, L. (1934) *History of the Russian Revolution*. London: Gollancz.

Walzer, M. (1992) *Just and Unjust Wars*. New York: Basic Books.

Episode I
The Armenian genocide

The killing of over a million Armenians in the Ottoman Empire in 1915 has been described as 'the first of the modern ideologically motivated genocides' (Chalk and Jonassohn 1990: 249). Throughout the nineteenth century, the Empire's writ had been maintained in Ottoman Armenia (part of what is now eastern Turkey) and other provinces through intermittent terror by irregular armed forces. 'Small' war, including attacks on civilian village populations, was a constant condition of Ottoman imperial rule. However, at the beginning of the twentieth century, the Empire was threatened from without by more powerful European empires and from within by factional struggle among elites as well as by autonomist movements. In the growing crisis, revolutionary Turkish nationalists (the 'Young Turks'), many of them army officers, seized power in 1908.

The radicalized Young Turks increasingly viewed the Christian Armenian population as an enemy, linked to the rival Russian Empire. The declaration of a *jihad* (holy war) sanctioned attacks on any enemies. When war broke out with Russia in 1914, the Ottoman army began to attack Armenian villages, its Turkish nationalist officers increasingly influenced by German 'total war' doctrines and their ethic of 'annihilating' the enemy. Applying these ideas to the Armenian population led to intensified attacks on civilians in areas far from the regular war with Russia.

The Turkish total war policy against the Armenians including forced deportations, death marches and large-scale killing. The genocide began after Armenian men were conscripted into the imperial army: the absence of these younger men made attacks on villages easier. The attacks were escalated into massive, bureaucratically administered abductions. The aim was to destroy Armenia before regular war began, by forcing its people to leave home, split apart and die. Typically the remaining able-bodied men in towns and villages were rounded up, then marched outside the walls to be shot or bayoneted to death. After this, the old men, women and children 'were forced to walk, endlessly, along prearranged routes, until they died from thirst, hunger, exposure or exhaustion' (contemporary account quoted by Graber 1996: 101). The 'caravans of death', escorted by soldiers who corralled, robbed, beat and raped the Armenians, were led to remote, inhospitable regions and lingering death from exhaustion, starvation and disease.

All this was directed centrally from within the state and executed over a period of barely four months in the middle of 1915. Under the cover, and with the excuse, of generalized war, an entire society was destroyed. Although large-scale mass killing of civilians was nothing new, in the total war of the twentieth century it had taken on a terrible new form. The perpetrators were Turkish nationalists, but the critical element in their ideology was a new kind of militarism. The genocide happened 'primarily because the military ethics of the time permitted generals to view civilians as valid targets of war' (Reid 1992: 21).

Armenia set a precedent for the horrendous slaughter that was to come throughout the century. Like the Holocaust, the Armenian genocide has become an increasingly significant issue in contemporary world politics. But, unlike the Holocaust, which the modern German state has fully recognized, what was done to the Armenians is still denied by the modern, supposedly democratic Turkish state, even though all the perpetrators are now dead.

Further reading

Chalk, F. and Jonassohn, K. (1990) *The History and Sociology of Genocide: Analyses and Case Studies*. New Haven: Yale University Press.

Graber, G. (1996) *Caravans to Oblivion: The Armenian Genocide, 1915*. New York: Wiley.

Reid, J. J. (1992) Total war, the annihilation ethic, and the Armenian genocide, 1870–1918. In R. Hovannisian, ed., *The Armenian Genocide: History, Politics, Ethics*, London: Macmillan, 21–52.

Sukru Hanioglu, M. (2001) *Preparation for a Revolution: The Young Turks, 1902–1908*. New York: Oxford University Press.

2

Genocide as a Form of War

The conventional definition of genocide can be summarized as the *deliberate destruction of a people, principally but not only by means of killing some of its members.* Uniquely, this definition of genocide depends heavily on an international legal document. The Genocide Convention (see box 2.1) was agreed in 1948 by the United Nations, which had been established three years earlier by the victors of the Second World War. The term 'genocide' had indeed been coined only recently, in response to the Nazis' extermination of the Jews. Accordingly, the International Convention took this as its basic standard, although it defined genocide in terms that would also qualify many less extreme episodes as genocide.

Box 2.1   The definition of genocide

The United Nations Convention on the Prevention and Punishment of the Crime of Genocide, adopted in 1948, states: 'In the present Convention, genocide means any of the following acts committed with intent to destroy, in whole or in part, a national, ethnical, racial or religious group, as such:

(a) Killing members of the group;
(b) Causing serious bodily or mental harm to members of the group;
(c) Deliberately inflicting on the group conditions of life calculated to bring about its physical destruction in whole or in part;
(d) Imposing measures intended to prevent births within the group;
(e) Forcibly transferring children of the group to another group.'

The following main issues arise from the definition and the rest of the Convention:

- The term 'genocide' (from *genos*, a people, and *-cide*, killing) was coined by the jurist Raphael Lemkin (1944). He stressed that genocide did not necessarily mean the immediate physical destruction of all members of a target group, but applied to a co-ordinated plan of different actions aiming at the destruction of the essential foundations of their life, with the aim of annihilating the groups themselves.
- In the UN debate before the Convention was agreed, Soviet representatives succeeded in excluding political groups from the list of those protected; as Leo Kuper (1981: 39) writes, this is a 'major omission'. Social classes were also left out.
- Nevertheless, the Convention's phrase destruction 'in whole or in part' left ambiguity about the extent of mass killing required for genocide to be established. Many adopted the term 'genocidal massacre' to refer to episodes of killing with genocidal intent that fell short of the wholesale destruction of a population.
- Others continued to regard only cases that approximated the maximum case of total extermination (as with the Jews) as genocide. This could be politically convenient, of course, if it excused politicians from regarding as genocide cases of mass killing about which they wanted to do nothing. This classification has also been adopted, however, by some some social scientists, such as Mann (2001).
- The Convention commits states to 'protecting' threatened populations and to 'punish' those responsible for genocide. But both commitments have been largely neglected by the United Nations itself and by major states since 1948.

Thus the definition of the concept of genocide, and the application of both concept and Convention to particular cases, remains highly controversial. Social scientists have often proposed refinements of the international legal definition, as I do below.

Destruction

The Convention's definition clearly limited genocide to the deliberate destruction of groups *as such*. It implicitly drew a particularly sharp line between genocide and other forms of mass killing. It separated genocide from even the most degenerate war, such as the annihilation of civilian populations for strategic reasons. As we have seen, this was what the Allies themselves had practised, and it was about to become the norm of the new nuclear age. It was clearly true that Germany (see episode III) and Japan (episode IV) had slaughtered those whom they regarded as inferior races; the

Nazis in particular had regarded these groups as distinct enemies whose destruction was desirable in itself. For the Allied governments, on the other hand, the destruction of Germans and Japanese as such was not an end in itself. But mass killing of civilians was an intended and desired consequence of the Allied bombing, carried out in order to defeat the Axis powers (episode V). This fine line, which separated Allied mass slaughter from Auschwitz, remained sacrosanct in the Convention.

The Convention said that genocide concerned the destruction of *national, ethnic, racial and religious groups*. It excluded the annihilation of groups defined by other characteristics, such as class or political affiliation – so that Stalin's liquidation of the *kulaks* (or 'rich' peasants: episode II) and eastern European political elites could not be counted. But in the same year that the United Nations adopted the Genocide Convention, it also adopted its Universal Declaration of Human Rights. From a universal human standpoint, it is clearly untenable to lay down that the destruction and mass killing of some sorts of human group (races, nations or religions) should be regarded as a particularly heinous crime, while that of others (classes, professions or political groups) should not. Yet the restrictive international defin-ition gives special status to the former groups. Given that perpetrators of mass killing often target both kinds of group, in some combination, the restriction often makes little sense in practice. Are we to say, for example, that when the Khmer Rouge targeted people because of their Vietnamese origins, they were practising genocide, but when they killed Cambodians because of their education or social class, they were not? Such a legalistic distinction would fragment the sig-nificance of the Cambodian 'killing fields' and prevent us from under-standing the criminal destruction of the Cambodian people as a single, if multi-targeted, process (as I explain in episode VII).

The Convention said, too, that genocide involved the destruction of groups *in whole or in part*, through a number of means (five were named, of which killing was the first and foremost). This phrase has been instrumental in much of the ambiguity surrounding the mean-ing of genocide. On the one hand, it reflects the valid and very important understanding that the process of destroying a group is the same, whether the perpetrators are wholly or only partially successful, whether they destroy the entirety, the majority or only a minority of the group. On the other hand, it reflects a central uncertainty, in all the literature about genocide, concerning the meaning of the *destruction* of a group. Moreover, the Convention's specification of genocidal means points, apparently, in contradict-ory directions. The primary criterion of killing points towards an understanding of genocide as the attempt to eliminate individual members of the group – indeed, another criterion refers to 'physical destruction'. However, the secondary criteria, especially the prevention of births and forcible transfer of children to another group, suggest that the destruction of group identity is genocidal even where its individual members survive physically.

Clearly, while the framers specified that 'any' of these acts was genocidal, they understood all the various means as driving towards the destruction of a group as such. So destruction cannot be understood *simply* in terms of killing people. Not even Hitler succeeded in killing all the Jews, even within German-occupied Europe, and it is not clear that he even intended this before 1941. Yet there was manifest continuity between earlier phases of violence against Jews, before mass killing became a systematic policy, and the final stage of mass extermination. The intention to destroy the Jews as an economic, political and cultural force in German and European society was manifested much earlier, and there is a sense in which systematic killing completed (as a 'final solution') a process begun through many other measures, less final and comprehensive in their violence. Moreover, Nazi violence against other groups, such as Poles, was also considered genocidal by the Nuremberg Tribunal, even though there was never any intention of mass extermination of the whole population. Subsequent debate has tended to emphasize the uniqueness of the Holocaust's horror, in comparison to other mass slaughters – even those committed by the Nazis. This has helped to enshrine a maximum concept of genocide as the complete extermination of a group, involving killing of almost all its members, in legal, popular and even academic understanding. But this is clearly mistaken.

To make more adequate sense of the idea of destruction in genocide, we need to grasp that it involves three elements:

1 The identification of a social group as an *enemy* in an essentially military (rather than merely political, economic or cultural) sense – that is, as a group against which it is justified to use physical violence in a systematic way.
2 The intention to destroy the real or imputed *power* of the enemy group, including its economic, political, cultural and ideological power, together with its ability to resist this destruction.
3 The actual deployment of violence to destroy the power of the enemy group through *killing* and physically harming a significant number of its members, as well as other measures.

Thus genocide as a destructive *process* can be developed even where the third element is not fully or successfully carried through. A major cause of misunderstanding in the discourse of genocide is its equation with the successful completion of the process in a maximum sense – that is, where all three elements are completely carried out. Genocide is then understood as a *state* of completed destruction rather than a process leading towards it. 'A genocide' as a discrete event is generally understood in this way, but it is misleading as it separates the result from the process that leads towards it.

Intention

The Genocide Convention clearly specifies that genocidal acts must be *committed with intent* to destroy the group. This is also a valid and essential element of any definition. Clearly, in the standard cases of genocide (and also, I shall argue, in others that don't fit the Convention's criteria) it is central to understanding mass killing that we grasp the intention of powerful, armed forces to destroy the power of an 'enemy' group through violence. Intention does not mean, of course, a clearly stated policy: on the contrary, since genocide is always and everywhere illegitimate, the destruction of civilian groups is almost invariably cloaked in subterfuge and euphemism. Orders are hidden and indirect, and the chain of responsibility needs careful elaboration before criminal liability on the part of leaders can be established. Intention may be inferred, moreover, from patterns of actions that would hardly have occurred in its absence. Where organized groups directly inflict terror and killing, intention is usually relatively easy to establish. Where people are dying from the indirect effects of policies, as in famines (see box 2.2), intentionality is more difficult to establish.

Box 2.2　Famine and genocide

One of the most basic ways in which the power of social groups is weakened is through deprivation of the means of life. A population which cannot find food to maintain itself will be forced to kill its livestock, use its housing for firewood, sell its property, migrate to other regions and even in extreme cases kill those it cannot feed – or who can provide food for others. In places like China, where famine has been endemic, cannibalism has been a regular resort in the most extreme crises.

Such experiences, whether or not they are the results of intentional policies, will break a society. Famines have occurred throughout history where crops have failed. But they have often been precipitated, or worsened, by war. In recent times, the 1984–85 Ethiopian famine that prompted the 'Band Aid' movement was represented as an outcome of drought; but behind this lay the bitter war between the Ethiopian regime and Eritrean secessionists. To the extent that leaders could have foreseen that widespread famine was the likely indirect consequence of their campaigns, their policies can be seen as genocidal.

Mike Davis (2001) has argued that nineteenth-century colonialism was marked by regular 'holocausts' of this kind. In the context of cyclical weather patterns that tended towards food crises, more or less conscious neglect and indifference on the part of colonial authorities contributed decisively to extensive, preventable famines. It is difficult to avoid the conclusion that there was a quasi-genocidal element in these events: colonial administrators and their masters saw an opportunity to weaken the colonial peasantry and increase their dependence on the imperial state.

Although strangely seen by Davis as exceptions, the rural holocausts of twentieth-century Communist empires were even more extreme cases. Stalin's early 1930s 'terror famine' in the Ukraine and elsewhere (see episode II) was the culmination of repeated campaigns of direct violence and killing of the peasantry. Hunger was clearly designed to break their independent social power and subordinate them to the party-state.

Mao's 'Great Leap Forward' of 1959–61 was in many ways a repetition of Stalin's campaign. This state-made famine was the worst episode ever recorded in rural China, and the largest single case of mass death in the twentieth century, with an estimated 30–40 million victims (Becker 1996). Uniquely, this famine was not confined to particular regions, but spread across the entire countryside of this huge country. While the scale of mass death was hardly intended, it was a direct and foreseeable consequence of Mao's attempt to subordinate the peasantry to his will. The 'Great Leap Forward' was a policy of do-it-yourself industrialization and agricultural change forced on the peasant class to destroy their traditional way of life. It centred on Mao's own fantastic ideas about agriculture, and imposed a programme derived from the pseudo-scientific ideology of Stalin's biologist, Lysenko. Mao continued his policy long after it was evident that millions were dying; he exported grain while refusing it to starving peasants, and he enforced his policies with brutal repression and killing of peasant resisters.

Echoes of such dangerous fantasies can still be found in state development projects in China and elsewhere (India, Turkey, etc.), where huge displacements of population (especially for dams) are being carried out. More directly murderous policies have also been practised recently against indigenous peoples – for example, Iraq's drying out of the wetland homes of the Marsh Arabs and commercial destruction of rain forests in Brazil and Indonesia.

'Complicity in genocide' is one of the acts punishable under the Convention. Modern Western governments and corporations have often been complicit in such destructive development policies. In the case of Iraq, moreover, a plausible case has been made that UN sanctions promoted by the USA and the UK have contributed to hunger and disease, which have weakened the population – policies continued even when the consequences were known.

However, the criterion of intention also leads, if interpreted one-sidedly, to the danger of taking the standards of the genocidists for reality. Certainly, we cannot explain what happens in genocide without grasping the perpetrator mentality that defines certain social groups as enemies, to be defeated by mass killing and other victimization. Yet genocide, like war, is not just a course of action pursued by one more powerful party, but a *clash of social power and experience between two social forces*. We should define genocide, therefore, *by the experience of the victims as well as the mentality of the genocidists*.

The common experience of genocide is of cumulative discrimination against enemies and targets leading to indiscriminate slaughter. For victims, the threat to their social, personal and physical existence is similar, regardless of the particular reasons for it in the minds of their killers. In practice, killing has a deeply arbitrary aspect, involving chance and uncertainty, and often appearing 'senseless' to observers as well as to those on the receiving end. If Nazism is our model of genocide, we need to put alongside the images of clinical selection for the gas chambers the roadside massacres and mass burnings of villagers – often Jews and non-Jews alike – by special commando groups in occupied Soviet territory, which preceded extermination in the camps. Whether the Nazis were killing you because you were a Jew, a Slav, a Soviet citizen or a Communist, or all or none of these, was not so important as the fact that you were going to be killed. Moreover, all genocidists kill for a range of reasons and, at the same time, seemingly for none in particular. As we shall see later in the book, they target young men because they are potential fighters or producers; old people for the opposite reason, their uselessness; women because of the significance of sexual power. But in the end, killing is killing, and tends to lead to more killing. Slaughter can appear utterly casual, arbitrary and senseless. There is (il)logic in terror and murder that surpasses the pseudo-rational discrimination dictated by strategy and political ideology, even as it fulfils them.

To understand genocide, we need to grasp how categorical discrimination in the minds of genocidal killers combines with relatively indiscriminate practice and results. We need to recognize how, in the way in which mass killing partially transcends political logic, genocide turns out to be very similar to war. Just as 'strategic' bombing has led to relatively indiscriminate mass slaughter, so has 'racial' targeting. It is rarely the case, moreover, that killers focus only on one kind of social target. The logic of terror tends towards *the multiplication of enemies*. Political enemies and social classes (commonly, educated elites) are often targets of genocidal regimes at the same time as ethnic or national groups. Thus Jews were not only a racial enemy for the Nazis, but represented social privilege and political opposition. At all stages they constituted only one among the social enemies of Nazism, and not always the most threatened. Since genocide frequently takes place in the context of interstate war, social enemies are often identified with international state enemies. The Nazis linked the Jews to international finance and Soviet Bolshevism.

These examples draw our attention to the issue of genocidal ideology. This is only implicit in the Convention, in the sense that racism is regarded as an inhuman and anti-scientific doctrine. But it is important to recognize that genocide generally involves *pseudo-scientific, irrational and fantastical beliefs*. Groups identified as enemies in the minds of perpetrators often comprise people who do not recognize themselves as a community, and whose imputed power bears little relationship to reality. Thus the Nazis defined 'the Jews' as a 'powerful' enemy, although they included among them many people of only part-Jewish ancestry who had become assimilated into German society, and whose wealth and power, such as it was, was hardly connected to their Jewishness. Stalin defined kulaks as an enemy of the state, designating certain peasants as 'rich peasants', although they often lived amidst other people described as 'poor peasants' and were often as close to the breadline as the latter. The Rwandan *génocidaires* defined 'Tutsi' as enemies, although the social distinction from 'Hutus' was often blurred, and its enforcement depended on the identity card system. Many genocides have involved schemes of social classification, embedded in fantastical belief systems, which themselves mutate rapidly according to the exigencies of the political struggles in which the perpetrators were involved.

A form of war

The many similarities between war and genocide are hardly coincidences. Most genocides take place during or around interstate and/or civil wars. Table 2.1 sets out selected major episodes of genocide in the twentieth century. It includes a number of cases that would not qualify as genocide according to the conventional international definition, because they were not directed against 'a national, ethnical, racial or religious group, as such'. These are Stalin's 'liquidation of the kulaks', the Nazis' euthanasia programme against the mentally handicapped, Mao's 'Great Leap Forward' and the Indonesian army's massacre of the Communists. It also includes the Cambodian

Table 2.1 The context of war (in selected genocidal episodes of the twentieth century)

Episode[1]	Perpetrator centre	Principal perpetrator organs	Constitutive war (or history/threat of war)[2]	Organized armed enemies (or perceived enemies)[3]	Enemy social groups
Armenian genocide, 1915 (I)	Ottoman state	army, police, paramilitaries	WWI	Russia, Britain, France	Armenians
Stalin's liquidation of kulaks, 1929–32 (II)	Soviet state	army, police, party	civil war 1919–21, 'imperialist' threat	Imperialism, counter-revolution	peasants, Ukrainians
Nazi euthanasia of mentally handicapped, 1930s (III)	Nazi state	police, party	WWI	International Jewry, Bolshevism	mentally handicapped
Rape of Nanking (etc.), 1937 (IV)	Imperial Japanese state	army	conquest of China	Chinese government, Communists	Chinese
German occupation of Poland, 1939–40 (III)	Nazi state	army, police, party	invasion of Poland	Poland, Britain, France	Poles, especially Jews
First phase, Holocaust, 1941–2 (III)	Nazi state	army, police, special paramilitary groups	invasion of USSR 1941	USSR and Allies	Jews, Slavs, prisoners, Communists
Second phase, Holocaust, 1942–5 (III)	Nazi state	army, police, camp administration	later stages WWII	USSR and Allies	Jews, Gypsies, etc.

Stalin's deportation of nationalities, 1941–2 (II)	Soviet state	army, police	WWII	Nazi Germany	Volga Germans, Chechens, etc.
'Great Leap Forward', 1959–61	Chinese state	army, police, party	*conflict with USA; Sino-Soviet split*	*USA, USSR*	peasants
Massacres of Indonesian Communists, 1965	Indonesian state (army)	army, police	*conflict with Malaya*	Indonesian Communist Party	Communists, Chinese
Occupation of East Timor, 1975–99	Indonesian state	army, police	conquest and counter-insurgency	East Timorese resistance (FRETILIN)	East Timorese
Cambodian genocide, 1977–9 (VII)	Khmer Rouge state	party, army	wars with USA, *Vietnam*	USA, Vietnam	urban-educated, peasants, Vietnamese, minorities
Yugoslav wars, 1991–9 (VIII)	Serbian-Yugoslav state + Serbian statelets in Bosnia, Croatia	parties, armies, police, paramilitaries	Yugoslav wars	Slovenia, Croatia, Bosnia, Kosovo Liberation Army, NATO	Croats, Muslims, Albanians, plural urban Bosnians
Rwandan genocide, 1994 (IX)	Rwandan state (ruling party)	army, police, militia, armed gangs	Rwandan civil war	Rwandan Patriotic Front (RPF)	Tutsis, opposition parties

[1] In this column, roman numerals refer to the episode sections of this book.

[2] In this column, italics are used for genocides that did not take place in an immediate context of war as such, but where earlier wars or threats of war provided important elements of context.

[3] In this column, italics are used where 'enemies' were defined ideologically, but where war was not actually taking place.

genocide, which would only partially qualify (because it was only partially directed against such groups).

Table 2.1 shows the social groups against which genocide was committed, and how in most cases there were three central connections to the state and war:

1   The genocidal episode was organized by a state, or a power centre within a state, that can be regarded as the primary perpetrator.
2   The principal organ which carried out the genocide was the army in conjunction with other state organizations such as the police, as well as party organizations and paramilitary groups.
3   The genocide took place in the context of a war between the perpetrator state and organized, armed enemies (often, but not always, other states).

The table suggests that in some cases, however, genocide was perpetrated outside a direct context of war with organized armed enemies. But in all these cases, the perpetrator states were militarized states with militaristic ideologies, and had recently experienced wars. Military and paramilitary organizations were still prime organs of killing in these episodes. The perpetrator regimes in these cases were often also totalitarian, with strong conceptions of external 'enemies' and general tendencies to designate internal 'enemies'. They often believed, in at least partially irrational ways, that they were threatened by world conspiracies combining these internal and external enemies.

This contextual evidence is strongly suggestive of connections between war and genocide. It is not sufficient, however, to represent the links between war and genocide as external, causal relations. *In no case does war simply cause genocide.* If that was the case, there would be far more major genocidal episodes. Rather, it is the case that when armed military force is being extensively used against organized armed enemies, then it is easier for leaders to take the extraordinary, generally illegitimate steps towards also using armed force against social groups as such. Militaristic and totalitarian ideologies that designate groups as 'enemies' are particularly likely to facilitate plans to destroy social groups as such through armed force. This is best shown by examining particular cases of genocide, as I have done in the episodes that interleave the main chapters of this book.

This argument suggests that the links between war and genocide are not simply external or causal, but are *internal* to the character of genocide. The simplest way to express this is to say that genocide can best be understood as *a form of war in which social groups are the enemies*. Table 2.2 shows how genocide can be seen on a continuum from war in general, through degenerate war (which was defined in chapter 1). The core linkages (and differences) between genocide and other forms of war, shown in this table, can be described as follows.

1   *Destroying the power of the enemy*. In war in general, the point of organized armed force is to destroy the power of another organized armed enemy together with its ability to resist (Clausewitz's definition). In degenerate total war, the destruction of the organized enemy

Table 2.2   Genocide as a type of war

Dimension	War	Degenerate war	Genocide
as a type of social action	destruction of the power of an organized, armed enemy	destruction of the power of social groups *linked to* an organized, armed enemy	destruction of the power of an enemy social group
as a conflict of actors	mutual contest of two organized armed forces	mutual contest of two organized armed forces *together with* targeting of enemy society	campaign of violence by an organized armed force against a social group as such, with resistance by the threatened group
legitimacy	generally legitimate; open ideological mobilization	contested legitimacy: illegitimate elements cloaked in general legitimacy; semi-open mobilization	illegitimate: mobilization gives way to denial and cover-up in critical stages
battle	armed clash with mutual killing of armed forces	armed clash with mutual killing of armed forces, combined with attacks on largely unarmed civilians	largely one-sided killing of largely unarmed civilians
outcome	victory of more powerful of two contending armed forces	victory of more powerful of two contending armed forces	victory of genocidists *unless* more powerful external armed force intervenes

is extended to include the destruction of the civilian population, but still as a means towards the defeat of the organized enemy. In genocide, organized armed force is used to destroy social groups as such (the Convention definition). What destruction means here is destroying the social power of a particular group – in economic and cultural as well as political senses – and usually eliminating or drastically reducing its presence in a particular territory. Destroying the target group's power also involves destroying its ability to resist.

2   *Killing*. In war, the destruction of an enemy's power involves killing some among its forces (but does not generally involve killing all its forces). In genocide, the deep destruction of the enemy group is defined by the mass killing of some among its members (but does not generally involve killing all of them). In both cases, the extent of killing depends on the precise aims of the parties, the means available and the course of the struggle.

3   *Relationship between killing and other means of coercion*. War is the extension of politics by other means, and typically includes economic, ideological and political coercion alongside military action. In genocide, killing is supplemented by other coercive measures. These include discrimination, robbery, expulsion and terror, as well as the transfers of population and control of births specified in the Convention.

4   *Nature of the conflict*. War in general, including degenerate war, is primarily conflict between two or more organized armed forces, although in degenerate war civilians are targeted as well. Genocide is conflict between organized armed forces, on the one hand, and civilian populations that are largely unarmed, on the other – although some among the latter may offer armed resistance, and the group may be more or less linked to an armed force. Many secondary differences of genocide from other forms of war flow from this difference.

5   *Legitimacy*. A crucial difference is that war is generally legitimate. Thus, although degenerate war breaches accepted standards of warfare, it masks itself in the general legitimacy of war. Because the enemy in genocide is defined as a civilian group, in contrast, it is by definition illegitimate. This has all sorts of ramifications, not least that genocide will tend to be presented as war whenever possible. Although perpetrating genocide usually involves special organizations developed for the purpose, it is often carried out mostly by or through the general state machine – especially the army – and other established institutions. Thus it generally utilizes the machinery of war and other organs of state power, and takes

place under their cover. It is in the interests of both genocidists and genocide deniers to claim the legitimacy of war. The close links between genocide and degenerate war mean that, to identify genocide, it is essential to clarify the difference between legitimacy and illegitimacy within war.

6   *Preparation*. Like war in general, genocide needs to be understood as a process. Because war is legitimate, long-term war preparations (e.g. organizing armies, making weapons, advocating military ideas) are generally open and explicit. Genocide is also prepared in complex ways within society, and the institutions and ideas that are mobilized by genocidists are also widely accepted in pre-genocidal periods – indeed, they are very much the same institutions and ideas as those mobilized for war. But genocide preparation, even more than revolution, takes place on the margins of social acceptance. The genocidal potentials of armies, ideologies, laws, racism, chauvinism, religious and class hostilities remain, for the most part, abstract. They are not seen as means of genocide. The direct preparation of genocide, in contrast to war, is generally semi-concealed. Therefore the specific machinery of genocide, like the machinery of insurrection in classic revolutions, is usually a novel construction, begun secretly, immediately prior to its use.

7   *Scope*. War is a pervasive and complex social institution, so that we refer to a wide range of practices as *military*, because of their connections with war, without assuming that they are homogeneous or that they are simply connected to a maximum case of warlike nuclear extermination. Similarly, the broad base of genocide, and the range of its expressions, means that we can also use 'genocidal', as an adjective referring to genocide, without assuming that its expressions are homogeneous or involve group extermination. *Genocidal practices* may be defined, therefore, as those that *treat social groups as enemies whose power and lives may have to be destroyed*. Clearly not all hostility towards other social groups, such as that manifested in racism and chauvinism, is actively genocidal. But such forms of hostility may be seen in certain contexts as pre- or proto-genocidal. These are the kinds of beliefs, ideologies and institutions that are likely to facilitate actively genocidal threats, when states or political movements begin to organize the conditions for widespread violence. In this context, any hostility against enemy groups may threaten genocide, hence pre-genocidal ideas may take on directly genocidal significance. For example, we know with hindsight that the previously abstract genocidal potential of German anti-Semitism started to actively threaten genocide when it was mobilized in the propaganda and street violence of the Nazis.

8   *Small-scale episodes.* Armed violence may be used against another armed force in a limited context, which does not lead immediately to a fully-fledged war. Likewise, such violence may be used against some members of a group, without leading immediately to an overall campaign against the group. Moreover, we can see now that such episodes, involving relatively small numbers of killings, often threaten the all-out destruction of a group's power and a much larger-scale slaughter. *Kristallnacht*, 11 November 1938, the 'night of broken glass' when ninety-one Jews were killed, is a good example of such a massacre. As a result of such experience, we can now detect genocidal tendencies in other movements, even if large-scale genocide may still be some way off. Genocide may be discerned, therefore, in relatively limited mass killing, short of anything that immediately threatens the destruction of the whole enemy group. The concept of *genocidal massacre* has been proposed to cover such smaller incidents, which are often a prelude to larger-scale genocide. These are particularly indicative when they are linked to other forms of targeting of given social groups. Understanding their dangers can help to identify the early stages of genocide, and halt the escalation in policies designed to destroy social groups – which may lead to extensive mass killing. Thus, in the sense of genocide proposed here, Nazi policy was already becoming genocidal in the 1930s, in relation to Jews, as well as to homosexuals and mentally defective people who were physically attacked in this period. It was clearly so during 1939–41, when Jews were transported across the territory of conquered Poland and forced into ghettos. Not only did maybe half a million Jews and many others die of ill treatment, starvation and disease during this period. These were already policies designed to comprehensively destroy the social power, and existing conditions of social life, of the Jews, well before any comprehensive plans for slaughter were evolved. Moreover, it was not only Jews, but Poles in general, who were targets of genocide in this period. (This multiply genocidal character of Nazi policies was accepted in the Nuremberg trials after the Second World War.)

9   *Extent of killing.* War can often achieve its ends without wholesale killing of the enemy. Likewise, genocide does not always involve the slaughter of the majority, let alone the entirety, of the 'enemy' group. This is because perpetrators can often achieve the destruction of a group through relatively limited killings, accompanied by other measures. For example, in March 1999 the Serbian regime of Slobodan Milosevic aimed to destroy the Albanian community within Kosovo, primarily by expelling large numbers of its members from the province. In this context, the killing of around 10,000 people, and the forcible eviction and deportation of many others, was more than

sufficient to terrorize over a million people out of Kosovo. Many who were not personally forced to leave nevertheless fled on hearing of the murder and terror that was being practised elsewhere in the province.

10   *Conflict.* War is, by definition, conflict between two armed powers. Genocide, likewise, is conflict. Although typically one side is initially unarmed, this may change, because genocide – even when successfully perpetrated in the short term – can never be uncontested. However unequal the initial struggle between the organized power that wishes to destroy and the group whose power and lives are attacked, in the course of time that struggle is likely to become more balanced. Groups targeted for destruction cannot but resist by whatever means they can find. However help-less most of the victims may be, much of the time, there are always passive resisters. There is also usually forcible opposition, sooner or later, either from the population that is directly attacked, or from other forces that see their interests implicated in what is going on. Since genocide usually occurs in the context of international polit-ical conflict and wider warfare, victim groups will look for, and often find, more powerful allies. All-out slaughter may be avoided because genocidal processes are halted. Indeed, genocide is *gener-ally* ended in war, by more conventional military forces, as Soviet and Anglo-American armies ended the Holocaust. This is another reason why we should understand genocide as a form of war.

What I have argued about the relationships between war and genocide was summarized in table 2.2, above. This shows the char-acteristics of genocide as a type of war, and shows how modern degenerate war combines characteristics of war and genocide and serves as a bridge between the two. Of course, as with any typology, characteristics are given in abstract forms: any real war will almost certainly combine the features of more than one type.

On slaughter

I have argued that war, revolution and genocide are closely related modes of organized political violence. In the end, revolution and geno-cide can be seen as distinct forms of war. The distinctions are often narrow, and they should not be regarded as absolute categorical differ-ences. Nevertheless, they have considerable continuing significance.

Between strategic bombing and the Holocaust, for example, there is not a simple difference between war and genocide. But there *is* a difference: between degenerate total war as such and genocide as a distinctive form of war in the context of degenerate war. The difference boils down to who the enemy was, and whose power the perpetrators of killing intended to destroy. For the Allies, the prime enemy remained other states; enemy civilians were derivative enemies, and their mass killing was (however terrible) incidental to the major goals of the war. There are strong echoes, of course, in the destruction of the 'derivative' enemy, of the genocidal attack on a civilian population as such. But there remained this slim difference: for the Nazis, Jews – and many other social groups – were enemies as such, whose destruction ranked as an aim alongside the destruction of the enemy states that the Nazis also fought.

This distinction is not one between right and wrong. Degenerate war, as well as genocide, clearly involves breaches of all the norms of war on an enormous scale. The importance of the distinction is, first, that it mattered in practice, and especially to potential victims – although we should note that it was less important to actual victims. When the Allies defeated the German and Japanese states, they stopped killing German and Japanese civilians. The Nazis would probably not have stopped killing Jews until they had eliminated virtually all Jews from Europe. Moreover, the Allies, through their degenerate war, stopped the open genocide of the Nazis. As I have suggested, genocide has often been halted by the military action of other states or armed groups. These have often perpetrated their own atrocities against civilians during their campaigns. However, the distinction between degenerate war and genocide clearly matters in such situations.

The other importance of the distinction is that it continues to reverberate. Directly genocidal policies have come to dominate the war strategies of many local states and state-like movements in the non-Western world. From Yugoslavia (episode VIII) to Rwanda (episode IX), genocide has become a large part of the practice of 'new wars'. A key aim of state elites has been to destroy the power of certain groups, plural urban as well as ethnic communities, and with this the lives of large numbers of their members. In Rwanda, this aim was unprecedentedly open, literally broadcast over the airwaves to simultaneously mobilize perpetrators and threaten victims. In other cases it has been only slightly veiled by more familiar practices of denial.

Post-degenerate, anti-genocidal war?

In contrast, the genocidal implications of degenerate war have stimulated attempts to escape from them, especially in Western military practice. Mainstream war preparation became exterminist in the preparation of all-out nuclear exchanges, and counter-insurgency war became brutally murderous in Vietnam. These led to powerful disarmament and anti-war movements that posed serious challenges to the legitimacy of war fighting and war preparation in Western states. But these controversies stimulated attempts by the West to renew military power in more limited forms of warfare, with more discriminating technology and strategies that avoid genocidal killing.

The contemporary argument about war is partly framed, therefore, by a new version of the mid-twentieth-century dilemma. In its simplest form, the question appears as: can new forms of legitimate warfare be the means to defeat illegitimate, degenerate war and genocide? We can reframe this categorical opposition: can one kind of war end another? It leads to further questions: can mainstream military forces genuinely create forms of war, or of military force short of war, in which its degenerative tendency is controlled? How else can genocide, the war of states against social groups, be halted? Underlying these specific questions is the deeper issue of whether the degenerative tendency of war can be overcome within the military tradition, or only by far-reaching political and social change that will gradually render war superfluous.

There are two main answers to these questions from within military thought and practice. One is the model of 'good' local war in non-Western regions, of legitimate defence against genocidal violence, that could re-legitimate warfare there. Some Western analysts, like Michael Ignatieff (1999), argue that reviving the 'warrior's honour' is an important component of restoring order. For them, recreating the institutions and possibility of legitimate warfare is a priority. Support for these arguments is provided by examples of military campaigns, by local states and armies, which have ended some of the most severe genocidal violence. Thus invasions by Vietnam and Tanzania ended genocidal episodes in Cambodia and Uganda, respectively, both in 1979. The military victory of the Rwandan Patriotic Front ended the 1994 genocide. The campaigns of the Croatian and Bosnian armies played a part in blocking genocidal Serbian rule in Bosnia in 1995. Likewise, the Kosovo Liberation Army played a role, albeit subordinate, in overthrowing Serbian rule in Kosovo in 1999. On the other hand many of these forces practised repressive violence of their own, committing in some cases massacres that may be described as genocidal, if not on the scale of those they defeated. These examples do not, therefore, provide a strong general counter to the perception of the illegitimacy of war.

The second answer comes from developments in the Western way of war. In Kosovo, the major role in defeating Serbian terror was played by NATO, and this campaign was claimed as 'humanitarian'. But this is only a strong version of the general case that the West has reinvented war in a form that escapes the degeneracy of total war and nuclear weapons. After its disgrace and failure in Vietnam, the USA faced the implication that war could no longer be successfully waged without unacceptable levels of casualties both among its own soldiers and enemy civilians. These would be reported by television and so de-legitimize the use of force. This led to the idea of the 'Vietnam syndrome', with its stark consequence that the West could no longer afford real wars. The only uses of force that would survive the rigorous new tests of instant media surveillance would be very limited, quick-fix operations, peacekeeping or at most 'peace enforcement', which would be more like policing than war. This view increasingly became the common sense of Western governments and societies in the late twentieth century. These were, in any case, 'post-military' societies in which mass military mobilization had been ended (Shaw 1991).

Early in the twenty-first century, however, the West was fighting its third war in little more than a decade. The new global era that opened with the end of the Cold War (1989) had produced the Gulf War (1991), the Kosovo War (1999) and the 'war against terrorism' which opened in Afghanistan (2001–2) and threatened to spread to other regions. In these conflicts, US-led, Western-centred coalitions fought a new kind of war, which represented a serious attempt to escape the Vietnam syndrome. New, more precise bombing appeared to bring war back within the limits of the 'just war' tradition, with 'collateral damage' to civilian lives that was merely 'accidental' and more 'proportional' to the advantages of ending or punishing aggression. What I shall call *risk-transfer militarism* (see episode X) appeared to overcome the visible degeneracy of earlier Western warfare. However, since much of the risk was transferred to civilians, there were still strong echoes of degenerate war.

The questions just posed will reverberate throughout this book. In showing how war degenerated and became linked to genocide, I have underlined the huge question mark that hangs over the legitimacy of war in human affairs. In the twentieth century, war was not just a fact of life. It became a huge problem. Mass killing as a key means of resolving political issues became ever more widespread and, simultaneously, increasingly unacceptable. 'War is over,' sang John Lennon: this was a statement of historic redundancy, despite the continuing empirical reality of violence. Is this situation changing in the twenty-first century? The attempts to reinvent legitimate forms of war, especially the new Western way of war, must be taken seriously. Do they represent a new, controlled use of force that will play a constructive role in resolving the most serious problems of our time? Or are they dangerous developments, which fail to overcome the degeneracy of war, and could even contribute to disastrous new escalations of violence? These are the challenges that we – worldwide humanity, including the readers of this book – will have to answer in the twenty-first century.

Further reading

Andreopoulos, G. J., ed. (1994) *Genocide: Conceptual and Historical Dimensions*. Pittsburgh: University of Pennsylvania Press.

Bauman, Z. (1991) *Modernity and the Holocaust*. Cambridge: Polity.

Becker, J. (1996) *Hungry Ghosts: China's Secret Famine*. London: John Murray.

Chalk, F. and Jonassohn, K. (1990) *The History and Sociology of Genocide: Analyses and Case Studies*. New Haven: Yale University Press.

Charny, I. W., ed. (1999) *Encyclopaedia of Genocide*. Oxford: ABC-CLIO.

Cohen, S. (2001) *States of Denial: Knowing about Atrocities and Suffering*. Cambridge: Polity.

Conquest, R. (1986) *The Harvest of Sorrow: Soviet Collectivization and the Terror Famine*. London: Weidenfeld & Nicolson.

Davis, M. (2001) *Late Victorian Holocausts: El Nino Famines and the Making of the Third World*. London: Verso.

Fein, H. (1993) *Genocide: A Sociological Perspective*. London: Sage.

Horowitz, I. L. (1997) *Taking Lives: Genocide and State Power*. Brunswick, NJ: Transaction Publishers.

Ignatieff, M. (1999) *The Warrior's Honour*. London: Chatto and Windus.

Kaldor, M. (1999) *New and Old Wars: Organized Violence in a Global Era*. Cambridge: Polity.

Kuper, L. (1981) *Genocide*. Harmondsworth: Penguin.

Lemkin, R. (1944) Axis Rule in Occupied Europe. New York: Carnegie Foundation for International Peace.

Mann, M. (2001) The colonial darkside of democracy. *www.theglobalsite. ac.uk/press103mann.htm*.

Markusen, E. and Kopf, D. (1995) *The Holocaust and Strategic Bombing: Genocide and Total War in the Twentieth Century*. Boulder, CO: Westview Press.

Roberts, A. and Guelff, R. (2000) *Documents on the Laws of War*. Oxford: Oxford University Press.

Shaw, M. (1991) *Post-Military Society*. Cambridge: Polity.

Strozier, C. B. and Flynn, M. (1996) *Genocide, War and Human Survival*. Lanham, MD: Rowman & Littlefield.

Episode II
Stalinism's mass murders

The regime of Joseph Stalin, who ruled the Soviet Union for almost three decades from 1924, was one of the bloodiest in modern history. The non-identical 'twin' of Nazism, Stalinism was the first totalitarianism. Often called 'bureaucratic', Stalin's rule is more precisely described as terroristic and lawless: he harnessed bureaucracy to the ends of arbitrary and violent power. The context of war was strong: the regime could be traced back to the convulsions that the First World War produced in Russian society and politics, and its terror was a kind of permanent war against society. It reached its peak in the Second World War in which the Soviet state fought for survival against Nazi German invasion.

The landmark in the development of Stalin's terror was the violent campaign known as the 'liquidation of the kulaks' at the beginning of the 1930s. This campaign was rooted in the history of the Bolshevik regime, which seized power in the Revolution of 1917. ('Bolshevik' meant majority, as the party had been the larger section of the Russian Social Democratic party at the time of its split from the 'Menshevik', or minority, faction.) During the Revolution, peasants – the overwhelming majority of Russian society, most of whom were very poor – seized large estates, expropri-ating the landowners. Thus the intellectual and worker revolutionaries who took power in the cities faced a large peasant mass, over 80 per cent of the country's population, whose hold on the land was strengthened by the Revolution.

Stalin's power originated in the military centralization of the civil war of 1919–21. The Communist Party (as the Bolsheviks renamed themselves) introduced 'war communism', with a militarized state and economy. The elimination of political opposition to the party, begun even before the civil war, was completed in this period. After the death of the Revolution's founding leader, Vladimir Illych Lenin, in 1923, Stalin succeeded him and carried this process further by eliminating organized opposition within the party as well.

Lenin's 'new economic policy', designed to counteract the over-central-ization of the war period, had allowed peasants to flourish outside party–state control. Gradual collectivization of agriculture, promoted during the 1920s, had only limited results, since the more successful peasants were improving their position as independent producers. By 1929 Stalin saw the peasantry as the central obstacle to his consolidation of total power and his grandiose plans for crash industrialization with the aim of making the

USSR a powerful military-industrial state. At the end of that year, he proclaimed the kulaks the 'enemy' of collectivization and the Soviet regime.

Pushing the party–state machine back into civil war mode, in early 1930 Stalin launched a military-style offensive to 'liquidate' the kulaks as a class. According to this policy, the richest and most 'counter-revolutionary' were to be put in prisons or concentration camps, their property confiscated and their families deported to remote regions. Others were to simply lose their lands and be deported, or moved within their district. In reality, specially constituted armed brigades packed destitute families into railway wagons for long winter journeys to Siberia, without provision for their survival en route. The mode of death recalled Armenia and anticipated the Holocaust. 'The mere sight of the trainloads of deportees, frequently referred to as "death trains", produced a shattering effect.... Crammed into goods wagons, the peasants died of cold, hunger and disease' (Lewin 1968: 506).

The events of the period were marked, writes Moshe Lewin, 'by a wave of disorder, violence, looting, brutality and debauchery which swept the whole country', producing 'an outburst of mass violence the like of which had not been experienced since the horrors of the Civil War'. Many were executed; the terror was hardly confined to kulaks, a category that naturally admitted no precise definition; old scores were settled. 'The entire peasantry felt that it was under attack, and that none could escape the hammer-blows of the anti-kulak campaign' (Lewin 1968: 499, 501). Some peasants protested violently, or by killing livestock to avoid handing them over to the party. Mass suicides, involving whole families, were common. The dispossessed contributed to armies of beggars. The countryside, especially in the Ukraine, the richest agricultural area of the Soviet Union, was devastated. (Stalin's campaign was directed against Ukrainian national feeling, as well as an independent peasantry.)

The excesses of this brutal campaign led to a retreat in mid-1930, but Stalin renewed his attack with even greater determination in the following two years. Through mass killings and deportations, the peasantry was destroyed as a class with a capacity for resistance, and agricultural production declined. At the same time, Stalin exported food from the main agricultural areas, compounding the peasants' defeat with a terrible state-made famine in 1932–3. In the 'terror famine', party and state officials seized grain, held it in secure stores, and even exported it, while millions of peasants starved. As one official is quoted as saying, 'It took a famine to show them who is master here. It has cost millions of lives, but the collective farm system is here to stay. We have won the war.' (Conquest 1986: 47).

It is estimated that at least ten million people died. Millions more were forced into the industrializing cities as well as the rapidly enlarged labour-camp system. The 'liquidation of the kulaks' did not just force peasants to accept collectivization and the destruction of private property. It signalled, before Hitler had even taken power in Germany, the arrival of the totalitarian state. The idea that certain political and social groups were 'enemies', to be 'liquidated' by terror and slaughter, had been established. Now its lethal discrimination was to embrace one social group after another, producing in the end a system of indiscriminate inhumanity in which no individual could feel safe.

From 1930 onwards, Stalin's rule took the form of an all-embracing, personalized, terroristic dictatorship, which claimed even more lives through a series of gigantic episodes of violence. This was a permanent war state, of the kind satirized in George Orwell's *1984*, which needed new enemies and new violence to feed its power. In the purges of the later 1930s, hundreds of thousands of party, state and army officials, as well as workers and peasants, were executed. Labour camps were developed into a gigantic system of institutionalized cruelty, in which millions died from overwork, disease and harsh conditions.

During the USSR's war with Germany from 1941 to 1945, German forces and their allies massacred millions of Soviet civilians and prisoners of war. However, Stalin killed his own citizens on a scale comparable to the Nazis. His camp system and terror swallowed millions of victims. Stalin deported supposed 'enemy' nations, such as the Crimean Tartars, Volga Germans and Chechens, from one end of the Soviet Union to another. As in the deportations of kulaks, so in the deportation of these nationalities, huge numbers died. Soviet victory in the war extended the system of terror to much of eastern Europe. Only after Stalin's death in 1953 did his successors begin to curb the system's arbitrary power, eventually trans-forming Soviet rule into the more routinized bureaucratic repression that lasted until its collapse in 1991.

Further reading

Conquest, R. (1986) *The Harvest of Sorrow: Soviet Collectivization and the Terror Famine*. London: Weidenfeld & Nicolson.

Conquest, R. (1990) *The Great Terror: A Reassessment*, new edn. London: Hutchinson.

Conquest, R. (1991) *Stalin: Breaker of Nations*. London: Weidenfeld & Nicolson.

Fitzpatrick, S. (1994) *Stalin's Peasants: Resistance and Survival in the Russian Village after Collectivization*. New York: Oxford University Press.

Lewin, M. (1968) *Russian Peasants and Soviet Power*. London: Allen & Unwin.

Viola, L. (1996) *Peasant Rebels under Stalin: Collectivization and the Culture of Peasant Resistance*. New York: Oxford University Press.

—— 3 ——

Organizing Violence

War and genocide are *organized* violence, and historically established states have been the major perpetrators of both. Evidently, however, it is not exclusively their work. Insurgents make up a large part of the armed forces actually fighting and killing across the world, today even more than in the past. Citizens armed in paramilitary groups have participated in many genocidal massacres, from the colonial settler extermination of indigenous peoples to the 'ethnic' killings of recent wars. And against such groups, central state power may be instrumental in preventing or controlling violence. Indeed, the right kind of state institutions may be the best guarantee against slaughter.

State power

Nevertheless, there is an intrinsic relationship between killing and state power. As the sociologist Max Weber suggested (see box 3.1), violence is part of what defines the state. A state is an organization that claims rights to exercise particular kinds of violence and to prevent others from doing so. States claim to control the legitimate use of force. As a matter of historical record, most of the mass killing of modern history can be laid at the door of state organizations. States are the practitioners of slaughter *par excellence*.

Box 3.1   Theories of the state

The most widely used definition of the state is Max Weber's (1978: i. 54–6):
'A compulsory political organization with continuous operations will be called
a "state" insofar as its administrative staff successfully upholds the claim to the
monopoly of the legitimate use of physical force in the enforcement of its
order.' His concept, sometimes referred to as the state's territorial *monopoly of
legitimate violence*, has been a foundation of modern thinking about the state.

Following Weber, Anthony Giddens (1985) has analysed the *modern nation-
state* as a 'bordered power container'. In his account, the state's monopoly of
violence is enhanced through other forms of power:

- In pre-modern times, armies fought warlords, bandits and rebels, as well as
  other state centres; internal and external war could not be so clearly
  distinguished. Now society within the state's borders is *pacified*. Violence is
  'extruded' from social relations in general, including the state's own methods of
  control.
- With extensive bureaucratic *surveillance*, states achieve increasingly homogeneous control of the population in their territories.
- The loose boundaries of pre-modern states are replaced by precise
  borders, which are securely policed. Interstate borders are *borders of violence*, demarcating the ordered world inside the nation-state – including
  what Marx called the 'dull compulsion' of capitalist relations – from the
  anarchy without.
- Relations beyond the bordered nation-state are characterized by precisely
  the violence that is overcome within. The flip side of pacification was
  therefore *increased violence between industrially militarized states*, culminating
  in the danger of nuclear war.
- There is a sharpening distinction between *policing*, within borders, and
  military force, without.

Michael Mann has a more flexible model. He sees states as internally
complex, contingent products of the interactions with nations and classes, in
power networks which are 'inside' as well as 'outside' the state. He offers a
looser version of Weber's definition:

1 The state is a differentiated set of institutions and personnel,
2 embodying centrality, in the sense that political relations radiate to and
  from a centre, to cover a
3 territorially demarcated area, over which it exercises
4 some degree of authoritative, binding rule making, backed up by some
  organized political force. (1993: 55)

Although these sociological accounts understand state institutions in
the context of wider social relations, they appear to some critics to encapsu-
late the old relations of a world divided into nation-states and to approximate
the conclusions if not the method of realists (see box 3.2). The character of
states has also changed in important ways (see box 3.5).

Conversely, state power is what war and mass killing are generally about, in the most immediate sense. Slaughter usually involves
the question of which rival state-like organization will prevail over
a given issue, and often which will control a particular territory.
Mass killing is central to what states do to prevail in these conflicts
over issues and territory. Likewise, state control over mass killing is
what happens when they do prevail. In the end, on a large scale, the
question of life and death and the question of the state are largely
the same. The way in which this question is answered is crucial to
the possibilities of peace and justice in the world.

For most international scholars, as well as statesmen, what
counts as a state is an organization recognized by other states as
the 'sovereign' power in a given territory. This concept of *exclusive
territorial authority* is the principal modern idea of the state. The
idea of states as self-sufficient, 'sovereign' entities has also been a
key organizing concept of the academic study of international relations (see box 3.2). Historically, however, different layers of authority often overlapped, and territorial boundaries were looser, so that
states were not such exclusive 'bordered power containers' (as the
sociologist Anthony Giddens (1985) has called modern nation-
states). Likewise, in the last half-century, 'global' ideas have made
'national' sovereignty increasingly contingent upon observing universal standards of human rights, so that sovereignty is not so
exclusive any more.

Box 3.2   International relations and war

The modern study of international relations has focused on power relations
between sovereign nation-states. The field has assumed that modern world
order is based on *anarchic* relations between such units. It has also assumed
that a sharp line can be drawn between 'international' politics *between* and
'domestic' politics *within* states. War has been understood, therefore, as the
ultimate expression of international anarchy. Civil wars within states have been
seen as a secondary category.

- A 'realist' tradition typified by the work of Hans Morgenthau (1985)
  dominated international relations as it emerged as a field of study (centred
  in Cold War America). It assumed that *states were unitary, power-maximizing
  actors competing with each other.*
- Realism mutated into a 'neo-realist' position, formulated by Kenneth Waltz
  (1979), which saw international relations as *a structured international system,
  with states' rivalries conditioned by their relative power capabilities.*

- An alternative 'English School' emphasized that underlying states' rivalries was a framework, however limited at times, of *international society based on norms and values to which all states subscribed* (Bull 1977).

International relations scholars have generally accepted the Treaty of Westphalia (1648) as marking the beginnings of the modern international system:

- Westphalia codified the competition of European dynastic states and the notion of separate international and domestic realms.
- In reality, however, modern international relations appeared only later, after the French Revolution had raised the *nation* as the basis of statehood.
- After 1789, sovereignty – understood as popular, democratic and national, rather than dynastic – became a powerful political ideal, which it had not been in the Westphalian era.

In reality, politics, including violence, within and between states were always linked:

- Interstate wars stimulated revolutionary upheavals, which, in turn, led to new wars – interstate as well as civil.
- As civilian populations became both participants in and targets of war, it became less and less possible to understand any war simply or largely as a matter of international relations.
- Revolution, genocide and war all involved power struggles that cut across the international-domestic divide assumed by international relations scholars.

International relations' constitutive idea of anarchy has been *further qualified by the development of relations between states since 1945*:

- Major West European nation-states and Japan were subsumed into a US-led bloc, strengthening co-operation, at the expense of anarchy, in international relations.
- Revulsion at the slaughter of the world wars increased support for the idea of a common global order. This was partially implemented through new international institutions (the UN system), although the Cold War held back the process for half a century.

Since 1989, there has been a new impetus to develop stronger legal, political and social, as well as commercial, global frameworks. War has increasingly centred on issues of the *violation and enforcement of global norms, expressed in international law*. In this new situation, academic international relations has itself undergone a major transformation. Its domain assumptions (sovereignty, the centrality of the international-domestic frontier) have often been questioned.

Although the authoritative side of the state has often been central to how it is understood, the real core of the state was always the organization of violence. The bottom line of political authority, territorial or otherwise, was the exercise and control of force. Authority was always intimately connected with the use of violence, since in order to become or remain legitimate, a state needed to be able to demonstrate its capacity to use force. It is thus no accident that in the world of modern states 'legitimate' holders of state power are recognized by their *de facto* control of territory. Possession is nine-tenths of the law, and usurpation is no barrier to legitimation. Augosto Pinochet Ugarte, dictator of Chile from 1973 to 1989, was brought before an English court in 1999 to begin answering for killing and torture carried out after he had made himself 'president' by murdering the legitimate, elected holder of the office. The hearings were a landmark, because the judges denied his claim to 'sovereign immunity' from prosecution for abuses committed during his rule. However, it was Pinochet's immunity that was denied; his claim to have been the legitimate 'sovereign' was not overruled.

Statesmen make the distinction between states, inherently legitimate through their mutual recognition, and governments, legitimate because of their factual control over state institutions. Hence the paradox that a usurper like Pinochet can be transformed into a sovereign statesman accepted by 'democratic' politicians. The distinction has actually been reinforced in recent years, as states have attempted to stem the fragmentation of existing states and the multiplication of new ones. Ultimately, however, the distinction is only partial. New states, once they exercise real control, are eventually accorded recognition. It is as true of states as such, as of governments, that their authority rests on force.

Two conclusions about state power follow immediately. First, state power is generally constituted through violence. Would-be state organizations, as well as would-be rulers of existing states, commonly establish their claims by demonstrating their superiority in the contest of force, within a given social space and territory. It follows from this that no fundamental difference can be made between established, sovereign states and insurgent forces. Armed movements that aspire to legitimate authority are state-like organizations. States, on the other hand, are in the end based on 'bodies of armed men', as Karl Marx put it. The difference between a marauding, murderous gang and the most lawful civilized state may be apparent, but they are polar forms of the common category of state.

Second, state power is ultimately maintained through violence. Established states uphold their claims by making apparent, and often by demonstrating, their ability to project force superior to that of other established and would-be state organizations. It follows from this that no fundamental difference can be made between contests involving sovereign versus insurgent forces and contests between two or more sovereign states. 'Civil' wars are as much wars as 'international' conflicts. Likewise, interstate, as well as civil, wars put in question states' fundamental control over society and territory.

Understanding that these categorical distinctions do not represent fundamental gulfs in social reality is highly important in practice. Wars always sharpen all the power relations in which states and state-like organizations are involved. War between one state centre and another intensifies the power relations between those centres and the societies over which they claim authority. War between an established state and a would-be state organization arising from society inevitably causes tensions with other states. Indeed, most wars involve both civil and international elements. This has never been more so than at the beginning of the twenty-first century. Today, the idea of the territorial nation-state is simultaneously universalized as the common goal of all nations and relativized by the growth of global values and internationalized power. The distinction between civil and interstate wars is deeply embedded in theories of war, but it is not always experienced as a fundamental division in practice. What we can say, more plausibly, is that wars remain centred on the contradictions and transformations of state power.

Systems and politics

The prime, interstate form of war is conventionally understood as emanating from international systems; the secondary, civil form from political conflicts within states. As I have suggested, it is more helpful to look at war in general, in the context of the relations and forms of state power as a whole. War is the ultimate way in which power relations are tested by, and conflicts resolved between, state-like collective actors. The character of the power networks in human society has changed over time, and forms of war have changed with them.

War is a near-ubiquitous feature of the more complex human societies that have developed over the last 10,000 years, and arguments about its origins are summarized in box 3.3. Modern ways of organizing and thinking about war as a way of resolving the *anarchy* of relations between different political communities can be traced back directly to Greek city-states – a group of, by modern standards, small communities, without any overarching authority structure, whose conflicts often took the form of war. However, another model of power relations across communities was that of the classic *empires*, like Rome and China. In these complex civilizations, authority relations spread across great distances. Power radiated from centres to peripheries, at which imperial writs ran more thinly and were often contested. War was also central to imperial systems of power. Border regions had to be continually pacified, and invaders repelled; conquest supplied captives who were sometimes sold as slaves and supported social hierarchy in central regions. War arose from several types of conflict: between factions within imperial elites, between centres and local client rulers, and from peasant or slave rebellions.

Box 3.3   War in the development of the state

Competition between human groups often gave rise to killing in the early stages of human history. However, the emergence of organized warfare seems to be linked historically to the development of more territorially fixed agrarian communities in the last 10,000 years.

- This new kind of human economy enabled surpluses, which supported, for the first time, the emergence of distinct groups of warriors. This was considered by Friedrich Engels (1970) to be the foundation of *class division* in general.
- The warrior class was, in turn, the social force that sustained coercive authority relations over large, geographically disparate populations. This was the basis of *statehood*.
- War continued to be the *main business of states* throughout recorded history. Up to the twentieth century, the vast majority of state expenditures were consistently devoted to military purposes.
- It is only in the last 200 years that *policing*, the coercive function within societies, has been separated from warfare between them.
- It was only in the twentieth century that the *social expenditures* of Western states began to overtake their military expenditures. Even then, war was actually a major stimulus to social welfare. States wanted their soldiers to be fit, and had to concede improved rights and living standards in return for military and wartime mobilization. So the *welfare state* came out of the era of world wars.

In the twenty-first century, many national states in the West appear more as agents of social welfare and global economic competition than as military institutions. But this is because national state institutions are integrated into larger Western military structures.

In the rise of modern Europe, the medieval patchwork (with its residual empire and myriad local rulers) was largely replaced, in the sixteenth and seventeenth centuries, by stronger absolute monarchies. Of course, society in general was hardly pacific: hierarchy was based on extreme inequalities; violence was a normal means of exercising power and subduing unrest; arbitrary and abusive power was common. Moreover, larger concentrations of state power grew with the expansion of European empires in the 'Orient' and the 'New World', accompanied by waves of slaughter of people who were often seen, in the religious ideology of the time, as less human than Christian Europeans. In the Americas, the most 'advanced' European societies waged genocidal war, wiped out whole civilizations and instituted the most extensive slave systems since antiquity.

Like their ancient predecessors, modern empires spread authority relations across huge distances, and they were greatly aided in this by improved means of transport and communication. At their centres were large 'pacified' areas of society. Although the development of industrial capitalism stoked up great social discontent in imperial heartlands, more sophisticated states were often able to control this mainly by non-violent means. War remained, however, the usual mode of expanding and pacifying the peripheries of empires and the normal way in which, ultimately, imperial states resolved their conflicts with each other. And war became a key method of overthrowing established state power, especially in the colonized world.

The pacified imperial metropoles, in which expanded middle classes and even parts of the working class were prosperous and more secure in their day-to-day peacetime existence, presented a deep paradox during the twentieth century. Ultimately, these most stable modern systems of power rested on immense organizations of war. Military networks were at the core not only of states but also of economies, societies and cultures. In the end, these returned to society, not only in two world wars but also in many other horrendous conflicts, bringing mass slaughter on an unprecedented scale.

World war to world order?

It is not possible to make neat separations between internal and external factors in the histories of twentieth-century slaughter. The rivalries between empires led in places to the most complete sealing off of national economies, societies and belief systems in modern times; but there were always acute connections between national and international politics. Total-war preparation produced national insulation, but the actuality of war also intensified political conflicts within societies. For a period, in extensive regions, war was increasingly the form of politics within as well as between states. *Totalitarianism* was the state form of total war (see box 3.4). Totalitarian states waged war on classes, races and any group they conceived as enemies; in their hands, more than any others, genocide became a new form of war. In the hands of the democracies, on the other hand, degenerate war – strategy by other means – was more common.

Box 3.4   Total war and totalitarianism

The slaughter of innocents has been practised by rulers throughout the ages and by all kinds of modern governments, including liberal democracies. But there were special links between total war, totalitarianism and mass killing. Totalitarian movements openly celebrated the absolute power of life and death which governments took in war. For them, *the total power of war became a model for power in general.*

- Fascist movements were consciously motivated by war experiences. Benito Mussolini (1995), founder of Italian Fascism, wrote of the leading role of the 'trenchocracy' – the 'aristocracy of the trenches' from the First World War. Hitler also exalted this martial solidarity in *Mein Kampf*.
- Both Fascism and Nazism were driven by desires to avenge their countries' war humiliations. Italy, although on the winning side, had lost on the battlefield; defeated Germany had suffered punitive terms from the victorious Allies.
- Fascists glorified military symbols, modelled their political organizations on armies and organized paramilitaries to smash their political opponents and seize untrammelled power.
- Fascist movements in power saw new wars as prime means to satisfy their national ambitions, and state violence as a means of destroying 'enemies' within society.

Communism, in contrast, had an *anti-militarist tradition*. Although Marx and Engels, founders of scientific socialism, took a pragmatic approach to military power, the horrors of total war for the working class spurred Marxists to organize against it at the turn of the twentieth century. Communists split from the socialist mainstream during the First World War, chiefly because Social Democrats were seen as compromised with militarism. The only successful proletarian revolution, in Russia, began with soldiers' revolts against military authority, which the Bolsheviks (as the Communists were then known) encouraged. However, the Communist tradition was thoroughly *militarized* after 1917.

- To consolidate their power, the Bolsheviks had to fight a bitter civil war, and quickly re-established a centralized army. Trotsky, Commissar for War, 'seemed to be burning all he had worshipped and worshipping all that he had burned' (Deutscher, n.d.: 406).
- The centralized military expedient turned into a model. Marxists eulogized military centralization as *war communism*, and applied it to all areas of life. Instead of workers' organizations gaining democratic control, workers were organized into labour battalions; trade unions were militarized.
- This model lent itself well to the total control that Stalin extended even to the party itself after he became its general secretary in 1924.

In both Fascist and Stalinist totalitarianisms, *militaristic command systems* spread throughout economy and society.

- The state was a *lawless* bureaucratic monster: power was often violent and arbitrary. Leaders perpetuated highly personalized rule through widespread terror.
- This terrorist rule had much in common with war: it thrived on the identification of *enemies* who were to be eliminated.
- In Stalin's Russia especially, these were found even at the highest levels of the state machine. In general, however, terror states identified *classes, social or national groups* in the general population as enemies, and waged war on them.
- This kind of policy was facilitated when social enemies were *linked to international enemies*.

Totalitarianism, like total war, was largely a twentieth-century phenomenon. At the beginning of the twenty-first century, surviving Communist states have mostly replaced universal terror with more limited repression, in the context of openings to the market. Nevertheless, the mass-murderous aspects of totalitarian rule remain options for authoritarian rulers, even in the context of less total control. They can even be part of a strategy of nationalist electoral mobilization, as they were for Slobodan Milosevic, leader of Serbian genocides in the 1990s.

The world of militarized empires and totalitarianism, revolution and counter-revolution – itself based, as we shall see, on a deep penetration of war preparation into economy and society – finally exploded in the generalized war of 1939–45. It is important to understand that this war was far more than the single conflict of two alliances that has entered into popular myth. World war was a general cataclysm in which states and proto-states clashed across the globe. It was many wars: wars of alliance versus alliance, state versus state, insurgents versus state, insurgents against each other and of course states against peoples.

Slaughter of combatants and non-combatants alike was universal, but it took many forms. Out of the killing, moreover, world, regional and local victors fashioned new relations of power, while the evils of the defeated, at least, were acknowledged in the new ideas of international justice that developed after 1945. Many old empires were felled, either through outright defeat (Germany, Japan) or through subordination to the newly dominant United States (Britain, France). The USA constructed a new Western bloc of states out of the wartime alliance. The Soviet Union, inheritor of the Russian Empire, created its own bloc out of the extended domain that it conquered in central Europe. The Chinese Communists continued their war to victory over the Nationalists in 1949, reconstituting a unified Chinese state and giving them complete control over the world's largest people.

Together the blocs dominated the world in the second half of the twentieth century. From their origins in the common victory of 1945, East–West relations combined overt rivalry with uneasy, sometimes latent co-operation. Although the Cold War was a real military contest, an 'imaginary war' as Kaldor (1990) called it, in which development and deployment of weaponry substituted for battle, it was also a political system. Bloc rivalry was managed short of all-out war, partly through luck, but also because its mutually destructive character was increasingly recognized. Growing co-operation between blocs complemented their internally co-operative character (especially in the West, where unity was essentially voluntary). Nevertheless the 'war' was for practical purposes won, politically, by one side (see box 3.5).

Box 3.5   From bloc-state to Western-global conglomerate

In the Cold War era, the main forms of state were no longer empires but two giant multinational blocs. The appearance of bipolar symmetry was deceptive, however. The Soviet bloc eventually collapsed, because it was fundamentally weaker than the West.

- Its geographical scope was regional rather than pan-regional.
- Its economic base was chronically backward compared to that of the West.
- Its technological dynamism was concentrated in the military sector and, across the broader spectrum of technologies, it was far behind the West.
- Its political coherence and legitimacy were weak, and it failed to modernize.
- It remained imperial, authoritarian and militarist, while the more advanced Western state was becoming internationalized, democratic and post-military.

In the end, the Soviet bloc fell prey to the twin pressures of Western superiority and democratic-national revolt from within. The Western bloc (North America–Western Europe–Japan) survived and formed the basis of an extensive conglomerate of state power that dominates at the beginning of the twenty-first century.

- Western nation-states have largely pooled their traditional 'monopolies of violence', so that the bloc (centred on NATO), rather than the individual state, is the primary organizer of legitimate armed force.
- There are overlapping layers of state power – e.g. European, Atlantic and global, as well as national – and the role of national state institutions has changed.
- The internationalization of the Western state means that many boundaries between nation-states are administrative conveniences, not borders of violence.
- Democracy has been normalized in the West, and formal imperial systems dismantled.

This Western conglomerate is also the main basis of the developing global layer of state institutions.

- Western states provide most funding and personnel, and define most of the direction, of the UN system – although non-Western states have significant voices.
- When local wars are defined as 'global crises', and UN-authorized interventions take place, it is usually because Western interests are engaged or Western public opinion mobilized, e.g. by media coverage of human suffering.

Thus the *pacification* of the industrialized North in the second half of the twentieth century grew, paradoxically, out of the most total armed rivalry ever seen. State institutions became preoccupied with economic growth and competition, even with social welfare, to the extent that some scholars argued, mistakenly, that 'complex interdependence' had pushed warfare out of its defining role in interstate relations. Within the Western bloc, internationalization proceeded apace, as durable military alliances (the North Atlantic Treaty Organization, the US–Japanese alliance, etc.) were complemented by a proliferation of economic institutions (including the Group of 7, the Organization for Economic Co-operation and Development and what was later to become the World Trade Organization). Democratization of national – and in Europe, to a limited extent, regional – state institutions, sometimes seen as the cause of peaceful relations, was in reality a part-consequence of internationalization, as political structures were standardized across the Western bloc.

According to conventional realist ideas of international order, the Western alliance should have gradually fallen apart once its Soviet rival was vanquished. However, despite economic rivalries between North America, Europe and Japan, a unified military-political West has survived into the twenty-first century. The rich West, with one-fifth of the world's population but nearly four-fifths of its wealth, trade and arms, has rediscovered its common interests *vis-à-vis* still powerful authoritarian or semi-authoritarian states like China and Russia as well as 'rogue' states like Iraq and Serbia and local warlords in parts of Africa. It has found its own internationalized institutions and even the layer of global institutions more, not less, useful in legitimating Western dominance and, at times, in actually managing new contradictions.

The demise of the bloc system has led, therefore, to new relations and forms of power, just as the crisis of the inter-imperial system led to the Cold War bloc system in the middle of the twentieth century. Although the United States remains the pre-eminent nation-state, it is not simply dominant. The 'American century' has passed; its high point was the decade after 1945. At the beginning of the new era, it is not a single nation that dominates, but an internationalized, pan-Western conglomerate. The West increasingly integrates not only the triangle of America, Western Europe and Japan, but also many medium-sized and smaller national states. It mobilizes global norms, based on universal democracy and human rights, but much of the running for these comes from popular movements and non-governmental organizations. On the other hand, the West is divided economically, politically and ideologically in its responses to the new demands placed upon it by global leadership. The United States has often acted unilaterally and preferred to work through bilateral relations with its allies and other important states, rather than develop the pan-Western and global institutions that European leaders tend to prefer.

The end of the Cold War has stimulated a *general crisis of state power* in the non-Western world, and not only in the former Soviet bloc itself. Across the Third World the Soviet Union no longer supported its former allies; the West too no longer saw a decisive interest in supporting authoritarian client regimes that jarred with its 'democratic' ideology. Indeed, the democratic revolutions in former Eastern Europe in 1989 led to a powerful surge of democratic movements, from South Africa to South Korea to Chile and Indonesia, that removed authoritarian pro-Western regimes during the 1990s (see box 3.6). The combination of Western victory and popular protest led to transformations of state power at three levels: the inter-bloc system itself, the blocs and states within the blocs. In the former Soviet bloc and in much of the Third World, state crisis took the widespread forms of fragmentation and partial collapse of existing state structures. As with earlier imperial collapses, these state crises led to wars. Sections of old state elites and would-be new elites mobilized support on the basis of nationality and tested their power through violence against each other and against the 'enemy' national groups. The general context of democratization, promoted by the West as well as by popular democratic movements, actually intensified conflict, especially where democracy threatened to lead to secession from existing states. There was a widespread outbreak of 'new wars', sometimes mislabelled 'civil' or 'ethnic' conflicts, in which state power was recomposed – often through genocidal reorganizations of society.

Box 3.6   *State crisis, democratic movements and genocidal war in the non-Western world*

In contrast to the internationalized Western bloc, non-Western states often maintain:

- authoritarian or (despite formal democratization) semi-authoritarian rule;
- huge gulfs of income and wealth between elites and the poor, both rural and urban;
- quasi-imperial forms of rule over minorities (indeed, many states, such as Russia, China, Turkey, Indonesia and Ethiopia, are based on historic empires).

In the last decades of the twentieth century, democratic reform spread across the non-Western world. Although often seen as an elite process (sponsored by the West), democratic change has often resulted from popular – even revolutionary – movements that have challenged elites and appealed to global human rights principles. There have been varied experiences of conflict:

- In some cases, as in East-Central Europe in 1989 and South Korea in 1994, movements have been peaceful, and old elites have surrendered power with minimal violence.
- In others, like South Africa in the early 1990s and Indonesia in the late 1990s, the handover of power has been agreed between the old dictatorship and new elected rulers, but accompanied by considerably more on-street violence in peripheral regions.
- In still others, such as Serbia, Rwanda and Zimbabwe, democratic transition has been strongly contested: old elites have clung to power and unleashed extensive violence against opponents.

Thus the new spaces for political and social conflict that democratic reform opens up can also lead to extreme conflict. Where democratization has allowed ethnic-national political movements to challenge the quasi-imperial character of the state, counter-revolutionary violence has often taken the form of *genocidal war*. Thus democratization has been accompanied by extensive violence in cases like East Timor (vs Indonesia), Bosnia and Kosovo (vs Serbia) and Rwanda. This is described as 'state fragmentation' or even 'state failure', but it often involves strong, repressive states – and the formation of new states.

There is thus a deeply unfinished global democratic revolution, as people, especially in the non-Western world, demand democratic rights and accountability and challenge quasi-imperial, authoritarian or semi-authoritarian states. Behind these demands, of course, lie, huge demands for socio-economic reform, as the billions of poor people aspire to the vastly higher living standards of the West and, indeed, of urban elites worldwide. In the world of the twenty-first century there is a profound turbulence in state relations, which is far greater than the ramifications of the end of Communism. Behind it lie continuing crises in the world economy and society and their inequalities. This turbulence could mean more, rather than fewer, occasions for war.

Future wars

Much writing about the future of war speculates about the possibilities emerging from how war is prepared, in military organization and above all technologies. At the beginning of the new century, as throughout the old, these are changing rapidly, and there is a temptation to think that war's future will be radically different from its past. More sociologically oriented thought focuses on changes in the world economy, the shifts in patterns of activity to the non-Western world and the possibly violent significance of the vast social inequalities.

Both kinds of speculation can tell us only so much about what is likely to happen. Technological changes open up possibilities in how people think about force; but they often remain at the level of ideas. Most war preparation remains just that; it stays unrealized in battle. On the other hand, although broader economic and social crises certainly lie behind continuing dangers of war, they do not generally translate directly into violent conflict. Likewise, shifts in economic power do not translate simply or automatically into new military relations. Although poverty cheapens lives and creates conditions in which states take them lightly, highly unequal societies can exist without mass slaughter.

War is still the continuation of *politics* by other means. We can identify the possible causes and courses of future wars only by examining fractures of political power – the prime contexts of violence. The emergent structure of world politics has already disclosed many possibilities of killing. 'New' wars have been phenomena of more than the disintegration of the Soviet bloc, communism or even the bloc system as a whole. They are symptoms of a new wave of political struggle across the world. Ideas of universal democracy, human rights and national freedom are taking new hold. But they are meeting with resistance, often violent, from rulers old and new.

The equation of democracy with peace (see box 3.7) has been lodged in thought since the writing of Immanuel Kant at the end of the eighteenth century. It was much revived as the Cold War ended, but it is obvious that it does not hold in any simple sense. As we have seen, democracy has been as much an effect as a cause of pacification in the modern West. Conversely, democratic movements, because they challenge established power, often provoke violent repression. If democratization is a turbulent process, then, like any revolutionary movement, it can be warlike. Moreover, we should not forget the sombre idea, first proposed by Carl von Clausewitz after the French Revolution, that the involvement of the people in war adds to its intensity.

Nor should we ignore the fact that national democratization often involves identifying people of different nationalities as

Box 3.7   A democratic peace?

International relations theory has traditionally argued that wars result primarily from the anarchic structure of the international system, not the 'domestic' characteristics of states. However, in the last decade, some American political scientists (e.g. Doyle 1983) have argued that democratic states do not go to war with each other. The fact that democracies like the USA and Britain fight a lot of wars is because, it is argued, they are involved in conflicts with non-democratic states and movements.

Certainly, totalitarian states like Stalinist Russia, Nazi Germany and Maoist China have shown a particular propensity to extensive, genocidal violence. But they are not always externally aggressive in the manner of Nazism: both Stalin and Mao avoided war with the West, in recognition of the latter's greater international power. Democratic America, on the other hand, sometimes upped the stakes in the Cold War because of its stronger position.

More mature democratic states have tended not to fight each other, on the other hand. But this is as much because they have formed military alliances (e.g. NATO, USA–Japan) as because of their political systems. Indeed, democratization has often been a consequence of military alliance rather than a cause of alliance or peace (thus formal democracy has become the political norm within NATO, whereas in the early days of the alliance it included authoritarian states).

Democratization has often been associated with violence: thus democratizing states, like Serbia and Croatia in the 1990s, often fought wars both against each other and against ethnic groups. 'Democratic peace' is too simple, as an empirical hypothesis, and we need a more complex historical account of the relationships between democracy and peace.

enemies. The depressing fact is that state elites have often been able to create democratic legitimation even for genocidal wars: Slobodan Milosevic, a war criminal to most of the world as well as to his victims in Croatia, Bosnia and Kosovo, remains a national hero to many Serbs. Worse, the idea that elections are essential legitimations of national projects has actually motivated much of the so-called ethnic cleansing. Driving out potentially disloyal national groups creates pliant, homogeneous electorates. International institutions, often more concerned with the form of democracy than its substance, may then be called upon to validate the results of the exercise.

If national democracy can be compatible with war and genocide, global democracy creates different standards. The powerful idea that human rights are universal provides a basis for opposing any violations. Those who appeal to it in support of their particular interest must, in principle, support it for others. In practice, of course, people are often very selective in their application of common principles. In political struggle, global norms (like national interests) require social force to make them viable. It is a sad reality that the global institutions charged with realizing these ideas are often inadequate. Neglect and even betrayal are norms: for example, the pattern of international forces handing over civilians to slaughter by genocidists is disturbingly well established from Rwanda to Bosnia and East Timor.

Thus transformations of state power have at best a double-edged significance for warfare. The pre-eminence of the West is such that it is unrealistic to think that Russia, China, India or any major non-Western country could make an overall challenge for world dominance. These centres are all greatly preoccupied with their own modernization, actual and potential internal challenges, and rivalries among themselves. Elites seek accommodations with, entry to and advancement through Western-dominated world markets and institutions. Post-military culture, with its de-legitimation of traditional military institutions, has made advances in many populations; people are not always as willing as before to see young men become cannon fodder.

Nevertheless, non-Western states possess the means of war in abundance, as well as a continuing capacity to mobilize troops and populations. As the Russian war in Chechnya showed right at the beginning of the new century, the largest states are able to prosecute brutal campaigns against civilian populations with almost complete international impunity. Although the West has fought wars against both Iraq and Serbia, even lesser states may calculate that the risk of serious Western military intervention in any given local war is low. After Yugoslavia, any optimism that the costs of war – isolation, sanctions, economic decline, mass emigration – will necessarily deter elites from war and genocide must surely be dismissed.

Worst cases for future war must therefore include at least war between major non-Western states, even up to and including the sort of nuclear exchange threatened by the arms race between India and Pakistan. Such wars, even if limited, or halted early by Western and UN intervention, could certainly involve catastrophic numbers of casualties. There were few major, old-style interstate wars in the latter part of the twentieth century. The long Iran–Iraq war of the 1980s, with its missile 'war of the cities' as well as its 1914-type trenches, can too easily be dismissed as the last gasp of an old way of war. State power, even in the Middle East, politically the least transformed region of the world, has certainly moved on rapidly since that time. But it is too early to say that we have seen off the danger of this kind of mass slaughter.

If worst cases include war between major non-Western states, they must also include war between the West and one or more of these states. Western leaders have mostly taken care to become militarily engaged only with smaller centres, categorized as 'rogue' states outside international norms, and which can be defeated with sufficient force and determination. Yet Western, especially US, military spending remains at Cold War levels, and under George W. Bush is pushing back towards the peaks of Ronald Reagan's 1980s rearmament. US forces are prepared to fight not merely Iraq or North Korea but, in theory, Russia or China – or even both. The oscillation between diplomacy and force, especially on the part of a USA that still resists extensive development of global state institutions, reminds us of disturbing potential for utterly disastrous conflict.

These darkest possibilities are much less likely, it is true, than the widespread recurrence of more localized wars, involving smaller centres, or the intervention of only one great power or global state force, that have been the norm both during and since the Cold War. Outcomes of both kinds will depend on how far, how fast and in what forms political transformation takes place. With the humbling of Russian power, China's modernization has been impressive, and it is no accident that new cold warriors in the West have found in China the surrogate Cold War rival that they have sought since 1989. Yet the crisis of Chinese authoritarianism, suppressed since the Tiananmen Square revolt in that year of change, remains latent. The promise, as well as the dangers, of a transition in the world's largest (and last big fully authoritarian) state has a profound significance for the future of war. Political change as much as old-fashioned interstate rivalries will dictate the kinds of war that take place in the century to come.

Further reading

Barkawi, T. and Laffey, M., eds (2001) *Democracy, Liberalism and War: Rethinking the Democratic Peace Debate*. Boulder, Co: Lynne Rienner.
Bull, H. (1977) *The Anarchical Society*. London: Macmillan.
Dandeker, D. (1990) *Surveillance, Power and Modernity*. Cambridge: Polity.
Deutscher, I. (n.d.) *The Prophet Armed: Trotsky 1917–23*. New York: Vintage.
Doyle, M. (1983) Kant, liberal legacies and foreign affairs. *Philosophy and Public Affairs*, 12 (3), 203–35.
Duffield, M. (2001) *Global Governance and the New Wars*. London: Pluto.

Engels, F. (1970) *Origins of the Family, Private Property and the State.* In K. Marx and F. Engels, *Selected Works,* vol. III, Moscow: Progress Publishers, 204–334.

Giddens, A. (1985) *The Nation-state and Violence.* Cambridge: Polity.

Halliday, F. (1994) *Rethinking International Relations.* London: Macmillan.

Hanson Davies, V. (2001) *The Western Way of War.* London: Faber.

Holsti, K. J. (1996) *The State, War and the State of War.* Cambridge: Cambridge University Press.

Howard, M. (1979) War and the nation-state. *Daedalus,* 108 (4), 101–10.

Kaldor, M. (1990) *The Imaginary War.* Oxford: Blackwell.

Kiernan, V. (1982) *European Empires from Conquest to Collapse 1815–1960.* London: Fontana.

Mann, M. (1986, 1993) *The Sources of Social Power,* 2 vol. Cambridge: Cambridge University Press.

Mann, M. (1988) *States, War and Capitalism.* Oxford: Blackwell.

Morgenthau, H. (1985) *Politics among Nations: The Struggle for Power and Peace,* 6th edn. New York: Knopf.

Murphy, C. N. (1994) *International Organization and Industrial Change: Global Governance since 1850.* Cambridge: Polity.

Mussolini, B. (1995) Trenchocracy. In L. Freedman, ed., *War,* Oxford: Oxford University Press, 28–9.

Reno, W. (1999) *Warlord Politics and African States.* Boulder, Co: Lynne Rienner.

Rich, P., ed. (1999) *Warlords in International Relations.* London: Macmillan.

Shaw, M. (2000) *Theory of the Global State: Globality as Unfinished Revolution.* Cambridge: Cambridge University Press.

Tilly, C. (1985) War making and state making as organized crime. In P. B. Evans, D. Rueschemeyer and T. Skocpol, eds, *Bringing the State Back In,* Cambridge: Cambridge University Press, 169–85.

Waltz, K. (1959) *Man, the State and War.* New York: Columbia University Press.

Waltz, K. (1979) *Theory of International Politics.* Reading, MA: Addison-Wesley.

Weber, M. (1978) *Economy and Society,* 2 vol. Berkeley: University of California Press.

Episode III
Nazism, war and the
Holocaust

The Nazi regime was murderous to an almost unimaginable degree. It is well known to have been responsible for the murder of as many as 6 million Jews. But it also perpetrated the genocidal killing of (according to the best estimates available) as many as 10 million Slav civilians (including Poles, Russians, Belorussians and Ukrainians), 3 million Soviet prisoners of war, 250,000 Roma, over 200,000 homosexuals and up to 100,000 people with mental and physical disabilities. What drove this regime to such a horrific orgy of destruction?

National Socialism was a lawless product of total war. This truly warful movement used force freely to win, consolidate and extend its power. From the beginning, the Nazis celebrated violence, glorified war and demonized their enemies, within Germany and without. They promised to restore German greatness, following their humiliation at Versailles, by defeating not only other states but those social groups that in their national-racist ideology they saw as hostile to the German *Volk*. *Vis-à-vis* state enemies, especially 'Bolshevik' Russia, this meant German military victory. For the 'non-Aryan' peoples and groups whom Nazism defined as inferior or hostile, it meant appalling oppression. But what determined the extent of the violence to which people were subjected? How and why did demonization lead to killing the members of enemy groups and eventually the deaths of huge numbers of people – indeed the destruction of whole populations?

From their beginnings, the Nazis had identified the Jews as both a particular enemy and a decisive element in the 'international conspiracy' ranged against them. From the early days of his movement, Hitler's anti-Semitic rhetoric was highly threatening, and violence against Jews as well as the Nazis' political enemies was an important element in Nazism's drive to power in Germany. From 1933, when Hitler gained power, he simultaneously introduced discriminatory legislation and orchestrated street violence against Jews. In 1935 the racist Nuremberg laws were enacted; in November 1938, on *Kristallnacht*, synagogues were destroyed, Jewish shops were looted, ninety-one Jews were killed and 30,000 were thrown into concentration camps.

However, it was supposedly mentally incompetent Germans who were killed in large numbers before the outbreak of war in 1939. Of the 500,000

Jews in Germany and 200,000 in Austria (which Hitler annexed in March 1938), state terrorism had driven out half by this time, but large-scale mass killing had not begun. But with the invasions of Czechoslovakia (March 1939) and especially Poland (September 1939), Nazi power demonstrated new depths of brutality. Special action squads were sent to kill thousands of Polish political and intellectual leaders. Millions of Poles, non-Jews as well as Jews, were transported. Jews from western Poland, which was incorporated into the German Reich, were expelled into the east, which was under direct military rule.

The war against the Jews

In Poland, the Reich conquered Europe's largest Jewish population (3 million). The Nazis entertained ideas for a 'territorial solution' in which Jews would be dumped on the island of Madagascar, part of the newly conquered French empire. But the course of the war prevented any serious pursuit of this proposal. Instead, Polish Jews were rounded up, transported (often without food or even water) and concentrated into swollen, disease-ridden, poorly provisioned ghettos in the major cities and in forced labour camps. Very many died, as was intended, through cruelty, overwork and starvation. These policies (directed against Gypsies as well as Jews) were already genocidal.

Through conquest, killing of political enemies, mass transportation, ghettoization and labour camps the Nazi state demonstrated that Jewish lives were especially cheap. While many Jews were killed in the targeting of Polish leaders, direct mass slaughter of Jews as such was still not widespread. But when the Nazis invaded the Soviet Union, in June 1941, they deployed extreme brutality against the entire population. Soviet military and civilian resistance was seen by Hitler as a licence to 'exterminate' enemies. Mass slaughter of prisoners, partisans and the general civilian population began.

As Christopher Browning puts it:

If the Nazi regime had suddenly ceased to exist in the first half of 1941, its most notorious achievements in human destruction would have been the so-called euthanasia killing of seventy to eighty thousand German mentally ill and the systematic murder of the Polish intelligentsia. If the regime had disappeared in the spring of 1942, its historical infamy would have rested on the 'war of destruction' against the Soviet Union. The mass death of some two million prisoners of war in the first nine months of that period would have stood out even more prominently than the killing of approximately one-half million Jews in that same period. (Browning 1992: p. ix)

It was in this context that the mobile killing groups slaughtered Russian Jews, chiefly through shooting, and even burying them alive in freshly dug pits. 'Within five *weeks* of the German invasion of Russia,' noted Martin Gilbert, 'the number of Jews killed exceeded the total number killed in the previous eight *years* of Nazi rule' (emphasis original, quoted in Markusen and Kopf 1995: 135, n. 46). Within eighteen months an estimated 1.4 million Jews had died. This extraordinarily brutal paramilitary campaign was almost as destructive as the more clinical mass extermination that succeeded it.

Just after the beginning of the war, Hitler had ordered a 'euthanasia' programme, designed to kill mentally handicapped people in Germany itself, in which gas chambers disguised as showers were first devised. Later, mobile 'gas vans' accompanied the mass killing in the east, and experiments with mass gassing began in camps. By late 1941, however, the Nazi elite had decided on a programme of mass extermination. Jewish ghettos across Europe were cleared, their populations relocated to the camps that became killing centres, with gas chambers and crematoria which 'processed' the victims. At Auschwitz-Birkenau alone, the largest and most notorious centre, 1.3 million Jews may have been killed from late 1941 to late 1944.

The Nazi state waged war on Jews and other civilian groups as part of its war against the Soviet Union and other state enemies. The war was the context in which the Nazis came to control a large Jewish population, so transforming the fantastical 'Jewish problem' of Nazi ideology into a threat to millions of lives. The context of overwhelming, all-round violence, especially on the eastern front, made it easy for the Nazis to perpetrate their crimes. Total political control enabled them to terrorize non-Jewish populations into accepting these crimes (indeed, many anti-Semites in Poland and elsewhere welcomed them and participated in the killing). It also helped the Nazis to hide the genocide, to some extent, from the outside world.

Some courageous Jews resisted the clearing of the ghettos, and others fought as partisans. But the genocide, which had developed within the Nazi war drive, was defeated only by the counter-offensives of the Soviet Union and the Western Allies. As the Red Army approached, camp officials began to dynamite crematoria and force-march surviving inmates to more westward camps, which in turn were also liberated.

Before long the Holocaust, as it eventually became known, was general public knowledge in the West. Western states had known of it for longer, but – despite the pleadings of Jewish organizations and others – had not seen either its exposure or its ending as a priority. In the aftermath of the war, however, this most heinous of the Nazis' crimes came to stand for all of them – a process which has been accentuated in recent years. In the short run, the crime of the Holocaust appeared to overshadow the crimes and failings of Stalin's Russia and the Western powers, and legitimated the new United Nations system. In the long run, it became the undisputed paradigm of the newly recognized crime of genocide and an inspiration for a global order based on human rights, in which state power would be universally accountable.

Further reading

Browning, C. (1992) *The Path to Genocide: Essays on Launching the Final Solution.* Cambridge: Cambridge University Press.

Davidowicz, L. (1985) *The War against the Jews.* London: Penguin.

Goldhagen, D. J. (1996) *Hitler's Willing Executioners: Ordinary Germans and the Holocaust.* New York: Little, Brown.

Gordon, S. (1984) *Hitler, Germans and the 'Jewish Question'.* Princeton: Princeton University Press.

Hamburg Institute for Social Research, ed. (1999) *The German Army and Genocide: Crimes against War Prisoners, Jews and Other Civilians in the East, 1939–1944.* New York: New Press.

Lipstadt, D. (1996) *Denying the Holocaust: The Growing Assault on Truth and Memory.* Harmondsworth: Penguin.

Markusen, E. and Kopf, D. (1995) *The Holocaust and Strategic Bombing.* Boulder, CO: Westview Press.

Mayer, A. (1989) *Why Did the Heavens not Darken? The Final Solution in History.* London: Verso.

— 4 —

Producing Destruction

Slaughter is mostly carried out by states and state-like organizations for their own purposes. It is prepared, however, through ever
more extensive networks within society. *Economies* of violence embrace millions of people who have never actually killed or seen
anyone killed. Although soldiering, making weapons and battle
have been some of men's major preoccupations for thousands of
years, only in modern times have they given rise to the extensive
social organization that we see today.

Industrialism and war

The way in which war is prepared in society is simplified when it is
reduced to explanations of the role of 'economic factors' in war (see
box 4.1). The role of the wider social organization that produces
war is more complex and indirect than many common ideas of it
suggest. What is most important is how the social organization and
fighting of war have been transformed in the nineteenth and twentieth centuries through the *industrialization of war*. This is generally
understood to refer to:

1 the transformation of war through the adoption of industrial
   technology in weapons design;
2 the employment of industrial methods of production, transportation and communication in the supply, deployment and organization of armies.

Box 4.1   Myths about 'economic factors' in wars

Ideas about 'economic' factors are strongly rooted in radical thinking about war, and supported by Marxist ideas of capitalism as its cause. However, these issues are often highly over simplified. We can identify several common myths, each containing elements of truth, but also capable of being seriously misleading:

Myth 1: The need of arms producers to profit from their activities is a prime driver towards war. What matters to arms (and other military equipment) manufacturers is that they can *sell* their products, not that these products are actually used to cause death. True, for weapons to sell, they must be *usable*, and to prove this, some weapons must be used somewhere at some time. Nevertheless, the vast majority of weapons are never actually used to kill people. This is especially true of the most expensive systems, which generate the largest profits for big corporations. Most victims are routinely killed with the cheapest, simplest kinds of weaponry, like rifles and machine guns. Therefore the producers' interest is a general, abstract one. It helps to explain the institutionalization of war in society, but, while it can provide an extra incentive, it does not explain particular wars or killings.

Myth 2: Calculations of economic advantage drive states towards war. Today the internationalized Western state generally fights major wars, in common with some kind of global (UN) legitimation, against secondary state centres or local armed movements. Its conception of its common interests certainly includes maintaining the general conditions for the functioning of the world economy – hence the perception of a threat to world oil supplies in Iraq's 1990 invasion of Kuwait. But common Western interests are also shaped by political values and strategic interests, which are often modified in the actual course of conflicts with other states. Economic interests are therefore only part of states' concerns. Common Western interests overlap, moreover, with competitive national interests. Yet today the main national economies compete with each other peacefully, in market-places, and use political power to gain advantage in this rivalry, rather than direct warfare. Leaders' conceptions of interests certainly include economic factors, like securing strategically important resources for 'their' economies, the success of nationally based corporations, and so on. Ironically, militarily dominant nation-states like the USA use wars to gain economic advantage over their allies, rather than enemies. For example, the USA got passive partners like Germany and Japan to help pay for the 1991 Gulf War, and then cleaned up itself on the contracts to restore Kuwait and re-arm Saudi Arabia. The maintenance of power is often more important to rulers than national economic interests. There are enough examples of state leaders pursuing war to the point of near economic ruin (e.g. Iraq and Serbia in the 1990s) to question the idea that economic rationality drives war. On the other hand, governmental and military elites in zones of conflict, as well as warlords and armed gangs, often have their own financial interest in perpetuating war even in the context of general ruin.

Myth 3: Economic strength determines the outcomes of war. Especially in a relatively symmetrical war between similar kinds of state organizations, the force that has the strongest economic base has a powerful military advantage. So, for example, the strength of the US economy was the prime motor of Allied victory over Germany and Japan in the Second World War. However, a state's *military* strength is not predetermined by economics. What matters in the end is how it mobilizes resources for, and actual deploys them in, military rivalry. A state with lesser overall economic strength may be more effective in mobilizing resources, may utilize them more effectively, or be more determined in its application of them. Many wars are deeply asymmetrical, and the conventionally weaker party may utilize unconventional forms of struggle to defeat its stronger adversary. There are sufficient cases of very powerful states being humbled by lesser adversaries (e.g. the USA in Vietnam) to oblige us to avoid reducing war to economics in this way.

A very obvious manifestation of these trends is the enormous importance of weapons development. Throughout history, the soldier was the key resource in war fighting, and weapons enabled him to kill and defend himself. In the last two centuries, however, the destructiveness of weaponry has increased exponentially through the application of mechanical power. The *machine* gun has provided hugely increased killing power to even the smallest armed force, while more complex weapons, up to and including nuclear warheads, have provided great states with previously unimaginable means of mass destruction. All of this has been accomplished through the gradual application of industrial technology in a relatively short period of time, historically speaking. It places a huge premium not only on access to technology but on the skills required to use and maintain it.

The production and maintenance of weapons systems have increasingly dominated warfare, but the significance of industrial technology has not been limited to weapons. From the first ironclad ships of the early nineteenth century, to the use of railways and telegraph in the American Civil War and of mechanized transport and field telephones in the First World War, improved transport and communications have made just as great a difference. In the twentieth century, these trends accelerated: from air power in all its forms to the computer electronics of recent decades, new technologies have been central. In the twentieth century, moreover, the integration of weapons and transportation became so important that we think not just of weapons but of *weapons systems*, which include the platforms (planes, tanks, aircraft carriers, missile launchers, etc.) from which weapons are launched, as well as the immediate means of destruction.

Many soldiers have become technicians servicing the equipment of war, just as workers in industry are harnessed to productive machinery. Indeed, a new social structure of war developed hand in hand with industrial capitalist society. From the seventeenth century, new methods of military discipline had anticipated the industrial discipline of the modern factory that became widespread from the second half of the eighteenth century. But, the social organization of the factory in turn had powerful implications for military power. It was linked in the early nineteenth century to the making of the working class as a new social force, linked horizontally across national and ultimately world society. Many observed the new class polarization; but Karl Marx was distinctive in believing that it would lead to social revolution and the birth of a new, socialist society. What all these arguments missed was that it was also the creation of a new social base for war. Although many of the soldiers in the new *mass armies* of the nineteenth century were peasants, at the core of the most powerful and successful armed forces were industrial workers. *Worker-soldiers* were the essential new social actors of modern war. Accustomed to the use of machinery and to industrial discipline, workers were the ideal fighters in the new armies – especially in navies and air forces, which often involved the most sophisticated weapons and platforms.

Moreover, since industrialized war needed mass-produced weapons, whole sectors of industry were devoted to it. In *military-industrial complexes*, people we might call soldier-workers produced these weapons. In the world wars, whole national economies became such complexes. Indeed, in totalitarian states, industrial workers – not just in arms factories but in every sector of the 'command economy' – were actually disciplined like soldiers. This kind of development was rationalized politically as, for example, 'war communism' or 'building socialism', or indeed 'national socialism'.

The ways in which armed forces were recruited also changed with industrial society. In the feudal era, soldiers were mostly peasant retainers who owed service to a particular lord. They were armed for particular campaigns, and it was difficult to make them fight away from their home regions. Armies fighting at a distance from their homeland lived off the land, pillaging from conquered people. In modern times, however, more disciplined, professional standing armies began to be created; initially made up of mercenaries, they were then filled with conscripts during the late nineteenth and twentieth centuries. They are now increasingly staffed entirely by highly trained professionals. (For further discussion of armed forces, see chapter 8.)

Armies and political leaders, steeped in old practices and trad-itions, have often been slow to adopt new ideas, technologies and ways of organizing. But military rivalry has eventually led them to turn each and every technological and social innovation to the ends of war. Arms technologies – from gunpowder to rifles and machine guns to chemical, biological and nuclear 'weapons of mass destruc-tion' – have developed exponentially. Means of delivering fighters and weapons have developed through steamships and railways to aircraft, intercontinental missiles and computer-directed 'smart' bombs. Indeed, military industry has become a major source of technological innovation in general, with many spin-offs for civilian production. From the nineteenth century too, with modern means of transportation, it became possible to constantly re-supply and re-equip standing armed forces over long distances. New means of communication facilitated more or less instant co-ordination be-tween governments, commanders and forces 'in the field'.

There is controversy about the causal significance of industrial capitalism for war (see box 4.2). But all agree that the development of capitalism provided states with the *means* of preparing unpreced-ented levels of death. It fed larger populations and kept more people alive longer, with the result that there could be larger numbers of soldiers and greater resources to support them. Capitalist industry accustomed a mass working class to a new kind of factory discipline, partly modelled on the discipline of early modern professional armies, which in turn helped twentieth-century states in moulding huge numbers of conscripts to their ends. Capitalism created mass-production industries, easily converted to produce munitions. It gave armies the technical means, first to mow down each other's expanded forces with unprecedented speed, and then to destroy whole populations more or less instantaneously. The organizational and communications infrastructure of industrialism gave states the new bureaucratic and ideological power of surveillance. With this they could mobilize not only their new mass armies, recruiting majorities of adult male populations, but also the rest of society in supporting roles. Industrial society has not determined new ways of slaughter, but it has certainly enabled them.

Box 4.2   Industrialism, capitalism and militarism

Early in the modern era, some social thinkers believed that the new industrial society would be more peaceful than the old feudal society. According to the early nineteenth-century sociologists Henri de Saint-Simon and Auguste Comte, a society based on science and technology would be a more rational order, in which the residues of war and militarism would increasingly be abolished (Aron 1958). By the end of the nineteenth century, it was evident that industrialism had actually fuelled a new stage of military rivalry between major states.

- The great European, American and Japanese empires used industrially generated wealth to build awesomely powerful armies and navies.
- Arms production became a state-protected sector (later to be called a 'military-industrial complex') within market economies (MacNeill 1982).
- By 1914 the new rivalries had pushed a large part of the world into the greatest war ever seen. This was followed by an even more global conflict in 1939–45. Industrialized war involved new levels of destruction.
- Late nineteenth-and early twentieth-century industrial societies were penetrated by military organization through mass conscription. Culture was penetrated through popular media that glorified armed forces and their imperial exploits. Politics was saturated with aggressive nationalist ideas that mobilized populations for war. Industrial society involved a new militarism.
- Marxist theorists like Vladimir Illych Lenin (1939) and Rosa Luxemburg (1963) argued that militarism was the inevitable outcome of industrial capitalism in its latest stage of empires competing for world markets.
- Later sociologists have questioned this, seeing capitalism as intrinsically neither peaceful nor militarist. Michael Mann (1984) has argued, for example, that capitalism arose within an interstate system already characterized by warfare. Capitalist industrialism, he argues, increased not the number of wars but their lethality.
- In the 'post-war' West of the period since 1945, and especially since 1989, we could almost believe that the idea of 'pacific industrialism' had come true. In the rich part of the world, nation-states no longer fight each other, but are increasingly integrated into a complex conglomerate of power, regulating a prosperous, interdependent consumer society. National state apparatuses are more vehicles of economic competition than military might, seeking not political empire but relative advantage in global markets.
- However, our 'peace' is not an automatic result of industrialism; it has been obtained through the blood-lettings of two world wars. Moreover, Western peace has been based on massive war preparation, as well as scores of smaller wars on the periphery of the Western world. Within the West and other power centres, most of the extreme destructive potential of Cold War nuclear arsenals remains. Managing local conflicts in the non-Western world has driven the West to war in the Gulf and Kosovo, as well as to a series of lower-grade military interventions. Industrialism and war remain linked at the beginning of the twenty-first century.

Not only did industrialism enable new kinds of war; economy and society were themselves transformed by military changes. The practice of war stimulated new technologies, new social relations and new politics. War is wasteful: it destroys rather than produces. But in a society based on expanded production for profit, even destruction creates new demand. Technologies of weapons and military communication could often be adapted to civilian uses, as well as vice versa. The expanded state organization, generated by war, could be used to feed and care, as well as to kill and starve. Wartime solidarity could lead to democracy as well as to fascism.

In modern society, the age-old requirement to prepare the means of war has insinuated itself into social organization in unprecedented ways. In the late nineteenth century, the growth of military organization and culture was a much-remarked phenomenon. By the turn of the twentieth century, the first 'military-industrial complexes', in which states protected arms production from market vagaries, fuelled the first modern 'arms race' over naval power between Britain and Germany. In the first half of the twentieth century, military organization moved to the centre of the economy, society and politics. Two world wars stimulated militarist, statist tendencies in economies and societies, which in turn supported unprecedented practices of mass killing. During these wars, the modern 'war economy' appeared (see box 4.3).

Box 4.3   Classical war economy

The modern Western economy has been pre-eminently a capitalist market economy. Theorists like Karl Marx (1976) assumed that capitalism was a system of generalized commodity production, in which production of exchange values prevailed over that of use values.

The development of large *military-industrial sectors*, in which market values were distorted by state subsidy, was from the beginning a departure from pure market capitalism. By the First World War, however, Marx's followers, such as Rosa Luxemburg (1963), argued that the military sector soaked up surplus capital and so stemmed the tendency for capital to exhaust its profitable sources of investment. Militarism, in Marxist terms, led to a displacement of capitalist crisis by military crisis.

During the First World War, military economy was taken further. Combatant states created the *classic modern war economy*, in which national production as a whole was temporarily subordinated to the demands of war. War economies were improvised in 1914–18 as the anticipated short war gave way to an ongoing system. Ownership of capital remained largely private, but alongside expanded state sectors there was state direction and control of both capital and labour. At the end of the war, states' economic roles contracted once more, but remained expanded as compared to 1914.

In the inter-war economic and political crises, states greatly expanded their control over national economies. In Soviet Russia, state ownership was extended by Stalin from industry to the land, so that the entire economy became what was called a *command economy* subject to military-style direction. In Nazi Germany, although capital remained privately owned, a similar system was developed by the time of the Second World War. In the democracies, state intervention, notably in the American New Deal programme of Franklin D. Roosevelt, was more modest. However, John Maynard Keynes (1919) had influentially advocated state management of demand as a solution for the economic crises of capitalism in the aftermath of the First World War.

The Second World War saw much more sophisticated war economies, in which production was comprehensively planned for war purposes, especially in the USA and Britain. In the aftermath of this war, *Keynesianism* became economic orthodoxy, and state spending on a variety of goods became normal. But the heavy-industrial and high-technology core of the state sectors remained military. In the new Cold War, the Western economy was seen as an *arms economy*, with the military sector driving growth in the economy as a whole (Kidron 1968), while in the Soviet Union the arms sector clearly dominated the economy. As war preparation involved ever more sophisticated technologies, the arms economy became more specialist and capital-intensive. Thus it was less of a driver of whole national and international economies, even if it still had important civilian spin-offs (e.g. the Internet).

Apart from the USA, Western nation-states could no longer sustain comprehensive arms industries; in Europe especially, internationalized arms production developed. Older versions of strategic economic thought, like state ownership, were discarded, as they became irrelevant to military power. An *excessively militarized economy* contributed to the failure of the Soviet bloc, and high arms spending partially disadvantaged the USA *vis-à-vis* Japan and Western Europe.

Since 1989, there has been a relative decline in military expenditure, although the 'pork-barrel' effect of military spending in particular regions, especially within the USA, remains important. In the West, especially Europe, there is greater emphasis on arms exports as a means of sustaining local industries (Lovering, in Kaldor, Albrecht and Schmeder 1998). Arms markets are arenas of state-subsidized international co-operation and competition. These new forms of arms economy in the West often supplied *parasitic* new war economies (see box 4.5).

The key changes were that whole economies and societies became part of the logistical chain supplying the fighting of war. Arms industries and supportive civilian populations were as important keys to military success as were mass armies. They made possible unprecedented 'total' slaughter on the battlefield. They became known as the 'home front', a recognized theatre of war. Not surprisingly, then, the domestic suppliers of war also became new targets: the battlefield came home. Clausewitz had originally argued that war was politics 'by other means'; now war itself was prosecuted by strikingly other means, the slaughter of civilian populations. With the incineration of cities, the mainstream of modern war became mass-murderous. (I explore this question further in chapter 6.) This coincided historically with the development of the direct form of modern genocide, the bureaucratic and industrialized killing of social groups as such for 'political' ends.

In these ways political economies became *economies of slaughter*. These were economies quite as dynamic as market economies. In the build-up to, and fighting of, the world wars, and in the Cold War, intense military competition led to rapid technological improvements and economic growth. 'Pure' genocides, such as the 'liquidation of the kulaks' (episode II) and the Holocaust (episode III), were in the end economically 'irrational', destroying production or diverting resources from economic and strategic goals. However autarchic, totalitarian militarism did force economic development. Hitler solved unemployment, made the trains run on time and built highways. With enormous brutality, Stalin created a modern industrial economy in the Soviet Union, one that could fight off the German invasion and later put the first manned satellite into space. Both used their industrial expansion to forge massive war machines. In their times these were vastly successful, even if Nazi Germany was crushed in 1945 and Stalin's totalitarianism fossilized into the failed Cold War bloc that finally crumbled in 1989–91.

More open, less commandist, economies thrived even more with the stimuli of war preparation. The biggest success of all, of course, was the United States, the ultimate victor of the period of total war. The Second World War turned the New Deal's slow recovery from the Depression of the 1930s into a runaway expansion. Americans lost hundreds of thousands of their menfolk in the war, but they thrived like no other nation in the boom it generated. The USA became a giant scientific, technological and above all mass-production power-house for defeating, first Germany and Japan, and then the Soviet Union. Its economy was best placed of all to exploit more broadly (in both geographic and socio-political senses) the wider benefits of arms-driven industrial strength. With its more open markets and political institutions, it avoided the extra costs of power projection that autarchy, totalitarianism and genocide imposed.

The Cold War thus institutionalized an arms economy both in the USA and in the wider Western bloc (Western Europe, Japan, Australasia) that clustered around it in the second half of the twentieth century. In the early decades after 1945, arms were the most dynamic sector of an expanding US economy, driving what Eric Hobsbawm (1994) called a 'golden age' of growth and prosperity. The USA fought major wars in Korea and Vietnam and supported client regimes in other conflicts. Given the potentially disastrous consequences of actual nuclear war, strategy became increasingly concerned with the balance and political meaning of weaponry, rather than its physical use. The superpower blocs fought what Mary Kaldor (1990) called an 'imaginary war' with their devastating arsenals. Britain, France and China kept, or obtained, their seats at high tables, partly through their nuclear power status; others followed suit, and nuclear weapons 'proliferated'. The USA fought political battles with Germany and, especially, Japan, to try to make them share the economic burdens as well as the gains of arms.

The paradox was that the pivot of the US arms system, its nuclear arsenal, was never used. Indeed, in the armed stalemate of the Cold War, many weapons systems were excessively complex and refined updates of 1939–45 technologies that would not be viable in battle. These relatively useless systems, pouring out of bloated arms industries, created a 'baroque arsenal' (Kaldor 1982).

New technology, new war economy

Deterrent purposes for weaponry could never be divorced from their possible use, so deficiencies demonstrated in actual wars had real meaning. The vulnerability of advanced British warships to relatively cheap Exocet missiles in the 1982 Falklands/Malvinas War symbolized the technological impasse of the Western way of war. But by that time, the USA's historic defeat in Vietnam was already provoking profound rethinking. All-out, mass-army confrontations were to be avoided; indeed, with no draft in the USA, the UK, Japan and Australia, the West 'offshore' of Continental Europe had already abandoned the mass army. Body bags were a real electoral danger, to be avoided at almost all costs. The West would rely on a combination of the 'deterrent' threat of massive force with high-technology fixes, which enabled real wars to be fought without risking large numbers of the West's own soldiers.

Military technology facilitated a new switch in the mode of war, with profound implications for the economy of slaughter. Air power was confirmed as the dominant branch of armed force, bombing ever more the pre-eminent application of fire-power, and the bomber the main delivery vehicle. Yet bombing was now enhanced in striking ways. Computer systems enabled pinpoint targeting. Manned bombers were supplemented by unmanned 'cruise' missiles – those much-sung villains of the 1980s Second Cold War were actually used (albeit without nuclear warheads) against Iraq and Serbia in the 1990s.

Although nation-states continued to foster and protect arms industries, arms were produced increasingly for international markets. Political rivalries continued to drive arms procurement, but economic changes fed them in crucial ways. The huge incomes of oil states in the 1970s enabled Middle Eastern rulers to spend on vastly enhanced armies and provided big new markets for Western and Soviet arms industries. It is no accident that two of the largest regional powers, Iran and Iraq, spent the 1980s locked in one of the most destructive wars of recent times, or that the dirtiest political-financial scandals of the Reagan and Thatcher regimes involved covert arms supplies to these states. The eventual fall-out between the West and Iraq produced major new wars from 1991 into the new century.

Although oil incomes no longer fuelled the rapid growth of the arms trade, the role of markets in arms production continued to expand, urged on by states. For the USA, arms sales cemented world dominance; for Britain, France and China they helped sustain national arms industries, and with them second-rank status; in the post-Soviet region, they helped stem the collapse of state funding. For smaller states, too, especially militarily challenged Western allies like Israel, South Africa and South Korea, exports bolstered national arms industries and secured political connections. Expensive weapons systems continued to make up the bulk of world arms sales measured in dollar terms. But burgeoning markets in small arms involved the most buyers and sellers, and these weapons played the most destructive roles in the new genocidal wars of the 1990s.

In the first half of the twentieth century, huge peaks of arms production occurred during world wars. Tens of millions of arms workers in the major states supplied their national war efforts. Producers did not know exactly when, where and who their weapons would kill, but they knew that they were supplying the millions of 'their' soldiers in a war that was ongoing or expected. At the beginning of the twenty-first century, there are still large workforces in arms industries; these are now spread worldwide, and in some cases production is internationalized. Connections with national military forces are still apparent, but much production is for sale in distant markets, its destination unknown or of little interest to the producers, the particular war in which it might be used usually unspecified.

Economy of slaughter zones

The economy of slaughter always looked very different close-up – in its climax, in defeat, at the points of maximum killing – than in overview. Attenuated survival, in the midst of highly visible death, contrasted sharply with the productive life of armaments workers in the heartlands of victor states. The brutalized half-life of the Jewish ghettos, still more of the 'labour' and death camps, or of the precarious Bosnian 'safe' areas, were worlds away from the 'normal' economies, in which both the forces that threatened them and the forces that might save them were produced. Moreover, genocide has its own economic logic, as perpetrators – especially their local auxiliaries and civilian supporters – eagerly prey on the land, homes and possessions of their victims (see box 4.4).

However, we can trace new patterns in the wars of recent times. The old war economy of all-out, total violence, with national mobilization, was productivist. Moreover, the distinction between where war was produced and where it was fought was partial and relative. Arms factories could become arms targets. Producers

---

Box 4.4   Robbery and genocide

This book has argued that genocide, like war in general, is the attempt by an organized, armed force to destroy the power of a social group through killing (and other means). Genocide is perpetrated primarily by state centres, their armed forces, police and local administrations, as well as paramilitary groups, for reasons of power in general – political, strategic and ideological, as well as economic. However, as the sociologist Michael Mann has emphasized, the role of civilian social groups is also very important in carrying out genocides.

If war and genocide are processes in which societies appear at their most state-led, and states as homogeneous and centralized, there is always an undercurrent of popular participation that adds an important element to their dynamics. In the Nazi Holocaust, there were plenty of local inhabitants – in Poland, the Baltic states and elsewhere – eager to settle scores against local Jews and profit from them. Even in Stalin's war against the kulaks, not only party officials but many peasants used the process for their own ends. While in colonial genocides, Mann (2001) shows, colonists were often more eager than colonial officials to wipe out indigenous peoples and thus steal their land.

Thus theft is often the sub-text of genocide. High officials, soldiers and local inhabitants alike seek to enrich themselves at the expense of the enemy group. Nazi concentration camps notoriously stripped the gold teeth and jewellery from their Jewish victims. Nazi leaders lined their own pockets on a huge scale. Jan Gross's *Neighbors* (2001), a study of a small town in German-occupied Poland, argues that its present inhabitants continue to deny their ancestors' genocidal massacre of the local Jews, partly because they have inherited the land and houses stolen from the victims.

'Ethnic cleansing' often involves civilian perpetrators and supporters moving into farms and apartments vacated. In recent times it has usually seen looting of consumer goods like videos. Often soldiers and paramilitaries have taxed terrified expellees: in 1999, Serbian forces widely demanded payment from Albanian civilians before allowing them to leave Kosovo for the safety of neighbouring countries.

could become victims. Home fronts could become battle fronts, if not through invasion, then through aerial bombardment. Of course this was true in grossly unequal ways. But in world war, everywhere and everyone was vulnerable, at least in principle.

In more recent wars, this unity of war preparation and battle-space has been increasingly broken down. We can increasingly distinguish between the general, worldwide economy of arms and the particular economies of slaughter in the *zones of war* themselves. Of course, the links between the two are important. Local protagonists rely on world networks of supply and support. Arms are bought, openly or covertly, on world markets; likewise, funds are raised from 'transnational' ethnic communities, diasporas and allies, rather than from local and national taxation. However, the main centres of arms production in the advanced West are virtually exempt – occasional terrorist bombs apart – from violent feedback.

In the zones of war, the new war economies are *parasitic* rather than productive (see box 4.5). Fighters are often not paid, but help themselves to the wealth and produce of victim communities – or misappropriate humanitarian aid. As we saw above, robbery is an inevitable accompaniment of genocide, and victims often count themselves lucky if they are allowed to buy their escape. International organizations, even if they intervene for the best of reasons, often find themselves sustaining thinly veiled or even overt economies of violence. Thus, although the political economy of war is now increasingly global, its fluid worldwide networks mock the universal values of 'global' institutions.

Box 4.5   *New political economy of war*

Wars in the early twenty-first century are mostly quite highly localized –
concentrated in specific *zones of war*. However, war frequently spreads across
locales, so that over a number of years chains of conflict create extensive
regions of war.

A paradigmatic region of this kind is the Balkans, chiefly former Yugoslavia, in
which war spread from Croatia to Bosnia to Kosovo to Macedonia in the
decade from 1991. A comparable new war region opened up in the same
period in the former Soviet Caucasus. The Middle East is a long-standing region
of war. In Africa, several such regions overlapped at the beginning of the new
century, with wars in many zones of North, North-East, Central and South-
East Africa interconnected in various ways, in addition to West African wars
linking Liberia and Sierra Leone. A particular concentration could be seen in
the Congo, dubbed by some 'Africa's Great War', where a multi-layered civil
war was compounded by interventions by states such as Rwanda, Uganda and
Angola, all involved in their own local wars, and Zimbabwe, where political
conflict threatened to produce civil war.

Writers like Kaldor (1999) and Duffield (2001) have identified a new kind of
economy in the war zones. The only productive activity tends to be extraction
of valuable primary commodities – above all, minerals and narcotics. Warring
parties, both recognized governments and warlords, prey on this to finance
their military campaigns. Thus the illegal sale of diamonds on world markets
kept Jonas Savimbi's UNITA in Angola and the Revolutionary United Front in
Sierra Leone in the business of war; right-wing paramilitaries and left-wing
guerrillas alike live off the drug trade in Colombia. As farmers are driven from
their land, and workers lose their jobs as factories close, populations – often
forced into refugee camps and other temporary accommodation – become
more and more dependent on humanitarian relief. Governments lose any
'normal' tax base, and become dependent on international support; warlords
and armed gangs sell protection, and prey on relief convoys. All armed factions
buy small arms on the international markets, which have become ever more
open since the end of the Cold War.

Governments and populations in regions surrounding the zones of war are
also drawn into the war economy, as well as often into the military struggle,
creating 'bad neighbourhoods'. War often deprives regional producers of their
markets and destroys tourism. Although Western attention focuses on refugee
flows into Western states, most refugees actually move into neighbouring
states. International assistance then provides partial compensation for market
losses – but widens the dependence on the West that results from wars.

Western state power maintains its own vast, part-national and
part-internationalized infrastructure of armed force, accounting in
total for well over half of world military expenditure. The purposes

of this war preparation are not altogether clear even to the politicians and planners. At worst, since the end of the Cold War the US leadership has still envisaged fighting major wars against Russia and/or China, as well as lesser 'rogue' states. Yet, there is a serious mismatch between the wars that militaries are preparing for and those for which politicians are preparing society. Some of the consequences of this disparity have been on view in the difficulties of mobilizing public acquiescence during the more serious, if still lesser, wars of recent times.

For neither state nor society in the West is war preparation such a strong symbol of national security as it used to be. Both state and society, indeed, relate equivocally to the new political economies of war. Western state power preaches non-violence and democratization even as it continues to supply states worldwide with lethal machinery of violence – as well as continually developing its own very large forces. Western society responds generously to 'humanitarian crises' as a result of distant wars, and the Western states sometimes intervene. At the same time, both society and state continue to welcome the benefits of the arms industries that remain at the centre of many local, regional and national economies, and which in turn supply these wars.

The chains linking war preparation and war are as real in the global world as they were previously. Indeed, they are more extensive and internationalized. But the loosening of the direct links between the supply and fighting of wars means that the full extents of these chains are less clear even to those directly involved. They are less visible still to larger publics, with considerable consequences for our awareness of the issues they raise.

Further reading

Aron, R. (1958) *War and Industrial Society*. Oxford: Oxford University Press.
Bayart, J.-F., Ellis, S. and Hibou, B. (1999) *The Criminalization of the State in Africa*. Oxford: James Currey.
Berdal, M. and Malone, D. M., eds (2000) *Greed and Grievance: Economic Agendas in Civil Wars*. Boulder, CO: Lynne Rienner.
Berghahn, V. R. (1984) *Militarism*. Cambridge: Cambridge University Press.
Bukharin, N. (1972) *Imperialism and World Economy*. London: Merlin.
Calvacoressi, P. and Wint, G. (1974) *Total War: Causes and Courses of the Second World War*. Harmondsworth: Penguin.
Carr, E. H. (1966) The Marxist attitude to war. In *The Bolshevik Revolution 1917–1923*, vol. 3, Harmondsworth: Penguin, 541–60.

Doorn, J. van (1973) *The Soldier and Social Change*. London: Sage.

Duffield, M. (2001) *Global Governance and the New Wars*. London: Pluto.

Ellis, J. (1993) *The Social History of the Machine Gun*. London: Pimlico.

Gross, J. T. (2001) *Neighbors: The Destruction of the Jewish Community in Jedwabne, Poland*. Princeton: Princeton University Press.

Hobsbawm, E. (1994) *The Age of Extremes 1914–89*. London: Joseph.

Kaldor, M. (1982) *The Baroque Arsenal*. London: Deutsch.

Kaldor, M. (1990) *The Imaginary War*. Oxford: Blackwell.

Kaldor, M. (1999) *New and Old Wars*. Cambridge: Polity.

Kaldor, M., Albrecht, U. and Schmeder, G., eds (1998) *The End of Military Fordism*. London: Pinter.

Kennedy, P. M. (1988) *The Rise and Fall of the Great Powers: Economic Change and Military Conflict from 1500 to 2000*. London: Unwin Hyman.

Keynes, J. M. (1919) *The Economic Consequences of the Peace*. London: Macmillan.

Kidron, M. (1968) *Western Capitalism since the War*. London: Weidenfeld.

Lenin, V. I. (1939) *Imperialism: The Highest Stage of Capitalism*. New York: International Publishers.

Looney, R. E. (1995) *The Economics of Third World Defense Expenditures*. Greenwich, CT: JAI Press.

Luxemburg, R. (1963) *The Accumulation of Capital*. London: Routledge.

MacKenzie, J. (1984) *Propaganda and Empire: The Manipulation of British Public Opinion 1880–1960*. Manchester: Manchester University Press.

MacNeill, W. H. (1982) *The Pursuit of Power*. Oxford: Blackwell.

Macrae, J. and Zwi, A., eds (1994) *War and Hunger: Rethinking International Responses*. London: Zed Books.

Mandel, E. (1986) *The Meaning of the Second World War*. London: Verso.

Mann, M. (1984) Capitalism and militarism. In M. Shaw, ed., *War, State and Society*, London: Macmillan, 25–46.

Mann, M. (1988) *States, War and Capitalism*. Oxford: Blackwell.

Mann, M. (2001) The colonial darkside of democracy. www.theglobalsite.ac.uk/press/103mann.htm

Marx, K. (1976) *Capital: A Critique of Political Economy*, vol. 1. Harmondsworth: Penguin.

Milward, A. S. (1977) *War, Economy and Society, 1939–1945*. London: Allen Lane.

Nove, A. (1992) *An Economic History of the USSR 1917–1991*. Harmondsworth: Penguin.

Overy, R. J. (1994) *War and Economy in the Third Reich*. Oxford: Clarendon Press.

Pearton, M. (1982) *The Knowledgeable State*. London: Burnett.

Semmel, B. (1981) *Marxism and the Science of War*. Oxford: Oxford University Press.

Smith, D. (1995) *The War Atlas*. London: Pan Books.

Episode IV
Japan's genocidal wars

Imperial Japan waged aggressive total war in an extremely degenerate, effectively genocidal manner. In the first half of the twentieth century, Japan's imperial nationalism glorified war above all else: 'war is the father of creation and the mother of culture' (Markusen and Kopf 1995: 96). Japanese imperialism was firmly based on ideas of racial superiority over Koreans, Chinese and other Asian and Pacific peoples whom it conquered. Total war, for Japanese armies, was war against enemy peoples as well as states. Conquests were accompanied by slaughter on a scale, and with a cruelty, that was matched only by the Nazis.

The most horrific of the genocidal massacres committed by the Japanese was the 'rape' of Nanking, then capital of China, in the weeks after its capture in December 1937. As Iris Chang (1998: 4) summarizes: 'Tens of thousands of young men were rounded up and herded to the outer areas of the city, where they were mowed down by machine guns, used for bayonet practice, or soaked with gasoline and burned alive. For months the streets of the city were heaped with corpses and reeked with the stench of rotting human flesh.' Tens of thousands of women were raped and killed. The slaughter repelled even Nazi observers. The International Military Tribunal of the Far East later estimated that more than 260,000 non-combatants were killed on the streets of the city – a greater death toll than at Hiroshima or Dresden.

The slaughter of Nanking was only the most prominent episode in a long history of extreme violence against civilians in Japan's wars. In their long war against China's Communists, the Japanese inverted Mao Zedong's dictum that 'the peasants are the ocean in which the Red Army swims' with the order to 'drain the ocean'. Their scorched earth policy, with the slogan, 'loot all, kill all, burn all', was total war against the peasants (Markusen and Kopf 1995: 102). As late as 1945, the crimes of Nanking were repeated in Manila, capital of the Philippines, where an estimated 100,000 were killed out of a population of 700,000.

The history of Japan's crimes underlines two connections in modern slaughter that have been widely missed. First, it shows how completely genocide was a form of total *war*. It is not possible, in this case, to draw a clear line between degenerate war and genocide, even to the limited extent that this distinction appears possible in the Holocaust. Second, genocide does not necessarily involve the extermination of a national group. There could never have been a question of wiping out hundreds of millions of Chinese in the way that the Nazis tried to exterminate European Jewry, or that colonizers more or less completely eliminated some indigenous peoples. Yet the extensive slaughter of Chinese people, simply because they were Chinese, at Nanking and many other places, was every bit as genocidal as the most complete extermination of a people ever carried out.

Further reading

Buruma, I. (1994) *The Wages of Guilt: Memories of War in Germany and Japan.* London: Cape.

Chang, I. (1998) *The Rape of Nanking: The Forgotten Holocaust of World War II.* London: Penguin.

Hicks, G. (1997) *Japan's War Memories: Amnesia or Concealment?* Aldershot: Ashgate.

Hsiung, J. C. and Levine, S. I., eds (1992) *China's Bitter Victory: The War with Japan 1937–1945.* Armonk, NY: Sharpe.

Lary, D. and Mackinnon, S. (2001) *Scars of War: The Impact of Warfare on Modern China.* Vancouver: University of British Columbia Press.

Markusen, E. and Kopf, D. (1995) *The Holocaust and Strategic Bombing: Genocide and Total War in the Twentieth Century.* Boulder, CO: Westview Press.

Tanaka, Y. (1996) *Hidden Horrors: Japanese War Crimes in World War 2.* Boulder, CO: Westview Press.

— 5 —
Thinking War

Human killing is a conscious act. Because it is committed in defiance of general taboos, it must be especially premeditated and justified. Of no killing is this truer than killing in war. Emotions are stirred by war, and especially by killing, but neither is simply an outcome of feeling. A warrior may feel intense hatred for his enemy; he may take an individual life apparently spontaneously in the 'heat' of battle; or he may kill in an apparently unintentional way by causing 'collateral damage'. But in all these cases and many others, killing in war is always intellectually prepared. Before men kill, they have to *think* that their killing will be acceptable. So before killers can be prepared to think killing, this activity has to be made acceptable in society at large. In a small-scale, simpler society, the intellectual preparation of killing may be a fairly straightforward outcome of shared values. In larger, more complex societies, with specialized military and state organizations, its intellectual preparation is as complex as these organizations themselves.

Ideas, of course, are central to how 'material' preparation for war takes place. Politics and economics are conscious activities. Yet, as we saw, the links between material preparation for slaughter and its actual practice are often indirect. Those who make bombs know abstractly that they can be used to kill people. But not knowing against whom, how, when and even if their particular products will be lethally deployed, they may absolve themselves from responsibility for any killing that may result. This kind of distancing is a central aspect of how war is intellectually prepared in complex societies. Distancing involves, crucially, separating actors morally, not just from unforeseeable and unintended, but also from generally foreseeable and intended consequences. Gaps between actions and consequences are covered by systems of ideas that generally justify the chains of war preparation and war practice. It is with these that we are most concerned in this chapter.

Broadly speaking, two different kinds of belief system are implicated in mass killing. First, there are belief systems concerned with war and peace themselves. For war to be maintained as an institution, it needs, just as much as religion, commerce or any other general type of social action, special ideas that explain and justify it. Thus traditions, handed-down ways of thinking about war, are highly important, and can be traced back hundreds or thousands of years. Moreover, like other important belief systems, military traditions do not just exist abstractly, but are fostered and developed not only in armies but in other social organizations where military values are inculcated – often including schools.

Secondly, there are more general belief systems in society, not principally concerned with war, through which war – both war in general and each particular war – is nevertheless legitimated. Given the inherently problematic nature of slaughter, military traditions alone are not capable of giving it full legitimation. They can do so only if they are thoroughly supported by pervasive sets of fundamental beliefs embedded in social structures. Indeed, particular wars are principally validated by political and cultural, rather than specifically military, beliefs. Since war has been a central activity of human society for thousands of years, all belief systems contain ideas about its role and practice. Almost all validate war to some degree and in some circumstances.

In this chapter I shall examine these two main ways of thinking war, in turn. In the light of what I have said about how ideas are embedded in organized social practice, I also look particularly at the role of the mass media of communication. These have become the main centres of daily reflection on social practice in modern society. As such, they have become the principal institutions through which people's intellectual relationships to mass killing are organized.

Ideologies of war and peace

Because of the peculiar sensitivity of killing, belief systems have always defined its proper role and limits. In some (but not all) small-scale societies war has had a highly restricted, even ritualized character, in which battle deaths are few. In ancient and medieval societies, thinking about war prescribed, at least in principle, considerable constraints. Military roles were the prerogatives of high-status social groups, and were surrounded by conceptions of virtue and honour that defined the legitimate scope of killing.

Nevertheless, in these more complex states, war long ago assumed much of the scale, complexity and murderous character of modern war. Western civilization developed through regular, extensive, highly bloody wars, both internally and in its relations with non-European powers. Given the categorical prohibition on killing in the Judaeo-Christian tradition, particular sets of ideas had to be developed to justify the pervasive role of war in Western society. Out of this came the 'just war' tradition, with its twin principles of *ius ad bellum*, concerning the conditions in which waging war could be just, and *ius in bellum*, concerning the conditions for just behaviour within war (see box 5.1).

Box 5.1   The just war tradition

First elaborated by Christian writers like Thomas Aquinas and Hugo Grotius, this classical tradition is the standard frame of reference for the justification of war. In its classic modern defence, *Just and Unjust Wars*, Michael Walzer (1992: 72) explains its fundamental idea, that aggression is a crime: 'The defence of rights ... is the only reason [for fighting].'

The theory's key contribution is its capacity to make moral distinctions between uses of violence. The tradition tells us that 'Just wars are limited wars; their conduct is governed by a set of rules designed to bar, so far as possible, the use of violence and coercion against noncombatant populations' (p. xvii). However, while this is certainly a crucial moral criterion, the fact that it has been violated more than it has been observed – even by liberal states – does raise fundamental questions about whether war *can* generally be regulated by moral principles. Walzer rightly insists that this is not a new problem: 'There never was a golden age of warfare when just-war categories were easy to apply and therefore regularly applied. If anything, modern technology makes it possible to fight with greater discrimination now than in the past, if there is a political will to do so' (pp. xii–xiii).

Walzer agrees that 'It is certainly possible to reinterpret or reconstruct just war theory so that no war could possibly be justified'. 'In one of its modes, just war theory would also abolish war by the (theoretically) simple method of calling unjust wars "crimes" and just wars "police actions".' But this requires more than just changing the names; it needs a 'thoroughgoing transformation of international society' (p. xxii).

> Just war thinking is tightly governed by the doctrine of non-intervention: 'Except in extreme cases, [just wars] don't legitimately reach to the transformation of the internal politics of the aggressor state or the replacement of its regime' (p. xvii).

The least that can be said in favour of the 'just war' tradition is that it meant that war had always to be justified. Accepted in broad terms throughout European society into modern times, the tradition seems often to have functioned in practice, however, as a source of justifications for war – rather than of objections to it. As with all abstract ideas, in the hands of practitioners, just war thinking has often become merely another tool for furthering their concrete requirements. The West's moral ideas enabled, as well as constrained, war.

At the onset of the modern period, two principal developments changed the terms of ideological debate about war, in ways that still resonate today. During the Enlightenment, people thought systematically – for the first time outside predominantly religious parameters – about the proper foundations of social and political order. The prevalence of war meant that the problems it caused could hardly be outside the scope of philosophy. Progressive thinkers grappled with the possibilities of a 'federation' that would enable co-operative relations between peoples. Thus a series of writers produced proposals for 'perpetual peace', the most lasting of which was Immanuel Kant's (see box 5.2). These ideas provided a critical framework of more universalistic values against which reality could be measured, but in the succeeding historical period they appeared as moral absolutes standing against the historical tide towards more and more total war. The main historical trend of the nineteenth and early twentieth centuries, towards a world of rival national empires, militated against the concrete implementation of these ideas.

Box 5.2 Perpetual peace and world government

In the eighteenth century, thinkers revolted for the first time against the idea of the *necessity* of war. The Abbé Saint-Pierre produced a proposal for 'perpetual peace' based on the idea of an alliance of nations. Jean-Jacques Rousseau advanced a more developed case for a 'confederation' of peoples. He had an optimistic faith in the human capacity to constitute a better world. For Rousseau, state independence – or, more precisely, autonomy – was valued in so far as it contributed to the welfare of the people. Where, however, the security and happiness of the people could be augmented, Rousseau accepted the need to renounce part, at least, of its 'independence'. The sovereign state built upon the social contract could enter into undertakings with others. A confederation would be 'a free and voluntary association'.

Immanuel Kant's *Perpetual Peace*, written in 1795, is the best known of all the proposals in this vein, and still forms the basis of 'cosmopolitan' thinking about international relations. For Kant, peace was not a natural condition: the state of peace had to be established. War itself drove man 'to leave the lawless stage of savages and enter a league of nations; where each state, even the smallest, may expect his security and his rights – not from its own power or its own legal views, but alone from this great league of nations, from a united power, and from the decision according to laws adopted by the united will' (Kant 1983: 115).

Writing in the context of the revolutionary wave, Kant saw the establishment of 'republican constitutions' as the basis of the state of peace. Other, more practical writers advanced the same beliefs: the Englishman Tom Paine, who participated in both the American and the French revolutions, argued in his *Rights of Man* that, 'As the barbarism of the present old governments expires, the moral condition of nations with respect to each other will be changed. Man will not be brought up with the savage idea of considering his species his enemy' (Paine 1994: 179).

In the event, the succeeding 200 years saw the rise (and fall) of many and worse new barbarisms. But the 'cosmopolitan' ideas of Kant and his co-thinkers have not only remained the foundation of an alternative, throughout this period, but have gained new life in the 'global' era since the end of the Cold War. In particular, their legacy is a new interest in flexible forms of global governance as a means of preventing war.

Indeed, the greatest early modern revolution, in France, which inspired thinkers like Kant and Tom Paine, also culminated in the first distinctively modern phase of generalized European war, over two decades from 1793 to 1815. Reflecting on this experience, Clausewitz produced the foundational modern theory of war (see chapter 1). His core insights were interpreted in the developing military academies and among the general staffs of Continental Europe as a recipe for what became known as 'total war'. With the aid of the technological, economic and political resources discussed in the last chapter, armies could plausibly expect to annihilate their enemies in conflicts of new destructiveness. Notoriously, these ideas informed not only the conventional war plans of Prussian generals, but also the thinking of the first modern genocidists, the Young Turk movement in the Ottoman Empire (see episode I).

The nineteenth-century 'long peace' was spattered with bloody confrontations, from the Crimea to Gettysburg and Paris, and across the colonial world. By its end, there was growing recognition that future wars would involve unprecedented slaughter, and that attempts should be made to constrain this. There was no shortage of pacifistic approaches, informed by universal values, which proclaimed the possibility of radically overcoming war. Liberals sought a world of international co-operation based on free trade in goods and ideas; socialists, a world commonwealth federating the associated producers of all nations. Labour movements conferred to pledge international resistance to war. Meanwhile, at the Hague in 1907, states developed the first modern conventions on war, laying down a minimal framework of rules for the world conflicts of the twentieth century (Roberts and Guelff 2000).

Despite all the warnings about future bloodshed (even the most pessimistic of which underestimated the slaughter to come), in the nineteenth century war had not always been identified as *in itself* a major social problem. Progressive thinkers such as Marx and his collaborator Friedrich Engels (a military analyst) saw war as a vehicle of social change, speeding up transformation – or, as their follower Leon Trotsky put it, war was 'the locomotive of history'. In the twentieth century such progressive ideas of the impact of war became more difficult to uphold. For many, during and after 1914–18, war itself was the problem. There was a generalized reaction to the way in which European civilization was mired in slaughter. The military tradition represented by Clausewitz was identified as a source of the blood-bath of the trenches. The 'liberal' militarism of Britain and the USA needed to differentiate itself from this experience and the understanding of war that had produced it. Militarism was defined, therefore, as the kind of glorification of military power associated with authoritarian empires. But, in a more fundamental sense, the problem of militarism was pervasive in 'liberal' as well as in authoritarian states. Militarism required a more generic definition, discussed in box 5.3.

With the failure of the inter-war attempt at inclusive international organization (the League of Nations), military defence – in the form of collective security – was widely affirmed as a necessity against the 'aggressive' militarisms of totalitarian powers. This understanding was further entrenched in the Cold War, despite the danger of all-out annihilation posed by nuclear war. The Western military tradition was supposed to have moved beyond Clausewitz: its new doctrine of *deterrence* claimed that war preparation would prevent war. In the Soviet bloc, where a Marxist-Leninist

---

Box 5.3   Defining militarism

Militarism has classically been understood as an ideology that positively evaluates military power. In this most common meaning, the glorification of war and war preparation, it has had a negative significance. Each side in a conflict has often described the other as 'militarist'.

However, for the term to have social-scientific value, it needs to be used in a generic sense, and be defined as about more than ideology. The term *military* describes all social relations, institutions and values relating to war and war preparation. *Militarism* can therefore be defined as the tendency of these relations, institutions and values to influence social relations, institutions and values in general. A highly *militarized* society is one in which military forms have very extensive influence. *Militarization* refers to an extension of military influences in society, and *demilitarization* to the contraction of these influences.

In these senses, militarism can be strong even when the glorification of military power is lacking. The liberal democratic states (USA, UK, etc.) were extensively militarized in the Second World War, because economy and society were mobilized for total war. This was, however, a 'democratic militarism' that utilized a very different set of values concerning the role of the military in society compared to, for example, Nazi Germany and Imperial Japan.

Military participation through mass conscription used to be a powerful indicator of militarism. With its decline, Western societies have become 'post-military societies' (Shaw 1991). However, militarism has not disappeared, but has taken new forms. For example, 'armament culture' (Luckham 1984), with its fetishism of high-tech weaponry, has been highly influential in consumer culture – films, games, etc. – and has to some extent replaced the influence of traditional military hierarchies and symbols. The media consumption of wars has led to what Mann (1988) called 'spectator sport' militarism in Western societies.

---

version of Clausewitz's ideas still prevailed in the military, war preparations and military institutions generally were justified as defensive measures against potential Western aggression. During the Cold War, therefore, both sides claimed to be in favour of peace, while remaining locked into the problematic of mass slaughter through nuclear war. These were the conditions in which the idea of peace was increasingly reclaimed by oppositional social movements (discussed in chapter 9). Yet, if the self-proclaimed 'peace movements' agreed in rejecting the pacific claims of the blocs, the meaning of peace was also highly contested within their own ranks, as box 5.4 shows.

> ### Box 5.4   Varieties of pacifism
>
> The French Revolution led not to the universal peace hoped for by thinkers like Kant and Paine, but to the most general pan-European wars seen before the twentieth century. From the end of the Napoleonic wars, writes Michael Howard in his seminal War and the Liberal Conscience, dates the modern 'peace Movement...the political organization of middle-class liberals on a transnational basis to secure, by education, agitation, and propaganda, the abolition of war' (Howard 1981: 36).
>
> Peace movements have taken many different forms, and have involved coalitions of different intellectual positions towards war. The complete rejection of war, pacifism, has generally been a minority position, justified principally by religious principles. Among Christians, it has been espoused mainly by denominations like the Quakers. The most positive version has been Gandhian pacifism (after Mahatma Gandhi), which advocates non-violent resistance.
>
> Most 'peace' thinking has constituted what Martin Ceadel (1986) has called pacificism rather than pacifism, seeking the conditions for more peaceful international relations rather than an absolute refusal of war. A major axis of differentiation in peace movements has been between the simple moral rejection of war and the emphasis on the political conditions for peace. Thus in the 1980s peace movements, some emphasized the need to abolish nuclear weapons, others the need for a post-Cold War European political order.
>
> Peace thinking has been linked to a variety of political traditions – hence there are not only liberal but socialist and latterly green and feminist pacifisms, stressing different kinds of social conditions for peace (political freedom, socialist transformation, environmental sustainability, gender equality).
>
> In the late twentieth century, much peace thinking was based on the rejection of nuclear war and weapons, the nuclear pacifism advocated by E. P. Thompson. Nuclear pacifism recognized the historical tendency of the means of war to outstrip any rational use. However, it narrowed this tendency by associating it with a particular kind of weaponry. I have suggested that a more adequate position would be historical pacifism (Shaw 1988).

Only with the end of the Cold War has the opportunity arisen to transcend the opposition of 'peace' and 'war' thinking. The lessons of the twentieth century, that war has become profoundly degenerate and has spawned genocide as a specific form of war, are now beginning to inform wider understanding. We can see the warfare practised by so many states as a supreme problem; but we can also begin to subject the means of controlling such war to more critical appraisal. The dilemma of the twentieth century can be seen in retrospect as whether Hiroshima was any kind of answer to Auschwitz. Throughout subsequent decades, Western cold warriors clung to the proposition that it was. Today that argument is no longer necessary or possible to sustain for the future.

Yet clear echoes of this dilemma remain in the twenty-first century. Western leaders seek military solutions that are ever freer of risk to their own soldiers, and hence of political risk with national electorates. This approach reinforces the supremacy of air war. Refinements in targeting and accuracy mean that extensive mass killing can be avoided. But high-altitude, long-distance bombing always involves some relatively indiscriminate killing. In the three-month Kosovo campaign in 1999, not a single Western soldier was killed by enemy action; however, NATO bombs killed hundreds of Serb and Albanian civilians. The scale of the direct slaughter was radically reduced compared to the world wars, Korea or Vietnam. Nevertheless, the core of the dilemma remained, reinforced by the problem of long-term damage to 'enemy' societies from sanctions. ('Risk-transfer militarism' is discussed more fully in episode X.)

The political problem of war, for the Western state, has been compounded by the growing application of law to war. Old ways of thinking separated the law-bound 'domestic' sphere from the anarchic, 'might is right' international realm. The new thinking, making defence of human rights a cause of war, inevitably brings rights back into its conduct as well. International law is no longer simply about relations between states, but is also about the common rights of people worldwide. Ultimately, law and war are opposite answers to the problem of order in human affairs. A fully lawful world must also be a warless one. We are, of course, a long way from such a state of affairs; but new and old ideas intermesh in increasingly contradictory ways.

The new century is already seeing greater recognition of universal norms and a global framework of society. Thus the challenge to war's legitimacy is likely to grow. In the short term, this poses problems of adaptation for military traditions, which must reinvent themselves in the spirit of peacemaking and peace enforcement. In the longer term, it will raise deeper issues about the justification of war preparation. We cannot assume that because in recent centuries society has nurtured mass killing in its core institutions, it will always continue to do so. (These issues are pursued further in chapter 10.)

Cultures of slaughter

It is shocking to think that *all* the values that people hold dear have been used to justify slaughter. Ideals for which people live are also those for which they kill. Ways of life that nurture are also those that destroy. Cultures, the symbolic frameworks in which people's lives grow, foster the death of others. So long as mass killing is an accepted aspect of human society, all our major value systems will continue to be implicated in it.

These reflections are undoubtedly sobering. We are used to thinking of other people's values as destructive – just as it is other people whom we destroy or whose destruction we condone. The gap between lofty ideal and murderous practice that we discern in others' beliefs is also, more than likely, part of our own tradition. Slaughter is so embedded in human society that its dilemmas are difficult to evade. Even total refusal of killing, the full pacifist stance, cannot avoid the charge that in some circumstances it allows slaughter to be perpetrated that could be prevented by the use of force. Any other position will have blood more directly on its hands, sooner or later.

These contradictions do not mean, of course, that human culture is irredeemably damned, or that we must simply accept slaughter's pervasiveness. They do mean that, in finding our way through the ethics and politics of war, we must be aware of slaughter's historic role in, and contemporary challenge to, our belief systems. As I remarked above, the tension between pacifist ideals and war-justifying reality has been a constant presence in the dominant Western religious tradition (see box 5.5). Although it has taken different forms, it has been present in other major world religions, too. Given the universality of both taboos on killing and practices of slaughter, it would be surprising if any major belief system did not embody contradictions around this theme.

Box 5.5   Christianity and war

On a literal reading of the Scriptures, Christianity appears to espouse an absolute rejection of killing. Christ abjured his followers to 'turn the other cheek', and the early Christians were outcasts in the Roman Empire. For most of its history, however, Christianity has been a state religion, and many of its leaders, Protestant bishops as well as Popes, have been wealthy and powerful in a worldly sense. Not surprisingly, Christian churches have placed more emphasis on another of their founder's injunctions, to 'render unto Caesar the things that are Caesar's'. The 'just war' tradition has therefore been invoked principally to sanctify war. Christian pacifism long ago became a minority, sectarian position, although influential religious leaders, such as Pope John Paul II, have continued to inveigh against war.

In early modern times, many wars were religious in character, with rival princes representing different Christian traditions. In the two world wars, bishops of the same church could often be found blessing rival armies as they went out to slaughter each other – and civilian populations. In Nazi Germany, many church leaders found nationalism and anti-Communism sufficient pretexts to endorse the war campaigns of the regime. Only a few courageous priests and lay people were openly defiant.

In late-modern wars, Christianity's role has often been no less dishonourable. The Orthodox and Catholic churches were closely identified with the excesses of Serbian and Croatian nationalism respectively in the 1990s. Catholic priests and nuns were among Rwanda's génocidaires, and the wider Church has sometimes sheltered them from international justice. Western church leaders have often maintained a studied ambivalence towards their own states' violence: my own study of the Gulf War found the position of the then Archbishop of Canterbury the least clear of the positions of all British public figures in the public perception (Shaw 1996).

Nevertheless, in some situations in Latin America, and in places like East Timor, church leaders, priests and lay people have been figureheads of resistance or, at least, of reconciliation and protection for victims.

The root of this problem is the tension between human society and societies, and between culture and cultures. Even when communities were much more separated in time and space than they are today, most people always recognized some degree of commonality with the human beings they met, or of whom they were aware. However, separations of, and within, human communities have always been such that 'others' were accorded different moral status. Inclusion within one society, status, or culture has implied (to a greater or lesser extent) excluding 'others' from equal moral consideration.

The radical character of differentiations within human society has therefore been used to justify inequalities, cruelties and ultimately killings. With the development of complex social organizations for war, any definition of certain people as radically 'other' could become, sooner or later, a pretext for killing them. We need to distinguish, of course, between the abstract potentials of differences *for* killing and their actual use *in* killing. Many adhere to beliefs that recognize certain differences as radical, without wishing or supporting, let alone being involved in, killing. Thus, anti-Semitic beliefs as such did not produce, and could not have produced, the Holocaust. It required Nazi ideas, politics and military organization to turn the belief in the otherness of the Jews into genocide.

We also need to distinguish between the killing potentials of various types of differences. For example, although supporting a particular football club against another has sometimes been a pretext for killing, in general this is not understood as the kind of affiliation in which slaughter could legitimately be implicated. Many people who would be scandalized by the idea of football killings find it acceptable that, for example, national or racial differences are pretexts for killing in war.

Yet even the sharpest national or racial differences are not, as such, grounds for slaughter at most points in time. People who become involved in killings based directly on such identities, in genocides, have often lived more or less peaceably alongside their victims, certainly without killing them, for decades. Indeed, their ancestors may have lived together for centuries. Even where histories of slaughter divide certain groups – and these are often powerful indicators of future killing – they often live in relative peace for decades. Thus Serbs, Croats and Bosnian Muslims had killed each other during the nationalist struggles of the Second World War, but then lived peacefully for almost half a century, often intermarrying, until mobilized by the new nationalist movements of the early 1990s.

Differences only become grounds of slaughter when they are mobilized as power. Although any collectivity or social organization can use the difference between itself and others as a basis for killing, mostly, as we have seen, differences are mobilized in this way only by state or parastatal organizations. Most, if not all, kinds of state, political organization and ideology are implicated in mobilizing social differences for slaughter, although we need to distinguish radically between different ways in which this is done.

One of the most radical indications of the potential for murderous perversion in *all* abstract thought is the history of humanistic science and medicine. The emergence of these secular traditions of thought, devoted to the causes of human knowledge and well-being, has often been seen by liberal internationalists as a reason for believing in a peaceful future. Yet the century in which modern science reached its highest achievements has also been the century in which it has been most perverted in the cause of war – and even genocide. Scientists and doctors working for genocidal regimes like

Nazi Germany and Imperial Japan carried out cruel pseudo-scientific experiments on living patients. In the Western democracies, scientists have developed the most hideous weapons known to man (see box 5.6), and in all states they continue to serve power in the cause of war preparation. Some scientists have been prepared to provide states with new methods of torture.

Box 5.6 Scientists and the bomb

From the earliest days of modern science, its findings have been harnessed in the cause of new weapons and technologies of war. This has resulted in a sharp contradiction between scientists' commitment to knowledge and the improvement of the human condition and the anti-human consequences of their discoveries. Scientists have often rationalized this conflict by separating their work in generating knowledge from the ways in which it is subsequently used by others.

This solution cannot work, however, when scientists are working directly within military machines. The most infamous case of the conflict concerns the development of the atomic bomb. The Second World War broke out when nuclear physics had reached the point of understanding that the atom could be split, and that an atomic bomb could be feasible. Physicists agonized over whether to proceed with their research and – even more – to enter the service of state efforts to harness the technology. Notoriously, scientists led by Robert Oppenheimer collaborated on the Manhattan Project, the US attempt to develop the bomb, because they feared that the Nazis might develop it first.

In the event, as Robert Jungk describes in his classic *Brighter than a Thousand Suns* (1958), Nazi Germany did not develop the weapons, but the USA decided to drop atomic bombs on Hiroshima and Nagasaki when it was already clear that it had won the war. Subsequently, many scientists have been in the forefront of campaigns to control and abolish nuclear weapons. Others, however, have continued to work to develop them, and some social scientists have been among those who have elaborated the nuclear war strategies that have justified this policy.

Nations and nationalism

In a long historical perspective, religious identity has been a primary mobilizing basis for killing, and it remains important to this day. The universalist tendencies of world religions, even where in principle they posit human brotherhood, have often been potent means of radicalizing difference, in the hands of political organizations. By assigning particular communities uniquely God-given roles and endowing leaders with supreme authority, religions have easily identified outsiders as 'others' unworthy of respect or even life.

Historically, the bounds of religion and large-scale community were often coextensive. In modern times, however, nations have become prime mobilizers of community, cutting across, as well as mobilizing, religious identities. Sociologists have made a key distinction between *national identity* and nationalism. We are conscious of particular identities, bounded by time and place, as outcomes of a shared history as well as ancestry. In modern times, these identities have become centred on nations. The nation has been the central 'imagined community' (as Benedict Anderson (1983) called it), the key intellectual basis for states. Through nations, therefore, the continuing significance of religious difference has been reconstructed.

National identities can be constructed in pacific ways. They may involve national peace cultures, according value to co-operative ideas of *inter*nationality, as for example in Sweden. The nation can be defined in an inclusive and civic – even cosmopolitan – rather than exclusive ethnic way. But when national identities are constructed through nationalisms, centring on the claims of nations to states, and of nation-states to empire and dominance, they are often taken in different directions. When identities are mobilized by national*ism*, they may become causes of violence. Nationalism, rather than national identity as such, is likely to be a pathway to slaughter.

Of course, nationalist ideas are involved in virtually every modern political programme, and do not always and everywhere lead to violence. Nationalism may be accommodated within 'normal' electoral politics within states, as well as in 'normal' international relations. But because nationalism, as a defining political idea, raises the claims of a particular community against others, and especially because it raises the claims of a particular state or would-be state against others, it has been particularly implicated in slaughter of all kinds.

To say that nationalism is especially linked to mass killing does not imply that it is simply bad. In a world of nation-states, national groups may have little alternative to nationalist politics, and even war, as means of defending or asserting themselves against more powerful (imperial) states. The claims that led early twentieth-century statesmen as diverse as Woodrow Wilson and Vladimir

Illych Lenin to uphold the right of nations to self-determination made good sense in their time, and are still potent today.

These claims, however, are recipes for violence in many circumstances. Asserting the claims to statehood of one national group against another, or against an existing state, commonly leads to war. Given that plural, multi-ethnic, mixed-nationality society is the normal context of life within any given territory, the assertion of the claims of one national party to exclusive control commonly leads to discrimination, violence and even genocide. This kind of nationalism means that minority, or even subordinate majority, national groups are at best second-class citizens; worse, no longer welcome within a given territory; and worst of all, at risk of their lives within it.

An abstract genocidal potential is thus implicit in nationalism as such, although it is often not realized. In particular, it may not be immediately evident in the nationalisms of the oppressed. Yet, even the most progressive nationalist movements almost invariably involve some kind of subordination of members of other nationalities. Where other nationalities are defined as 'enemies', persecution and killing are never far away. It may not be so obvious that this is true of constitutional nationalisms. But this is to forget the central feature of modern international war: that not only enemy soldiers, but also 'enemy civilians' (the term speaks volumes), are considered legitimate, if regrettable, targets.

Nationalism is thus centrally implicated in the modern prevalence of slaughter. When apparently progressive politics, whether of revolutionary movements or of liberal constitutional states, engage in and justify mass killing, national justifications are usually involved. It is too easy to say that nationalism is responsible for how twentieth-century democracy, liberalism and socialism became mired in blood. Yet the embrace of nationalism by these movements and ideologies was central to their practice and justification of extensive mass killing. Saving the lives of the nation's own soldiers, at the expense even of killing far more civilians of opposed nationalities, has been one of the West's principal rationales for killing others – from Hiroshima to Kosovo. This is a central idea in the degeneration of war, still strong in the risk-transfer militarism of our own times.

Likewise, nationalism was central to the degradation of the socialist tradition from its early twentieth-century pacifism to militarist and ultimately genocidal ends. The abandonment of co-operative internationalism at the outbreak of the First World War consigned the socialist mainstream to nationalist interpretations. The surviving internationalist tradition then itself became revolutionary, in the context of world war, but out of the Russian Revolution came new wars against counter-revolution. In these contexts, democratic impulses were snuffed out, and foundations were laid for the centralization of power in the hands of Stalin, who in turn proclaimed the new nationalist doctrine of 'socialism in one country'.

Thereafter, nationalist ideas were at the heart of many mass killings by Communist states, both in genocide and in war. As Stalinist parties seized power in Asia and the Balkans after 1945, they each proclaimed their own national ideology. Each 'great leader' claimed to represent his fatherland, and many were prepared to kill extensively in the leader's name. After this, nationalist militarism became the model for revolutionary movements across the Third World. Whatever other ideological elements and alliances the insurgent forces claimed, their killing was invariably in the name of national liberation.

The 'killing fields' of Cambodia (episode VII) represented the nadir of this kind of nationalist Communism. In the former Soviet and Yugoslav areas after 1989, many former Communist elites reinvented themselves as ethnic nationalists. In some cases, they launched genocidal wars in the name of their new creed, to renew the foundations of their power. Nationalism made democratization a sick joke in war zones – the incentive to manufacture ethnically homogeneous electorates became one of the driving forces of expulsion and slaughter (see episode VIII).

If nationalism has been a key ideological component in the militarized degradation of socialism, it has been the central idea of modern counter-revolution and fascism. Faced with democratic movements, every authoritarian regime has cloaked itself in the colours of the nation. In the most brutal counter-revolutionary episodes, new dictators and military regimes have invariably used nationalist justifications. Fascism has taken these tendencies to their greatest extremes. Hitler and Mussolini, like Stalin and Mao, presented themselves as embodying the greatest ideals of the nation, and urged their people on to war and genocide in its name.

Race and gender

Since nationalism has been central to all militarist and genocidal practices in our time, other ideological strands are often best understood as contributing to its doctrines. Racism has generally been a component of nationalism, even if to greatly different extents. Chauvinism towards other nations has found its most extreme justification in pseudo-biological explanations of cultural difference. The rival nationalisms of the European and Japanese empires were fed by conquests of supposedly racially 'inferior' people. Thus empire was accompanied by generalized racism. Nazism involved an extreme, formally ideologized rationalization of this general tendency in modern nationalism, but it was not unique. Pseudo-scientific ideas of race existed everywhere in the nineteenth- and early twentieth-century worlds. The Nazis were above all German nationalists, seeking to expand the German state and mobilize the *Volk*, and racist and anti-Semitic ideas underpinned their nationalism. Nevertheless, we must not fall into the trap of over-estimating the ideological coherence of Nazism or other militarist and genocidal movements. Their ideas are essentially tools for power.

Just as nationalism and militarism feed on national culture and racial identity, so too they feed on deep-rooted *gender cultures*. These have defined killing as a proper activity for men, and women's role as to support male warriors. Gender beliefs have not provided the principal, direct rationales for killing, but they have been integral supports for all its ideologies, with a profound influence on who is killed and how, as we shall see in chapter 8.

The significance of gender, like racial, beliefs has been twofold. First, they have legitimated the view that men kill. Being prepared to carry out slaughter is often presented as part of what it means to be a *man*. Second, they have defined widely shared ground rules about who can be killed. Men can legitimately kill other men, whereas women and children are generally excluded as legitimate objects of slaughter. In developed ideologies, this understanding is more commonly defined as a principle that soldiers must not deliberately kill civilians or non-combatants. Non-combatants are often thought of primarily as 'women and children', although in theory men who are non-combatants are also excluded from the category of those who can be killed.

In practice, of course, such attempts to build discrimination into the killing business are often attenuated or simply bypassed. In particular, all men of combat age are often regarded as legitimate targets, whether or not they are actual combatants. Even young boys are often killed as potential combatants; old men too may be included in the slaughter. And of course national and racial views of the enemy, as well as the cold logic of high-altitude strategic death, often define whole populations as targets. In these cases gender discrimination, while not vanishing, becomes subordinate in practice.

Thus core belief sets of modern societies, such as those about nation, race and gender, are deeply implicated in practices of mass killing. We can truly call such societies *cultures of slaughter*, contexts in which practices of mass killing are generated and sustained. At the same time, as we noted above, these are also contexts in which life is nurtured and organized. Gender beliefs typify these contra-dictions. Mothering is manifestly the most life-giving of all social roles: understandably, it has been claimed for pacifist purposes. Yet mothers have nurtured the warriors and killers of the next gener-ation: they have often imbued boys (and girls) with beliefs about men's soldiering roles. Historically, both sides of mothering are real; one cannot claim that either is more natural than the other. Killing has become a fundamental part not just of men's, but of our common (social) human nature. The contradictions of motherhood can stand for the general problem that slaughter poses for human culture. Culture's central role in the legitimation of slaughter neg-ates its core meanings as nurture and life context. We cannot but expose these contradictions; yet exposing them does not in itself solve the problem.

The depths of the difficulty over the roles of beliefs in war are further underlined by the fact that it does not go away when universalist, humanist values are foregrounded. Human beings rarely, if ever, act solely from general principles. Our particular, self-interested selves are 'in there' in our actions, and particularistic interests always cloak themselves illegitimately in universal values. These contradictions are especially apparent when it is claimed that universal human values are being given precedence over mani-festly particularist interests or ideology.

The problem is not that an idea such as 'humanitarian war' is oxymoronic. In a world where slaughter is pervasive, its prevention and control pose real dilemmas. Killing some people may indeed save the lives of others. Where it is only the killers who may have to be killed, culture provides almost universal justification. But this is rarely the case. The military prevention of slaughter almost always involves new risks of killing innocent civilians. As we have seen, part of the problem of contemporary Western arms is the prefer-ence for means, such as aerial bombardment, which minimize risk to military personnel rather than risk to civilians. Yet, even if this bias were overcome, the general dilemma would remain. All modern weaponry has the potential to be used indiscriminately. And all killing, however targeted, has the potential to go further than planned. Moreover, in a war-ridden world, even pacific, humanist ideas can become justifications for killing. A reductionist interpretation of this situation would be that the abstractions of politics and ideology themselves lead to violence. An alternative conclusion, recognizing that abstract ideas are a necessary part of complex social life, is that we need to work through these dilemmas towards a point at which we make killing less pervasive.

Media of war

It is not simply in the world of abstract ideas – whether about war and peace, or about nation, race, gender and humanity – that we think war. Such ideas are embedded in culture (the symbolic framework of social life) and in social institutions (its organizational frameworks). To understand how we think war, we need to grasp not just what we think, but the ways in which we come to think it. In part, this involves the specialized military culture and institutions that I discuss in chapter 7. But it also involves more general mechanisms, or media, through which culture works.

The term 'media' is widely identified with certain institutions of mass communication. But, however important these are (I discuss their role further below), 'media' has a more basic meaning. Cultural media are simply the ways, or forms, through which ideas are thought and communicated. To think war, we need first to utilize the more basic media of all thought and action. The pervasiveness of mass killing has meant that its ways of thought have become fundamental to human culture.

We can start with *language*. Slaughter has been so universal that its ways are thoroughly embedded in the ways we think and talk about the world. The language of strategy has become part of everyday life, routinely diffused in all rational, goal-oriented activity (especially in bureaucratic organizations), in contexts such as education and art, as well as commerce and marketing. Words like 'kill' have enormous ranges of use, far beyond the context of physical violence: 'the kill' is the end-point of many social activities. The most shockingly violent language is used in very mundane contexts: 'I could kill him' may be a fairly modest expression of disapproval; 'they should be lined up against a wall and shot' may be only a little bit stronger. Of course, the users of such language would be horrified if the objects of their ire were actually murdered, let alone taken out *en masse* before a firing squad. But the taste for violent language reflects the pervasive influence of organized killing. This is indulged, above all, in film and television products that circulate and resonate throughout the emergent global culture.

Actual practices of killing, in war and in genocide, have their own language, which is in many ways the opposite of the 'up front' violence of general culture. The always problematic legitimacy of killing lies at the heart of the studied ambiguity that has been much noted in military language. 'Positions' are 'taken out', rather than people killed. Civilian victims of military action are – in the phrase that has come to stand for military euphemism – 'collateral damage'. This covert language is generally maximized in genocide. Generally violent language towards target groups, which defines them as subhuman, is matched by coyness about the specific violence and killing that is being inflicted. Thus *denial* is a general feature of all politically organized killing, part of the way in which it is perpetrated, rationalized and even experienced (see box 5.7).

Box 5.7   States of denial

The sociologist Stan Cohen writes in his new standard work *States of Denial* (2001: 1): 'One common thread runs through the many different stories of denial: people, organizations, governments or whole societies are presented with information that is too disturbing, threatening or anomalous to be fully absorbed or openly acknowledged. The information is therefore somehow repressed, disavowed, pushed aside or reinterpreted. Or else the information "registers" well enough, but its implications – cognitive, emotional or moral – are evaded, neutralized or rationalized away.'

Thus denial is neither a single psychological mechanism nor a universal process, but comes in three main forms:

- literally denying that something happened or is true (no one was killed);
- giving the facts a different meaning from what seems apparent to others (yes, many people were killed, but it was not genocide);
- and denying or minimizing the implications that conventionally follow (it isn't necessary or legitimate to do anything about this episode of killing).

All kinds of belief systems can be used in denial. The language of strategy systematically converts war and killing into an abstract exchange of power. Genocidal killing, because less legitimate, is even more comprehensively denied. However, as Cohen points out, there is now a *double discourse*: 'No country today combines . . . total internal repression and external isolation.

This is why the *simultaneity* of literal denial and ideological justification is essential – for perpetrators at the time, for later official rhetoric, and for bystanders' (2001: 82). Minimizing the facts of war and genocide and minimizing their significance go hand in hand, in often complex ideological contests involving all sides in contemporary conflicts. In 'an atrocity triangle' of *perpetrators, victims* and *bystanders*, all engage in denial for their own reasons. Denial is part of the commission, the experience and the historical, cultural and political interpretation of violence. But 'Denial is always partial; some information is always registered. This paradox – knowing and not knowing – is at the heart of the concept' (Cohen 2001: 22).

While the practice of violence is generally embedded, it is simultaneously connected to particular narratives and causes. Each people has its own history of conflict, in which victimization is even more commonplace than victory. In every society, what is often called *collective memory* is a potent part of imagined community. Real, lived, individual experiences and memories are only small parts of such constructions. Historic events of centuries past, often long outside the range of any person still alive, play pivotal roles: the Serbs 'remember' the Battle of Kosovo Field in 1389, Ulster Protestants the Battle of the Boyne in 1689. In contexts like these, new and recent violence is easily interpreted within a well-established cultural framework, in which the roles of different ethnic and national groups are thoroughly defined. Individual 'memories' are informed by these cultural mechanisms.

Such mechanisms of memory are often informed by diffuse means of education and artistic culture. School textbooks, novels and films (among other media) build up broad frameworks of understanding in which individuals and families participate. Steven Spielberg's film of *Schindler's List*, for example, provided a powerful, graphic articulation – and reinforcement – of the story of the Jews' destruction by the Nazis. The film was not made primarily for Jews, or indeed in support of their organizations, but in order to reinsert this narrative of victimization into wider American, Western and world culture.

At the same time, however, mechanisms of memory are often directly politicized and propagandized. In every active conflict, states, parties and movements construct and disseminate their own, highly partisan versions of history. Some sort of historic narrative is conjured up in every attempt to mobilize power – and especially to organize violence. In modern history, most such narratives have been national. Typically the story concerns the horrific crimes that they, the 'other', have inflicted on 'us', as well as the heroic story of 'our' resistance. The point of the story is invariably that 'we' need to stand up to, teach a lesson to, resist, fight or kill 'them'. These kinds of narrative have always been developed; but in pre-modern times they were transmitted primarily by word of mouth, through social hierarchies, from pulpits and by those recruiting soldiers from village to village.

In modernity, the powerful new media of communication have been harnessed everywhere to support both war and genocide. The *mass media* are therefore the principal means whereby society is mobilized for killing. The mass circulation press, cinema and radio, the three principal media of the late nineteenth and early twentieth centuries, emerged from developments and inventions sponsored first by private firms in Europe and North America. They emerged, however, in the period of the most intense competition between imperial nation-states. In 1914–18, as rivalry turned to war, governments everywhere sought to control the press and utilize it for war propaganda. In the inter-war period, the new totalitarian states in Russia, Italy and Germany pioneered a more comprehensive propaganda of everyday life, using cinema and radio as well as newspapers to reinforce ruling parties' manipulation. In the Second World War, governments in the Western democracies also mobilized cinema newsreels, feature films and radio to propagate their war policies and sustain public support for their wars. It was not for nothing that George Orwell's bleak vision of *1984* grafted totalitarian power on to wartime English society.

The *propaganda* mobilization of mass media is the basic model of the media role in conflict. Authoritarian states and parties – a large proportion of those involved in wars and genocides – still exert more or less direct control over mass media. In formally democratic but semi-authoritarian states – like Slobodan Milosevic's Serbia in the 1990s and Russia during the Chechen wars – the principal media usually remain state-controlled. Even in privately owned media, or where state-owned media are formally independent of government, editors and journalists know what is expected of them, and generally deliver a reliable propaganda product. However, in an increasingly globalized media environment, even the most authoritarian states cannot achieve the degree of control that was normal for mid-twentieth-century totalitarian regimes. Independent and international media are generally marginalized, by limiting access and blocking distribution, if not by terror and direct repression, but they usually have a presence. Generally, authoritarian and genocidal states fight media wars as though they had the power that states had in an earlier period; but increasingly they do not.

In the West, changes in media and in war have come together to produce a new pattern of media politics in wars. Media are more complex and internationalized, and less easily centralized under governmental control. Television was the paradigmatic medium of the second half of the twentieth century: compared to the media of the Second World War, its management posed new problems for governments. Newspapers had lent themselves to direct censorship; cinema newsreels were pre-packaged; radio was a verbal, not a visual, medium. The context in which television was viewed and its capacity for 'real time' coverage made old techniques of control less viable. By the end of the century, moreover, television was no longer a stand-alone medium, but the centre of a more complex, decentralized media world of video and the Internet.

Controlling media is more difficult, too, because Western military campaigns are now generally limited: often 'interventions' rather than 'wars'. Even the largest-scale campaigns, like the Gulf War, are fought in conditions of 'normal' economics and political pluralism in the Western heartlands. The option of overwhelming direct control of the media, still available to many authoritarian and semi-authoritarian powers, cannot be used by Western governments. While propaganda is far from dead, it must now be waged in the context of *media management*, recognizing a substantial degree of real as well as formal journalistic autonomy.

Shared cultural assumptions, as well as more practical financial and political pressures, generally push journalists towards positive relationships with their national militaries, and therefore with international deployments in general. However, this is only one kind of factor in a more volatile interface between media and governments. In limited international missions, where humanitarian values are at stake and national investments are often modest, journalists may appear as champions of 'universal' values, highlighting the plight of the most vulnerable civilians and the failures of the West or the UN to protect them. Western governments' and militaries' relationships with media in war situations have developed considerably from the paradigm of crisis in the Vietnam War to the new media management of the Gulf, Kosovo and Afghanistan wars (see box 5.8).

Box 5.8   Television wars

Vietnam crystallized a new stage in the Western media–war relationship. In the 'first TV war', cameramen roamed across war zones freely enough for the some damaging images of US atrocities and defeat to be beamed into American homes. TV didn't cause the USA's failure – critical coverage developed *after* the war became militarily and politically controversial – but it did feed and publicize opposition (Hallin 1986). Politicians and the military therefore 'learnt' from Vietnam the need to 'manage' TV coverage. In the lesser military interventions that followed in the 1980s (Grenada, Panama, etc.), US authorities restricted journalistic access and heightened information management. An early example of media management was the British operation in the 1982 Falklands / Malvinas War. In an exceptionally isolated battle zone, coverage was restricted to a selected band of entirely British reporters who were logistically dependent on the military 'task force' (Morrison and Tumber 1988).

This trend culminated in the most successful 'media war' in the Gulf in 1991 (Taylor 1992). Here a five-month build-up enabled the USA to plan a complex media management operation. Falklands-style dependence on the military was reproduced by isolating journalists at a news conference centre in Saudi Arabia, away from the combat zones, and implementing a 'pool' system in which they were rotated with combat units according to military decision. Only a few 'independents' broke away. This system resulted for the most part in highly supportive coverage and strong opinion poll ratings for the Western war effort.

But at the end of the war, rebellions inside Iraq (unforeseen by Western planners) were crushed with appalling human consequences, leading to huge refugee flows. Television journalists waged a concerted campaign to highlight Western responsibility for the much-filmed suffering (Shaw 1996). This contributed to the precedent-setting 'humanitarian intervention' in Kurdistan in 1991 (Wheeler 2000). This has been seen as the paradigm case of the 'CNN effect' – popular demand for intervention stoked by film of atrocities competing with the fear of body bags as a media influence on Western policy regarding globalized local wars and genocides.

The contradictions of media management are only the global-era manifestations of the historic problem of war's legitimacy. To make people believe that killing people can be right, against the backdrop of fundamental prohibitions on killing in human society, has always been a core problem in war. This problem became much sharper in the twentieth-century era of total war and genocide. It remains central today.

Further reading

Anderson, B. (1983) *Imagined Communities: Reflections on the Origin and Spread of Nationalism.* London: Verso.

Audoin-Rouzeau, S. (1992) *Men at War 1914–1918: National Sentiment and Trench Journalism in France during the First World War.* Oxford: Berg.

Becker, A. (1998) *War and Faith: The Religious Imagination in France, 1914–1930.* Oxford: Berg.

Bourke, J. (1999) *An Intimate History of Killing.* London: Granta Books.

Ceadel, M. (1986) *Thinking about Peace and War.* Oxford: Oxford University Press.

Coates, A. J. (1997) *The Ethics of War.* Manchester: Manchester University Press.

Cohen, S. (2001) *States of Denial.* Cambridge: Polity.

Elshtain, J. B. (1992) *Just War Theory.* New York: New York University Press.

Glasgow University Media Group (1984) *War and Peace News.* London: Routledge.

Hallin, D. C. (1986) *The 'Uncensored War': The Media and Vietnam.* New York: Oxford University Press.

Herman, E. and Chomsky, N. (1988) *Manufacturing Consent.* New York: Pantheon.

Horne, J. N. and Kramer, A. (2001) *German Atrocities, 1914: A History of Denial.* New Haven: Yale University Press.

Howard, M. (1981) *War and the Liberal Conscience.* Oxford: Oxford University Press.

Johnson, J. T. (1984) *Can Modern War Be Just?* New Haven: Yale University Press.

Jungk, R. (1958) *Brighter than a Thousand Suns: The Moral and Political History of the Atomic Scientists.* London: Gollancz.

Kant, I. (1983) *Perpetual Peace and Other Essays.* Indianapolis: Hackett.

Kaye, H. and MacClelland, K. eds (1990) *E. P. Thompson: Critical Debates.* Cambridge: Polity.

Lifton, R. J. (1989) *Thought Reform and the Psychology of Totalism: A Study of Brainwashing in China.* Chapel Hill: University of North Carolina Press.

Lipstadt, D. (1996) *Denying the Holocaust: The Growing Assault on Truth and Memory.* Harmondsworth: Penguin.

Luckham, R. (1984) Of arms and culture. *Current Research on Peace and Violence,* 7(1), 1–64.

Lunn, K. and Evans, M. eds (1998) *War and Memory.* Leamington: Berg.

Mann, M. (1988) *States, War and Capitalism.* Oxford: Blackwell.

Mercer, D., Mungham, G. and Williams, K. (1987) *The Fog of War: The Media on the Battlefield.* London: Heinemann.

Morrison, D. and Tumber, H. (1988) *Journalists at War.* London: Sage.

Orwell, G. (1949) *1984.* New York: Harcourt.

Paine, T. (1994) *Rights of Man.* London: Everyman.

Roberts, A. and Guelff, R. (2000) *Documents on the Laws of War*. Oxford: Oxford University Press.

Shaw, M. (1988) *Dialectics of War: An Essay as the Social Theory of Total War and Peace*. London: Pluto.

Shaw, M. (1991) *Post-Military Society*. Cambridge: Polity.

Shaw, M. (1996) *Civil Society and Media in Global Crises*. London: Pinter.

Smith, A. D. (1991) *National Identity*. Harmondsworth: Penguin.

Taylor, P. M. (1992) *War and the Media: Propaganda and Persuasion in the Gulf War*. Manchester: Manchester University Press.

Walzer, M. (1992) *Just and Unjust Wars*. New York: Basic Books.

Wheeler, N. (2000) *Saving Strangers*. Oxford: Oxford University Press.

Episode V
Allied bombing in
1939–45

Aerial bombardment developed in the First World War and was used in wars of the inter-war period, from British attacks on rebels in Iraq to the notorious destruction of Guernica by Hitler's *Luftwaffe* in the Spanish Civil War – immortalized in Pablo Picasso's most famous painting. By then the mass-murderous danger of air power was well understood, and there was widespread fear of its consequences in the coming world conflict.

In the early stages of the Second World War, both sides exercised some restraint in the use of air power. 'British bombing policy was rigorously discriminatory – even to the point of putting British aircrews at great risk' (Markusen and Kopf 1995: 152); and Nazi Germany initially reciprocated *vis-à-vis* Britain – although it reduced much of Warsaw to rubble in 1939. Britain interpreted this as a violation of restraint and, after the German bombing of Rotterdam in 1940, began to attack 'strategic' industrial targets in German cities, a policy that (especially with poor accuracy and visibility) led to increasing civilian casualties.

Although the aerial Battle of Britain in the same year was largely confined to military targets, later German bombs dropped accidentally on London provoked attacks on Berlin and other cities, reciprocated by Germany in the 'Blitz' of English cities. This was to prove a fatal escalation: 'On September 7 [1940] the Germans sowed the wind of which they were to reap the whirlwind some years later. It was the start of indiscriminate air warfare – the end of the road to total war' (Sallagar, quoted in Markusen and Kopf 1995: 154). The British bombardment of Germany was renewed in early 1942 under the command of Sir Arthur ('Bomber') Harris and a new policy directive that stated explicitly that the 'primary objective' was 'the morale of the enemy civilian population and in particular, of the industrial workers' (Markusen and Kopf 1995: 156). A report based on the experience of Hull – after London, the most bombed British city – emphasized the 'strains' that were showing after only one-tenth of the city was destroyed. 'On the above figures', Churchill's advisor Frederick Lindemann wrote, 'we should be able to do ten times as much harm to each of the fifty-eight principal German towns. There seems little doubt that this would break the spirit of the people' (quoted in Hastings 1979: 141).

This policy culminated in the devastations by fire-storm of Hamburg in 1943, in which an estimated 45,000 people died, and of Dresden in early 1945, for which figures of 70,000 and upwards have been posited. US planes were involved in the latter, and Britain's destruction of German cities was followed by the US incendiary attack on Tokyo, in March 1945, for which the US Strategic Bombing Survey itself estimated 87,793 deaths. Thereafter US planes systematically destroyed Japanese cities, ending in the atomic bombings of Hiroshima and Nagasaki in 1945.

Unlike the Nazis' killing of the Jews, the killing of Germans and Japanese by the Allies was not an end in itself, but a means to the military defeats of the Nazi German and Imperial Japanese states. Nevertheless, British and US (as well as German and Japanese) air strategies involved the deliberate mass slaughter of civilian populations on the basis of their nationality. This killing was quite as intentional as the Nazis' overtly genocidal policies, even if the rationale was clearly different. It is, as Markusen and Kopf (1995: 252–8) argue, difficult to avoid the conclusion that in these actions of the Allies, war had become genocidal in a fundamental way. In international law and politics, however, genocide was defined by the victors, in a way that reified the line that separated their own policies from those of the losers.

The genocidal potential of total war had now been frightfully realized. Allied strategic bombing defined a new standard of barbarity that became the bench-mark for the new nuclear era.

Further reading

Hastings, M. (1979) *Bomber Command.* London: Joseph.
Hersey, J. (1946) *Hiroshima.* Harmondsworth: Penguin.
Lifton, R. J. and Mitchell, G. (1995) *Hiroshima in America: Fifty Years of Denial.* New York: Putnam.
Markusen, E. and Kopf, D. (1995) *The Holocaust and Strategic Bombing: Genocide and Total War in the Twentieth Century.* Boulder, CO: Westview Press.

— 6 —

Killing Spaces

If slaughter is the crux of war, all the preparation leads – as Clausewitz taught us – to battle, and hence to killing. The violence of war had, he believed, no intrinsic limits. It was restricted only by its political goals, on the one hand, and the friction involved in its preparation and prosecution, on the other. As we have seen, the political goals of war have widened, so that civilian populations have been defined as enemies in their own right, as well as surrogates for state enemies. As the logic of violence has expanded almost exponentially, external limits on war have been transformed. With the possibility of instantaneous annihilation of national populations, traditional kinds of friction have diminished (even if new forms have developed in the social preparation of war, e.g. media and political surveillance). In these circumstances, where is the modern battlefield? The short answer is, potentially, anywhere and everywhere.

Historical battlefields

As a general understanding of the social and physical location of killing, the idea of battle*field* is anachronistic. This is partly because battle has transmuted into extensive killing of civilians as well as soldiers. It is also because killing can extend into every area of social structure, and therefore also every physical location of society. However, the historical idea of separated 'fields' of slaughter still has real meaning in some conflicts.

In order to understand what has changed, we need to consider the classic meaning of 'battlefield'. From ancient times until the twentieth century, the core idea was an open space where two armies met each other in combat. Throughout most of this period, combat was conceived basically as hand to hand. But from early times, projectiles of one kind or another introduced an element of physical distance into the battlefield. This meant that killing already involved more (and less) than the direct, personal slaughter of one human being by another. Moreover, the idea that the decisive encounter of arms took place in a special kind of space was always qualified. From ancient times, the conquest of one army by another involved the capture of settlements. Battle was centred not only on separated fields but also on cities, the physical centres of power. From their beginnings, urban spaces were fortified, because they were often besieged.

The *siege* was the ultimate expression of the fact that war was a decisive contest of power between two centres. A power centre might survive defeat on the battlefield; but, overcome in a siege, it could be overwhelmed to the point where it ceased to exist as a separate centre. Further, the city was not merely a military power centre; it was always a concentration of social activity. The flip side of this was that when fortified cities were besieged and conquered, entire populations were at risk. Starvation, rape and massacre, sack and pillage, can be found in sieges throughout the history of warfare (see box 6.1). Nor were these forms of violence confined to fortified centres. As armies moved through the countryside, people living in villages and farms along the way were fair game for the same horrors that were inflicted on the city.

Box 6.1   Sieges, ancient and modern

From ancient times, the core idea of the siege has been what would now be called genocidal. As Michael Walzer summarizes: 'The death of the ordinary inhabitants of the city is expected to force the hand of the civilian or military leadership. The goal is surrender; the means is not the defeat of the enemy army, but the fearful spectacle of the civilian dead.' As he points out, 'These are intentional deaths' (1992: 161–2). Besieging forces generally block the escape of civilians from the city, as the threat of their mass death is essential to the siege.

   It is very difficult to reconcile sieges with the just war tradition's ban on violence against civilians. Yet, historically, they have been accepted as legitimate, underlining how far the practice of war has been from a serious application of just war principles. Thus the Nuremberg Tribunal acquitted the Nazi commander responsible for the siege of Leningrad (1941–3), in which more than a million civilians died of starvation and disease, although he had ordered the forcible prevention of civilian escapes.

The siege remains one of the most shocking features of late-modern war, in which the mass killing of civilians is commonplace. Cities are no longer fortified places; even capitals are essentially centres of civilian population. In conditions of modern urban warfare, besieged populations are targets for the sniper – producing a daily toll of civilian death – and for artillery bombardment – periodically inflicting larger massacres, as we saw in the sieges of Vukovar, Dubrovnik, Sarajevo and East Mostar during the Yugoslav wars. Large-scale massacre may also follow the conclusion of a siege, as at Srebrenica in 1995.

The siege, however, is no longer the only or often the principal form of violence against urban centres. States may flatten a city with long-range artillery, as the Russians have done to Grozny, or destroy its power centres selectively with sophisticated air power, as the West has done to Baghdad and Belgrade. Behind all these methods lies the continuing threat of total annihilation in the manner of Dresden and Hiroshima.

Thus the idea of laying waste, or *devastating*, fields and settlements – the archetypal spaces of settled, agrarian societies – was central to warfare historically. The extent of both killing and the destruction of settlements in ancient, medieval and early modern wars should put paid to any simple idea that modern and late-modern war is uniquely violent. Relative to the material conditions of the time, armed force was often appallingly destructive. Nevertheless, smaller populations and agricultural surpluses combined with limited means of transportation and communication to restrict capacities for slaughter. The horrors of ancient and medieval war were nothing compared to what was to come. As long as there has been war, any physical arena of human activity could become a place of battle. But only in modern and late-modern war has the idea of the battlefield been transformed into one of *complex, multiple, overlapping spaces of violence*.

The modern revolution in slaughter took the new technologies of production, transport and communications and turned them into means of killing. By the same token, it took the ever-ramifying social and physical spaces of industrial societies and made battlefields of them. This process has now gone so far that contemporary military thinkers are abandoning the idea of battlefield for that of *battlespace*. But decisive transformations in the location of battle had already occurred in earlier stages of modernity.

Modern killing spaces

The implications of industrialism for war have usually been understood in terms of technology. We saw in chapter 4, however, that industrial society also gave war a new social base. With the changing social structure of war came new battlespaces. War economies and societies were seen, at first, as *home fronts*, where goods were produced for the 'real' front where battle was still located. It was then an obvious extension of military logic, aided by new technologies of aerial bombardment, which transformed the home front into an actual battlefield. National economy and national society became battlespaces. This was not merely a technical shift with human consequences, but a shift in the military significance of society. Bombing targeted not just *industry* but also *morale*. It aimed to destroy not only the physical infrastructure of enemy arms production, but also its social, political and mental basis.

Precedents for this new targeting can be found, of course, in social and psychological aspects of warfare throughout the ages. But a new way of producing war, new social forces and new technologies (of surveillance as well as destruction) combined to produce distinctively modern battlefields. National economies and societies were regarded as key components of war machines: they were central parts of the enemy power that needed to be destroyed. Thus, however much the idea of attacking civilians contradicted all known norms of war, economy and society became in the minds of leaders and generals legitimate targets of war.

With the idea of economy and society as part of the enemy, their distinctive physical spaces became battlespaces. The *factory*, as an organization of war production, became a prime bombing target. However, in the middle and even late twentieth century, the accurate targeting of individual industrial plants remained difficult. Moreover, urban-industrial populations were key concentrations of the enemy population as a whole, whose morale was seen as a crucial element. It was not a large step for military planners, but a decisive one in the breaching of moral codes on the targeting of civilians, to make *the industrial city* in its entirety a space of war. Within a few years in the Second World War, bombing moved from the selective destruction of key sites within cities to extensive attacks on urban areas and, finally, to instantaneous annihilation of entire urban spaces and populations. Total destruction was first achieved through extensive bombing that created fire-storms, which consumed entire populations in places like Dresden and Tokyo. Destruction was then perfected into a single strike with the atomic bomb. This aerial bombardment of cities was different from historic sieges, because cities were no longer fortified spaces: everywhere they had long since outgrown the spatial limits of medieval fortifications, and had become places primarily of industry and commerce. As it moved beyond the direct targeting of munitions factories, urban bombing became indiscriminate slaughter of civilians: the quintessential form of degenerate war, tending towards genocide. Further, the aerial onslaught on the city was often matched by rapacious slaughter on the ground (see box 6.2). Towns, villages and farms were reduced to rubble by advancing armies. Populations were slaughtered in cold blood, often in vast killing ditches in the countryside, or in mass burnings in villages. Great cities were destroyed by siege as well as by air power.

Box 6.2   *Slaughter in total conquest*

Civilian death in modern war is overwhelmingly associated with aerial bombardment, and in genocide with special systems such as the Nazi extermination camps and the Cambodian 'killing fields'. Historically, however, the degenerate tendency in modern war, which links war and genocide, often emerged as part of *armed conquest* on the ground. Today it is still a common component of armed struggle, by both armies and irregular forces.

Two land campaigns of the Second World War stand out for their enormous brutality against civilian populations. The Japanese conquest of China, together with the subsequent struggles with both Kuomintang and Communist forces, was marked by extensive and indiscriminate violence against civilians (see episode IV). The Nazis' conquest of the western Soviet Union in 1941 was a campaign of extreme brutality, even by the standard of their prior advance into Poland. The slaughter of Jews (along with Communists, Soviet prisoners and others) in ditches and forests was the moment at which a generally *genocidal* campaign turned into a war of *extermination*, setting the scene for the 'final solution' (see episode III).

Many late-modern wars have been genocidal in similar ways, but not on the same scale. Conquests have been marked by roadside massacres of civilians as well as brutalized prison camps. However, the physical destruction, dispersal and demoralization of the enemy have often been undertaken with the aim of expelling a population from a territory – so-called ethnic cleansing.

Conquered populations were concentrated in the remnants of cities, in makeshift conditions where death from starvation, disease and bombardment was common. Particularly noxious examples of this were the *genocidal ghettos* into which the Nazis herded Polish Jews in 1939–41. Here the conquered civilians – men, women and even children were considered enemies by the Nazis – were concentrated, confined by guards and barbed wire, weakened by miserable, over-crowded conditions and inadequate food, and worked and destroyed at the same time. These ghettos were transitional killing spaces in a double sense. Their inhabitants were on the border between life and death, with the result that many died of hunger and disease. And these makeshift adaptations of existing urban quarters were precursors of the special new killing camps of the 'final solution', to which the remnants of the ghetto populations were eventually transported.

Increasingly, indeed, modern war and genocide had already produced grisly new spaces of systematic violence and death, of which the archetype was the *concentration camp* in its various muta-tions. Although warfare had always produced prisons, as enemies were incarcerated, concentration camps were novel places. Here vast numbers of mainly civilian enemies as well as captured sol-diers were imprisoned, forced to work, killed through overwork, cold, hunger, disease and brutality, and sometimes slaughtered (see box 6.3).

Box 6.3   Concentration and death camps

Concentration camps were originally devised to hold prisoners of war. The British used them in South Africa at the turn of the twentieth century to contain captured Boer fighters. But even in this early instance, camps contained many non-combatants – women and children whose homes had been razed to destroy the base for the Boers' irregular war (Spies 1977).

As the enemies in modern war became national, class, racial and other social groups, so the camp was developed as its distinctive military-political space. By the late 1920s Stalin had already incarcerated thousands of political opponents in camps. Thereafter, in his 'great terror' – a veritable war against large sections of society, peasants, workers and even bureaucrats (see episode II) – vast numbers were forced into a huge *labour-camp* system. Here people lived in terrible conditions, and many died; but they also worked – the camp system became a sizeable element in the Soviet economy. The vast 'gulag archipelago' of punishment and death (Solzhenitzyn 1974) lasted for more than a decade after the Second World War.

The Nazis also used concentration camps at first to incarcerate political opponents. During the war, however, their role was vastly expanded, to receive 'enemy' populations of all kinds, above all Jews. Within the Nazi camp system there was also an 'industrial' element, as in Soviet camps; but with the all-out war in the east, as the campaigns against Jews and other civilian enemies were intensified, the camps' main business became industrialized killing. Camps like Auschwitz-Birkenau were great metropoles of cruelty and killing, veritable cities of death. With the perfection of the gas chambers, these main Nazi centres became *extermination camps*.

While genocidal war produced these new killing spaces, modern war was generally turning existing social spaces into fields of death. Within two decades of 1945, nuclear war planning and missile technology created a situation in which every city was a potential Hiroshima. Nearly every sizeable urban area in the northern hemisphere was a planned target of nuclear missile attack. Without conquering or moving 'enemy' populations, nuclear-armed states would be able to produce the industrialized mass slaughter of each population concentration throughout enemy territories. The exponential growth of 'kilotonnage' in nuclear weaponry soon led to the conclusion that whole nations could be more or less instantaneously liquidated in a single exchange. The physical correlates of this were such extensive blast, fire and radiation that most human beings would be killed, and most physical structures destroyed. The very environment of life on earth was at risk. Except, of course, that there would no longer be battle other than in a very attenuated sense: only more or less complete mutual annihilation. The battlefield was everywhere; everywhere was the battlefield.

This distinctively modern trend towards more extensive battle-spaces, culminating in the totality of nuclear extermination, was complemented, however, by trends towards more *intensive* violence. The 'abstract' slaughter of the bomb and the missile was matched by new methods of terror and killing that took war inside the human body and mind. Of course, calculated physical and mental invasion had many precedents in the history of power. Torture, mutilation and indoctrination were commonplaces of medieval war: the Spanish Inquisition was the prototype of a modern torture organization. But with modern science and technology, killer states now had many new means of attacking the person.

Practitioners of genocide transformed mind and body into battlefields in the most gruesome ways. They deployed modern scientific and medical knowledge to inflict cruelty on individual human beings; but they also practised cruelty in the name of a perverted science and medicine. Defining certain populations not only as enemies, but as less human than others, totalitarian regimes saw people's bodies and minds as raw material for 'experiments', which destroyed them while they were still alive. During the Second World War, infamous medical practitioners in the Nazi camps and special units of the Japanese army exemplified this intensification of slaughter. During the Korean War, Communist North Korea became a byword for mental indoctrination. But the idea of the individual body and mind as battlefields has not been confined to the killing machines of overtly genocidal powers. Western militaries have been front runners in psychological warfare, as well as in bombing and nuclear weapons.

Extensive and intensive war are not opposites, but two sides of a process whereby violence claims every social space. The abstract annihilation of masses and the surgical-psychological destruction of the individual are polar cases of the same ultra-destructive tendency of modern war. Bombing kills many people simultaneously; shooting kills many serially; machine gunning makes serial killing virtually instantaneous. Radiation attacks many people more or less simultaneously; biological weapons work through serial infection. Gas chambers destroy many simultaneously; torture and pseudo-medical experiments work on individuals. These differences matter, but not excessively. In the end, the distinctions involved are partly about the specific motives for different kinds of killing, partly about the technologies involved. But whichever ways states kill, in the end people die, die in large numbers, and suffer enormously. In both extensive and intensive slaughter, the battlefield is society and the individuals who make it up.

Guerrilla war has involved parallel transformations of battle-space to those of more 'conventional' war. Indeed, the very point of guerrilla struggle is to avoid battle with superior forces in a battlefield. Military struggle is taken instead into every pore of society. While guerrillas and counter-insurgents deal in abstractions of class and nation, they also fight for the hearts and minds of each villager. For each side, enemy-controlled populations are both extensive and intensive targets. The people, and where they live, are the battlefield. Villages and villagers are burned.

Counter-insurgents especially fear the peasantry among whom the guerrillas hide. Governments frequently attempt to deprive insurgents of their support by concentrating the population in fortified settlements (the Americans in Vietnam were notorious for their 'strategic hamlets', but they have been used much more widely).

Global era slaughter spaces

Transformations of social structure produced the horrific killing spaces of the mid-twentieth-century world. However, social, as well as political, changes in the last half-century have continued to produce new ramifications of killing space. 'New wars' in the global era have inherited basic patterns of violence from twentieth-century total war. But rapid social, political and technological changes have produced new late-modern mutations: distinctive killing fields of our times.

The umbilical link between killing machines and class structure has been broken. Advanced armies no longer depend on mass recruitment of workers, or on labour-intensive arms industries. High-technology militaries don't need to organize whole urban economies: they are as likely to depend on scattered smaller firms in post-urban settings. By the same token, economic-strategic rationales for counter-industrial and city-to-city targeting have been undermined. Similarly, political contexts of interstate and inter-bloc rivalry have subsided, if not disappeared. Great states that were formerly rivals, like the United States and Japan, Britain and Germany, are enmeshed in ever deeper and broader co-operation in the Western power conglomerate. Between the West and its former Communist enemies, Russia and China, there has been rapid growth in co-operation and interdependence, even if tensions remain. With an ever more integrated global state framework (centred on the West) reinforced by a legitimate global layer of state institutions (centred on the UN), the political rationale for all-out war between major centres of state power is generally weaker. In this context, the idea of all-out totally destructive war, of the kind envisaged by nuclear planners during the Cold War, appears increasingly unreal – although by no means can it be ruled out.

With these social, political and military changes, the plausibility of many ideological concepts of 'enemies' has weakened. Particularly in the West, but also to some extent elsewhere, the development of more open, plural media has made it more difficult (although not impossible) for states to mobilize national societies for the limited wars that strategy and technology dictate. Thus the mass mediation of war reinforces the tendency towards more limited conceptions of battlespace.

Wars have tended to be either between lesser state centres or parastatal organizations, or between these and one or other of the great powers. They often arise out of the contradictions of democratization: to win or hold electoral power, a ruling group often needs to mobilize an ethnic base – against supposed ethnic enemies. In these contexts, genocide has become a common mode of war. States' enemies are social groups as much as other states. Yet the structures of the killing fields differ from those of earlier genocides. Ethnic-national dominion is still imposed militarily, but in a democratizing era it needs to be legitimated by electoral means. Nationalism can succeed only by manufacturing a largely homogeneous electorate, eliminating groups that will not support the national project. The homogeneity of the dominant national group is also reinforced by intimidation – and often by participation in bloodletting and robbery. Thus patterns of killing are determined largely by political mobilization in the killing zone itself.

The genocides of great centres have always depended on local auxiliaries – for example, the Nazis employed Latvian and Ukrainian nationalists and Polish anti-Semites. In today's genocides of lesser states and parastatal groups, the relationship has been tilted further towards local participation. The Serbian state relied heavily on Bosnian-Serb and Kosovan-Serb politicians, police and paramilitaries in its killing-sprees; the Croatian state relied on its ethnic base in the zone of conflict to do the dirty work in Bosnia. With this *localization* of genocide, the battlespace has switched to land, houses, goods and votes.

These processes intensify the killing. If slaughter is a local political-economic process, it is more often personal. The Nazi Holocaust was carried out in Poland and eastern Europe – most people in Germany itself knew only indirectly what was happening. Contemporary slaughter in former Yugoslavia, the Caucasus and many parts of Africa often occurs within a smaller region, and is often committed by people who are in closer relationships with their victims. *Neighbour killing* has become common. The direct, personal humiliation of the enemy is more important to the destruction of their social power. *Robbery* has become an even more important part of genocide, as perpetrators steal the homes, consumer goods and cash of the victims. *Rape and sexual slavery*, ever accompaniments of war, have been identified now as policy instruments. Likewise, *mutilation*, by hacking off of limbs, has become common in some wars. Violation of the body, with maximum pain, has become a common method of slaughter.

In the practice of many local regimes, therefore, killing spaces have enveloped the physical and emotional well-being of the killed in new ways. In the practice of the major powers, by contrast, killing spaces have become ever more abstract and general, so death is further distanced from the policies that produce it. The role of air power as the primary mode of war has been reinforced. Certainly, at the beginning of the twenty-first century, the Russian air force flattened Grozny in a manner reminiscent of Berlin in 1945. But the USA and the West bombed Baghdad and Belgrade with 'smart' weapons, precision-targeting barracks and bridges, ministries and munitions dumps. In these new Western campaigns, the physical battlefield has been inserted more selectively into the complex structure of an urban area, only indirectly and 'accidentally' including residential sites. Nevertheless, even selective bombing can have major life-threatening consequences, quite apart from the consequences of targeting errors. The firing of oilfields (which Iraq did in Kuwait in 1991) and chemical plants spreads dangerous pollution. The destruction of sewage or electricity facilities (as the West did to Iraq in 1991) threatens the infrastructure of modern life. It has long been recognized that the bombing of nuclear power plants could have the same effect as nuclear bombing.

If the physical battlefield has become more specialized, the psychological battlefield remains broadly conceived. Civilian morale has been targeted not with fire-storms or atomic annihilation, but with the drip-drip of bomb-induced intimidation, dislocation and economic sanctions. In all-out, generalized total war, such limited damage was judged insufficient to break morale. In contemporary limited war, it is still unlikely to produce surrender. It may be enough, however, to weaken the legitimacy of enemy regimes. This has often been the limit, in any case, of the West's active ambitions for political change.

Another attenuation of the battlefield results from the fact that war is often pursued by other means. From selective physical targeting, the West has moved to increasing use of economic and political *sanctions* as a complement to military force. Extensive economic and political controls are combined with limited demonstrations of military superiority. These economic and political regimes imposed by international institutions can constitute indirect killing fields (see box 6.4). Western-global state institutions aim to weaken enemy states, but find it difficult to avoid harming civilian populations whom they profess to protect. Thus indirect slaughter, from war- and sanctions-induced poverty and disease, becomes a larger part of the death toll than the numbers killed directly by bombs and missiles. Moreover, genocidal states and parastatal groups often exploit sanctions regimes strategically, to concentrate social resources in their hands at the expense of the population, while blaming the West.

Box 6.4   Sanctions: war by other means

Historically, sieges and blockades have often caused huge casualties. 'More civilians died in the siege of Leningrad than in the modernist infernos of Hamburg, Dresden, Tokyo, Hiroshima and Nagasaki, taken together,' Walzer (1992: 160) points out. 'They probably died more painfully too.' The global-era version of the siege or blockade is systems of *economic sanctions*, which have been imposed on far more states since the end of the Cold War.

Imposed by the UN, sanctions invoke international authority and demonstrate international power without overt violence. They have traditionally been supported by the pacific left wing in Western states: 'sanctions not war' was a cry of anti-war activists prior to the US-led attack on Iraq in 1991. Indeed, sanctions have traditionally been derided by many on the political right as an ineffectual response to international aggression.

At the beginning of the twenty-first century, the terms of the arguments about sanctions have changed. Faced not with great-power aggressors but with so-called rogue states and local genocidists, in many cases Western elites are increasingly unwilling to invoke military power. In the era of televised bomb blasts and body bags, the advantage of sanctions for Western power is that they impose a price on recalcitrant opponents without producing pictures of bomb victims or demanding the supreme price from their own soldiers. Although it is far from clear that economic sanctions, by themselves, have decisive effects on determined local forces, they can achieve some containment and they give the appearance of action.

Sanctions have not been deployed as simple alternatives to military force. Against Iraq, comprehensive sanctions were agreed in 1990, as part of the build-up to the Gulf War, and were continued afterwards, combined with military measures like 'no fly zones', supported by intermittent bombing. Against Serbia, years of sanctions had limited political effects until after the Kosovo War, when they helped to put pressure on a weakened

Milosevic regime, and the prospect of their removal provided incentives to its successors to co-operate with the West and international justice.

Controversy over sanctions has centred on the case of Iraq. The USA insisted that the UN maintain tight sanctions when other policies failed. The Iraqi regime largely protected itself and its armed forces from their effects, allowing the population to suffer and using this as a propaganda tool. The combination of sanctions with these regime priorities produced widespread suffering, which in turn led to controversy about the genocidal effects of sanctions and their general discrediting.

However, narrower political and military sanctions, aimed more specifically at elites rather than broadly at the economic basis of a state, could still be important measures for the UN in the future. This kind of 'smart' sanction, supposedly dispensing with the indiscriminate effects of measures like trade embargoes, is becoming more popular in Western policy circles early in the twenty-first century.

Media as battlespace

The other major transformation in late-modern war is that mass media have become a major battlespace. Although media do not constitute a killing field in a direct way, media war and physical war are intimately interrelated. Genocidal states use radio, television and video to arouse national and ethnic hatred, mobilize killing gangs and justify slaughter. Most notoriously, Radio-Télévision des Milles Collines called the Hutu population to participate in the killing of their Tutsi neighbours in Rwanda in 1994.

The principal media battlespace, however, has been the *globalized Western mass media*. It is not that war is now purely virtual, as the post-modernist Jean Baudrillard notoriously suggested during the 1991 Gulf War. But the new Western way of war, based on risk-transfer militarism (see episode X), is premised on taking direct killing out of view. Visible death, especially of Western soldiers and of civilians, is avoided. It follows that death that is less visible is more acceptable; death from hunger, in remote places and from causes that are relatively obscure, is less troubling to power than death from bombing by easily attributable sources, in places where it can be instantly filmed and transmitted around the world.

This sanitization of death in the media exemplifies a larger promise of non-war in the new Western way of war. Cyberwar promises, we are told, to replace the tearing apart of human bodies by the blocking of computer systems. In the robotic battlefield, as in the missile attack, machines will replace human beings. 'Non-lethal' weapons are being developed. And in peacekeeping and peace enforcement, soldiers become more like armed policemen than fighters. In all these developments, traditional battlefields are displaced. Yet, so long as contests of power between separated centres remain, physical force will continue to remain their central manifestation. Non-lethal war represents at best the attenuation, at worst an extension, of violent struggle – not its opposite.

Sanitized media coverage places a new premium, moreover, on any successful intrusion of violence. Thus media coverage of war is not a one-sided process, but a conflict in which anti-Western forces will attempt to disrupt the appearance of pacified conflict. The media battlespace centres on the attempt of the West's enemies to inflict sufficient casualties to dent the image of a smoothly managed, relatively painless, military process. This has been the central media process in recent wars with conventional state enemies, as box 6.5 shows.

Box 6.5 Global media war

Local states and movements often try to use the physical battlefield to damage their Western opponents in the global media war. The Vietnam-derived 'body bag' syndrome – killing enough Western soldiers to foster anti-war opinion in the West – has become a strategic imperative for the West's enemies. Both Saddam Hussein in 1991 and Slobodan Milosevic in 1999 believed that Western determination to wage war was not strong enough to withstand significant numbers of military casualties. At the same time, they tried to exploit Western global media coverage of their own civilian casualties as a result of Western bombing.

For Western governments and militaries, the media war has increasingly been combined with an attempt to maintain a 'surgical' use of physical force, which destroys enemy assets, minimizes embarrassing enemy civilian casualties and above all reduces losses of Western lives to very small numbers. They attempt to manage media coverage in a way that sustains public support for their political goals. In recent wars, they have generally managed this balancing act successfully. Coalition casualties of 250 in the Gulf, compared with tens of thousands of Iraqi deaths, proved compatible with 'public opinion' constraints. In Kosovo, there were, astonishingly, no Western combat deaths at all, and in Afghanistan few, making media management in these wars relatively easy.

The most striking example of a local movement's success with respect to this issue was the humiliation of the United States when its soldiers were killed in Somalia in 1993. Here, however, US determination to win the conflict was weak, and public opinion was unprepared. In more crucial conflicts, where Western powers are more committed and plan their media management better, they are more difficult to defeat. Authoritarian states may be relatively inept at media management – Iraq first antagonized Western media with crude manipulation of hostages, and then expelled journalists, having to invite them back in when civilian casualties became an issue. Serbia was more sophisticated in its approach, and more successful than Iraq in exploiting NATO targeting errors. But overall, the domestic and international political costs for its regime proved greater than those for the West.

Moreover, media war gives high priority not just to violence and death, but to dramatic acts. Even relatively small groups can make very successful propaganda by violent means, thus balancing out their weaknesses in conventional political and military terms. Not only is violence more dramatic than peaceful protest: but the bloodier the presentation of violence, the greater the media, and therefore political, effects.

Modern terrorism depends heavily, therefore, on mass media for its effect. Explosions, killing and maiming create dramatic images linked to emotions of horror and fear. The targets, and victims, of terrorism are overwhelmingly civilian, however. Civilians are easier to attack; their deaths are in many ways more shocking than those of soldiers; they symbolize the powerlessness of the enemy state in a key area, its inability to protect its own citizens; and their suffering puts intense political pressure especially on democratic states. Terrorism is usually a highly degenerate form of war, incipiently genocidal because it attacks civilian social groups in a more or less indiscriminate manner. But the ever more central role of media in conflict has provided increasing incentives to propaganda of the violent deed.

The planes crashing into the World Trade Centre on 11 September 2001 created an unforgettable violent spectacle, which will symbolize conflicts of international power for a generation. This was above all a *symbolic* action. The simultaneous destruction of the World Trade Centre (physical symbol of US economic power) and part of the Pentagon (centre of US military planning) with hijacked planes (symbols of global transportation) powerfully challenged American confidence in its way of life as well as its world supremacy. This terrorism converted office blocks into killing spaces and passenger planes into weapons. The perpetrators of these acts could never defeat the USA by more conventional military means. They rejected the slower, more painstaking routes, both of conventional international politics and of peaceful social mobilization. Their propaganda act depended on violence: not just the destruction of powerful physical structures, but the slaughter of thousands of office workers and others. Drenched in blood, the terror and shock that the action engendered increased its propaganda value enormously. Peaceful propaganda by deed, such as the dramatic gestures of Greenpeace, has never had the same effect.

Terrorism stands to propaganda, therefore, as war does to politics. Terror is certainly a normal component of war and genocide (hence state terrorism is also commonplace). But *terrorists* are warriors who make terror into a specialized struggle with propaganda goals. Like guerrillas, they typically draw on a wider social constituency, but, unlike guerrillas, they neither wage a direct struggle for all-out victory, nor actively mobilize their base. Terrorist groups are typically small, secretive organizations, which use their audacious deeds as propaganda to generate indirect political support. In global mass media they have found a powerful battlespace, in which they have many advantages.

Further reading

Arkin, W. M. and Fieldhouse, R. W. (1985) *Nuclear Battlefields: Global Links in the Arms Race*. Cambridge, MA.: Ballinger.

Arnove, A. (2000) *Iraq under Siege: The Deadly Impact of Sanctions and War*. Cambridge, MA.: South End Press.

Benard, C. (1994) Rape as terror: the case of Bosnia. *Terrorism and Political Violence*, 6(1).

Chan, S. and Cooper, A., eds (2000) *Sanctions as Economic Statecraft: Theory and Practice*. Basingstoke: Macmillan.

Chasdi, R. J. (1999) *Serenade of Suffering: A Portrait of Middle East Terrorism, 1968–1993*. Lanham, MD: Lexington Books.

Drezner, D. W. (1999) *The Sanctions Paradox: Economic Statecraft and International Relations*. Cambridge: Cambridge University Press.

Duffy, C. (1996) *Siege Warfare: The Fortress in the Early Modern World, 1494–1660*. London: Routledge.

Ehrlich, P. et al. (1984) *The Cold and the Dark: The World after Nuclear War*. London: Sidgwick and Jackson.

Guelke, A. (1995) *The Age of Terrorism and the International Political System*. London: Tauris.

Jasani, B. M. (1978) *Outer Space – Battlefield of the Future?* Stockholm: International Peace Research Institute / Taylor & Francis.

Katz, A. M. (1982) *Life after Nuclear War: The Economic and Social Impact of Nuclear Attacks on the United States*. New York: Ballinger.

Keegan, J. (1976) *The Face of Battle*. London: Cape.

Keegan, J. (1993) *A History of Warfare*. London: Hutchinson.

Krell, R. and Sherman, M. I. (1997) *Genocide: A Critical Bibliographic Review*, vol. 4: *Medical and Psychological Effects of Concentration Camps on Holocaust Survivors*. New Brunswick, NJ: Transaction Publishers.

Lifton, R. J. and Markusen, E. (1990) *The Genocidal Mentality: Nazi Holocaust and Nuclear Threat*. London: Macmillan.

MacNeill, W. H. (1982) *The Pursuit of Power*. Oxford: Blackwell.

McInnes, C. and Sheffield, G. D., eds (1988) *Warfare in the Twentieth Century: Theory and Practice*. London: Unwin Hyman.

Moser, C. and Clark, F., eds (2001) *Victims, Perpetrators or Actors?: Gender, Armed Conflict and Political Violence*. London: Zed Books.

Nacos, B. L. (1994) *Terrorism and the Media: From the Iran Hostage Crisis to the World Trade Center Bombing*. New York: Columbia University Press.

Onwudiwe, I. D. (2001) *The Globalization of Terrorism*. Aldershot: Ashgate.

Simons, G. (1999) *Imposing Economic Sanctions*. London: Pluto.

Sofsky, W. (1997) *The Order of Terror: The Concentration Camp*. Princeton: Princeton University Press.

Solzhenitzyn, A. (1974) *The Gulag Archipelago: 1918–1956*. London: Collins.

Spies, S. B. (1977) *Methods of Barbarism*. Cape Town: Human and Rousseau.

Walzer, M. (1992) *Just and Unjust Wars*. New York: Basic Books.

Ware, J. and Posner, G. (1987) *Mengele: The Complete Story*. London: Dell.

Watson, P. (1978) *War on the Mind: The Military Uses and Abuses of Psychology*. London: Hutchinson.

Weiss, T. G. (1997) *Political Gain and Civilian Pain: Humanitarian Impacts and Economic Sanctions*. Lanham, MD: Rowman and Littlefield.

Episode VI
Nuclear war preparation

The atomic bombings of the Japanese cities of Hiroshima and Nagasaki brought the destructive bombing of the Second World War to its logical conclusion. With the atomic bombs, a single weapon and delivery system achieved instantaneously what previously required a large number of bombs and planes. Whole cities were blown up, tens of thousands killed and many more burnt and irradiated. People died from the cancers caused for decades afterwards.

However, with the subsequent development of weaponry, nuclear war threatened far worse: the destruction of whole national societies, of the industrialized world, of worldwide human society, even of life on earth. The open questions about nuclear war were, and are, only about the extent of the mass killing it would cause, within this mind-boggling range. Developments in technology, the size of arsenals and strategy have all modified the terms of the argument. The Soviet atomic bomb made a prospective nuclear war two- rather than one-sided. Hydrogen bombs greatly increased the scale of probable destruction from a single weapon. Intercontinental ballistic missiles consolidated these changes, by the late 1950s, into the prospect of comprehensive mutual destruction of the warring states.

From the 1940s, there had been widespread recognition that nuclear weapons would change the terms of argument about war. 'Thus far the chief purpose of our military establishment has been to win wars,' wrote the strategist Bernard Brodie. 'From now on its chief purpose must be to avert them. It can have almost no other useful purpose' (Brodie 1946: 76). But it did not follow from this that nuclear war could not happen: the danger was built into deterrence. 'Weapons deter by the possibility of their use, and by no other route,' the senior British official Michael Quinlan pointed out, so 'the distinction sometimes attempted between deterrent capabilities and war-fighting capabilities has in a strict sense no meaningful basis' (Quinlan 1997: 15).

Indeed, as the nuclear strategist Colin Gray says, 'history would seem to show that deterrence is exceedingly unreliable'. The 'commonplace' view that 'for much of the Cold War the strategic balance between the superpowers was metastable' is wrong. 'On balance we did well to avoid allowing a World War III to terminate the Cold War. The non-war outcome was probably attributable at least as much to luck as to good political and strategic judgement, but still the occasions for possible folly were strewn with almost liberal abundance through the first two decades of the conflict' (Gray 1998: 324, 308, 347).

What kind of war would this have been, and what would it have meant for society? Gray writes that '[n]uclear war must always be a terrible event. But there are degrees of terrible, and those degrees could matter'. 'Statesmen and strategists of the nuclear era are trapped', he therefore argues, 'in the existential conundrum that they may be obliged to wage a form of war – nuclear war – that they believe unlikely to have any outcome other than bilateral disaster' (Gray 1998: 307, 315). During the 1970s and 1980s American planners devised schemes for 'flexible' or 'graduated' nuclear response, implying the possibility of a 'limited' or European 'theatre' nuclear war. Soviet planners never accepted this premise; in any case the law of escalation in war made it inherently problematic.

Critics of strategy attempted to find language to comprehend the awful prospects which nuclear war would bring. It would be at the same time *genocide*, the slaughter of the other side's population, and *national suicide*, given the likelihood of destruction of any society whose state used nuclear weapons. It could be *omnicide*, the destruction of all (or almost all) human life, and possibly of most non-human life on the planet – for example, through a 'nuclear winter' comparable in its death toll to those of mega-volcanoes and asteroid collisions. According to Edward Thompson (1982), it reflected an *exterminist* society, which consciously produced the means of its own destruction.

Further reading

Aronson, R. (1983) *The Dialectics of Disaster*. London: Verso.

Brodie, B., ed. (1946) *The Absolute Weapon: Atomic Power and World Order*. New York.

Gray, C. (1998) *Modern Strategy*. Oxford: Oxford University Press.

Lifton, R. J. and Markusen, E. (1988) *The Genocidal Mentality: The Nazi Holocaust and the Nuclear Threat*. London: Macmillan.

Quinlan, M. (1997) *Thinking about Nuclear Weapons*. London: Royal United Services Institution.

Thompson, E. P. (1982) Notes on exterminism, the last stage of civilization. In New Left Review, ed., *Exterminism and Cold War*, London: Verso, 1–32.

— 7 —

Combatants and Participants

If killing and killing fields have been transformed, who today are combatants? What are the roles of armies and other organized bodies of fighter-killers? What are the relationships between them and civilian populations? How far *can* we distinguish combatants and non-combatants? After a century notorious for the breaking down of this distinction, the answers to these questions are by no means simple. Moreover, we need to be careful in our answers, since broad designation of combatants could legitimate the wider identification of targets and thereby threaten the creation of even more potential victims of war.

Combatants and non-combatants

Combatants are men in arms, and are most simply defined as those who fight and kill. They conventionally include all those who give manifest token of their preparedness to fight through membership of an armed force. Most obviously, therefore, combatants are members of formally constituted armed organizations – that is, armies. In actual war, combatants have nearly always included men (and some women) who were not members of such bodies. But even if combat involvement is defined in this broader way, in any war, usually a majority of society – notably the young, old men and most women – are non-combatants.

Non-combatants are essentially *civilians*. As the term suggests, historically citizens have been distinguished from soldiers in this way. Of course, people moved between civilian and military roles in the course of a lifetime, even in the course of a war. Particularly at the rank-and-file level, armies have usually been composed of men who had other social roles, most commonly as peasants, to look back on and forward to. Standing armies were always expensive to maintain, and had to be paid for out of general production. In pre-modern periods the surplus was not always so great, nor the ability to tax so constant, nor the willingness of peasants to leave their fields sustainable for long periods – whatever the coercion applied. But even if combatant status is changeable, at any given moment it is reasonably clear: someone who bears arms or who is a member of an armed force is a combatant. A person who doesn't bear arms and isn't in an armed force is not.

The distinction becomes less clear, however, when we consider the relationship between combat and other forms of war participation. Non-combatants are not necessarily non-participants. In all wars, many contribute to the prosecution of a campaign without actually fighting, killing or being a member of an armed force. As I have argued, war is prepared politically, economically and ideologically. All who participate in war preparation can be viewed, in principle, as *participants* in war. In this broad sense, virtually all members of societies involved in wars, especially modern societies, may be participants to some degree. Nevertheless, to participate is not necessarily to be fully *responsible*: this is proved by the limiting case of children, who may participate in wars but cannot be held responsible for them. Even among adults, types and degrees of both participation and responsibility vary greatly – and not necessarily in the same way. Much war participation is coerced, and coercion certainly affects the context of individual responsibility.

This general character of war participation is not distinctively modern. In pre-modern societies too, war often involved whole communities, rich and poor, men and women, old and young alike. But the modern transformations of the politics, economics and ideology of war, discussed in earlier chapters, have all extended the framework of war participation. *Military participation*, in the narrow sense of membership of armed forces, has typically been organized through universal male conscription across society. *Participation in war preparation* has been organized through arms industries, mass politics and secular as well as religious ideology. Likewise, actual *war participation* has embraced mass civilian populations in these new ways. Although participation in, and responsibility for, war may be differentiated, near-universal participation does raise disturbing questions. The link between society as participant in war and society as its victim is strong. If society in general – and many groups within it – directly sustain war, is it surprising that society in general, and the same groups, have become targets and victims? There is thus a vicious cycle of participation and victimhood.

In order to clarify the nature of participation, I look first at the nature of armed forces, and then turn to wider social participation in war. Processes of victimization will be discussed in chapter 8.

Armed forces

Armies are bodies of men (and sometimes women) organized to fight and kill. Whatever else they do, armed forces (including naval, air and paramilitary forces) are organizations constituted for this purpose. Both war and genocide are carried out principally by armed forces. Armies are as old as war, but their character and role have changed in modern, compared to pre-modern, societies and are undergoing further transformation in the global era.

The classic modern armed force has been the *mass army*. Armies on a large scale relative to the general population existed earlier in history. But the mass army can be traced to France in the Revolutionary era, when a huge armed force was assembled using, for the first time, a recognizably modern method of conscription, the *levée en masse*. Similar systems of universal male military service in peacetime were standardized later in the nineteenth century, starting in Prussia and then spreading throughout Continental Europe. Typically, all young men served a year or two in the armed forces, and then remained available as members of a trained reserve until they reached middle age.

With this type of army, European empires and states developed capacities to mobilize very large numbers of men. A substantial standing army could be supplemented in war by a larger body of men who had undergone military training earlier in their lives. Supported by production surpluses, expanded bureaucracy, political organization and media power, the mass army enabled states to project much greater violence over longer periods than ever before. The peasantry and, increasingly, the industrial working class formed the core of mass armies: the latter thus became the main social force of total war.

In the nineteenth and early twentieth centuries, mass armies depended on sheer numbers of men, able to operate simple machinery and weapons and comply with discipline. Armies paralleled industries in being based largely on concentrations of relatively unskilled workers with basic mechanical skills. Soldiers were disposable commodities, easily replaced by new recruits from the rural poor and the unemployed. In the aftermath of the Second World War, we tend to think mainly about the vast scale of civilian slaughter inflicted by mass armies. However, the American Civil War and the First World War demonstrated above all that soldiers' lives were expendable on a shocking scale (see episode 0).

Soldiers were 'cannon fodder', because armies were the most authoritarian institutions of all in societies that were themselves still largely authoritarian. The progress of democracy and socialism led to only patchy challenges to the authority of military elites. During the First World War, even 'democracies' like Britain still shot deserters. During the Second World War, American forces were still racially segregated. During both world wars, even these liberal states introduced conscription and sent millions of men to fight, kill and die across the world. Early twentieth-century conscript armies were 'national', bonding together men from disparate regions and backgrounds, and 'democratic', but only in the minimal sense of representing cross-sections of societies. They embodied national beliefs in the rightness of inflicting and enduring immense slaughter, ideas that do not hold so clearly in Western societies today. Conscript armies were vehicles for total war, enabling states to inflict and sustain massive levels of killing – levels that Western society is widely believed to be incapable of tolerating today.

In totalitarian states especially, mass conscript armies were also instruments of genocide. The official myths of the successor armies (in today's Germany, Japan and Russia) try to separate the roles of regular armed forces from those of the special forces, party and paramilitary organizations that were particularly implicated in atrocities. But in reality the regular German, Japanese and Soviet armies also joined in mass deportations, killings and other abuse. Since genocide occurred largely in the context of interstate war, conventional armed forces both participated directly in the slaughter of civilians and collaborated with paramilitary killing activities. This pattern has continued to this day – for example, in the genocidal wars of Serbia-Yugoslavia. In such armies, young men have often been conscripted almost directly into the most brutal killing sprees.

Western armed forces also perpetrated genocidal massacres sometimes in colonial and post-colonial wars, at least up to the Vietnam War. In the West, however, with the growing technologization of force and the ending of colonial struggles, armed forces began to change from the 1960s. Although still large in historical terms, Western armed forces were no longer 'mass armies'. According to Jacques van Doorn (1975), the *decline of the mass army* had qualitative as well as quantitative dimensions. The new military involved not only relatively smaller numbers, but also a greater reliance on professional soldiers and advanced technology. Nevertheless, the key change was that armies were no longer 'mass' in the sense of compulsorily involving the majority of adult males. Conscription was phased out in Western states offshore from Continental Europe: by the end of the 1970s, the USA, Japan, the UK, Canada and Australia all had 'all-volunteer' forces. The change only really affected Continental Western states after 1989, when the end of the Cold War removed the threat of land invasion by Soviet forces. States like Belgium, the Netherlands, Spain and (symbolically very important, given the historical role of military service in its national culture) France then abolished conscription. Italy is set to follow.

Even where Western states, and former Soviet-bloc states in Central Europe, retained conscript armies at the beginning of the twenty-first century, the role and conditions of service were changing. Alternatives to military service were much more generally available, and in some states were widely taken up – in Germany, around half of all young men chose *Zivildienst* (civilian service), even though it involved a longer term; their labours were an essential support for the social services. Rights of conscientious objection were generally liberalized, although still variable. Moreover, Western states did not actually send conscripts in combat roles, if at all, into international military interventions.

Soldiering in Western armies became more like other jobs: it was professionalized and even occupationalized. Fewer, better-paid soldiers had to be more technically skilled. More of them, indeed, were paid to maintain complex weapons systems than to operate them. Fewer risked their lives; after Vietnam, it became a priority of US and other Western governments to avoid serious loss of life among their own forces, at almost all costs. Latterly, soldiers could often expect semi-civilian conditions of life even in wartime: for example, Western soldiers in the Gulf War phoned home almost daily; nowadays they may have email connections. Where soldiers were captured, killed or exposed to health hazards, military authorities were increasingly held accountable for apparent mistakes. The lives of Western soldiers (at least) were valued: no longer 'cannon fodder'.

Western, and to a lesser extent other, armies were increasingly involved in peacekeeping or peace enforcement operations in third-party wars. Not only was the West's willingness to risk its soldiers' lives even less in these situations: in the 1999 Kosovo War, the success of this policy reached the point where not a single Western soldier was killed by Serbian forces. The skills required in 'peace' operations were often more political and policing than military in a classic sense. The 'post-modern' military emphasized flexibility and judgement in what the military sociologist Charles Moskos and his co-authors (2000) called its increasingly 'soldier-statesman' or 'soldier-scholar' officer elite. Women were recruited on more or less equal terms with men into some branches of armed forces, if not always into combat roles, where they tended to have a largely token presence, if any. Civilianization meant that civilians became a major component of military forces. Soldiers' private lives became less of a concern: even gays began to be tolerated in some armies, although this remained a controversial issue, especially in the US military.

Non-Western armies, by contrast, still often fight classically genocidal wars at the beginning of the twenty-first century. Many conscript forces, including the Russian, Turkish, Iraqi, Indonesian and Serbian, have been employed in ruthless slaughter of civilians. Mounting popular dissatisfaction is increasingly voiced over conscripts' death tolls – but less often about the atrocities the soldiers committed – as political conditions become more democratic and media slightly freer. But these armies are still able, in most cases, to expose their troops to considerable losses. They remain highly authoritarian organizations, often brutal environments for their recruits as well as for the victims of their wars. The Russian army, for example, is a byword for bullying, which many young soldiers regularly fail to survive.

Advanced Western ideas of reliance on technological fire-power and professional militaries are certainly influential throughout the world's armies. States with large financial resources and small pools of manpower, like Saudi Arabia, mimic the Western model. Even in Russia, politicians and generals sometimes pay lip-service to the idea of a fully professional armed force. Not all non-Western armies are conscripted, in any case – in poor peasant societies armies can often recruit widely without direct coercion, as soldiers are fed better and are usually paid more regularly than under-employed rural workers.

Generally, however, conscription remains a relatively cheap way of maintaining the large armed force that big, quasi-imperial states still believe they need – for crushing secessionist and democratic movements, as well as for interstate war. There is only limited space for the new 'professional' Western ideas, and still less for the more liberal concepts, especially regarding gender roles and sexuality, that are developing in Western armed forces. While some Western armies have become more genuinely plural, opening up to ethnic minorities, the old multinational Soviet and Yugoslav armies have given way to increasingly ethnic-national armies, sometimes charged with 'ethnic cleansing', in post-Soviet and post-Yugoslav states.

New killing forces

In zones of war, alongside repressive conventional armed forces, a variety of less conventional forces exist. Old-style guerrilla forces, informed by 'progressive' military-revolutionary ideas, were becoming less common by the end of the twentieth century. Those that had succeeded in seizing power, from China to Cuba and Zimbabwe, were running more or less authoritarian regimes, increasingly challenged by democratic movements. Others were making the move to democratic politics themselves: the most successful was the African National Congress in South Africa, which achieved a negotiated handover of power from the apartheid regime.

Nevertheless, the classic contradiction of military-revolutionary movements, between loosely democratic national-liberationist ideologies and authoritarian practice, has been resolved in a repressive direction in many new irregular forces. Often alongside the conventional armies of authoritarian states, more or less private armed groups, unofficially bankrolled by states, are often at the cutting edge of the killing and terror activities involved in ethnic 'cleansing', as box 7.1 illustrates.

In genocidal slaughter, the relations between conventional armed forces, police, militia, that are formally constituted, and more informal gangs are constantly shifting. State leaders and military commanders often encourage or condone the worst atrocities – but

Box 7.1   Paramilitaries and warlords

Many kinds of new killing force have emerged. The idea of guerrillas as ideologically committed revolutionaries – never a very accurate picture of many irregular armed forces – is increasingly outdated. In Balkan, former Soviet and African war zones, militias are often based on an ethnic nationalism and organized by parties or local state authorities. But alongside more formally constituted militia, with the uniforms and insignia of armies, we find less formally organized bands.

- In the Bosnian wars, the army of the Serbian statelet (itself reconstituted from elements of the Yugoslav National Army, a tactical move by Serbian leaders) worked with local militia and with killing gangs like the Tigers of the Serbian warlord Arkan.
- In the Rwandan genocide, organized militia set up by elements in the old ruling party and armed with machine guns went on to spawn more *ad hoc* killing groups that recruited young Hutu men to kill often just with machetes; later, these militia operated in Congo as well.
- In the West African wars, the Liberian warlord Charles Taylor succeeded in leading his private army to take over the state, and then went on to sponsor 'rebel' militia in Sierra Leone.

These examples show the fluid relations between different groups. The term *warlord*, historically associated with China in the early twentieth century, indicates the more personalized mode of power of many *paramilitary* leaders. Robbery, crime and illicit financial dealings often finance their rule. However, lawlessness and self-aggrandizement are often found among the leaders of recognized states too: the regimes of Milosevic in Serbia, Hussein in Iraq, Mobutu in Congo-Zaire and Suharto in Indonesia are major examples from the late twentieth century.

The internationalized nature of the new killers can be seen in how they operate widely across borders, and mobilize extensive worldwide networks of exiles in the rich world. In these senses, the terrorist network co-ordinated by Saudi-born millionaire Osama bin Laden, which carried out a series of worldwide attacks on US interests culminating in the atrocities of September 2001, was not so dissimilar from more territorially based armed groups.

leave their execution to the ancillaries. The more informal groups are often recruited from the section of the general population that is ethnically aligned with the genodical state. As we saw in chapter 6, it has been characteristic of genocide in the global era that it is carried out by forces close to the victims.

The *génocidaires* of the current era, directed by a nucleus of politically organized militia, usually include people recruited more or less spontaneously into killing operations. Those directly involved in killing are mainly, but not only, young men – often so young as to be still children. But older men and women also take part in support activities. Genocides are political processes, not spontaneous outbreaks of mass hysteria. Whole layers of society are drawn into treating other groups as enemies and denying their civil and political rights: the preliminary stages of genocide. They are also involved, more or less actively, in the more dramatic, often physically abusive processes: notably robbery of cash, goods, houses and land; destruction of buildings; and expulsion, bodily harm, rape and killing.

Social groups and war participation

These contemporary involvements in genocide are the culmination of two centuries of societal participation in the machinery of mass killing. Modern society has been, as we saw in earlier chapters, a society in which slaughter has been extensively prepared and legitimated. But the ubiquity of war participation should not hide differences between social groups in their relationships to war, or lead us to embrace simple sociological equations of social stratification, war and peace.

Some social theories have presented war and genocide as particularly perpetrated by *ruling* classes, by men, and so on. However, this is an almost tautological argument. Ruling social groups – monarchical, landowning, industrial, party and bureaucratic – have always been those who have organized war preparation and initiated wars. Men have dominated in ruling groups as well as in armies, so it was axiomatic that men directed as well as fought wars. But, as we might expect, ruling groups did not themselves fight wars. The truth is that wars have generally involved *all* subordinate classes, and women as well as men at least in supporting roles. Few sections of society have *not* been caught up in processes that have led to mass death. Mass armies were staffed by the peasant and working classes. Coercion – which included imprisonment of conscientious objectors and execution of deserters – did not by itself explain ruling groups' successes in recruiting and motivating the largest, most destructive armies ever. Nationalist, racist and militarist ideologies (see chapter 5) were as strong among subordinate as ruling classes. Despite Marx's belief that the workers had 'no fatherland', they embraced mass killing for king and *Führer*, empire and party-state alike.

Clausewitz has thus not been alone in seeing extensive popular involvement as the key to the destructive character of modern war. Certainly, intensely held national beliefs and political mobilization could motivate modern soldiers, as religious beliefs had motivated earlier fighters. Class hatred and Communist politics have also fired people to kill. Nevertheless, many studies have argued that such convictions by themselves hardly explain why men kill. If 'the people' can be a destructive force, it is because of social pressures – peer expectations as well as discipline, as Browning (1992) showed in a classic study.

These pressures can also work *against* killing under the right conditions. Working-class solidarity sometimes produced opposition to nationalism and militarism, where these were seen as deriving from the ruling class. But it also produced support for nationalism and militarism, where socialist and communist ideologies translated 'the people' into 'the nation', in the service of state power. In the national-international era, socialism was more often national than international. And this was also for more practical reasons. Once large sections of workers were recruited into mass armies, their families and communities had an interest in their survival, which was more likely to be assured in victory than in defeat.

Thus class and national solidarity often became aligned: but this was a contingent agreement. There was often a cyclical pattern of support for, and opposition to, war among the popular classes. At the onset of war, nationalist and militarist opinions usually predominated. But once losses of soldiers' lives mounted, often compounded by impoverishment at home, subordinate classes turned against war. In defeat, an alternative, anti-militarist class solidarity often flourished. This cycle has been most powerful in total war, where popular involvement and its stakes – even including risk to the civilian population through bombardment or invasion – were at their maximum. The pressures stoked up by the First World War led to revolutions in states like Russia, Italy and Germany, whose armies had been defeated, and severe unrest even in victorious states like Britain.

This cycle has been much weaker in more limited wars. Nevertheless, there are some notable examples in recent times. Prolonged, unpopular and unsuccessful colonial wars precipitated the Portuguese Revolution of 1974. The impasse of the US war in

Vietnam provoked one of the most significant anti-war movements of recent decades. The trick for Western governments in the post-Vietnam period, when popular awareness of war has been heightened by television and other media, has been to foreshorten the cycle, cutting out the later stages. Governments have looked to military power for 'quick fixes' in distant locales, with minimum casualties and minimum disruption to normal social life in the West, allowing little scope for anti-war sentiment to gain hold.

In total war, the contradictions of mass militarism sometimes exploded in revolution. The people turned the arms and training that they gained in conventional armies against their officers and rulers. Many popular revolutions of the twentieth century began with soldiers and sailors shifting their allegiances in this way. By removing the armed supports of the existing state, rebelling soldiers opened the way for workers and peasants to rise up. However, the dissolution of militarism quickly turned into its opposite, and forms of violence quite as destructive as in any other kind of war (see box 7.2).

Box 7.2   Class war

'Class war' as a slogan has often meant little more than intensified class struggle, i.e. uncompromising political and industrial conflict. Socialists who used this slogan argued simultaneously that the working class was not interested in the wars of the ruling classes, but only in pacific international co-operation to defeat war.

Yet, when class politics did produce revolution, it often led to class-polarized civil war. In Russia in 1917, counter-revolutionary armies attempted to overthrow the fledgling Communist state. The revolution in turn was militarized. As war, class war was therefore much more than class struggle – it was ferocious civil war, pursued without mercy against all enemies. Out of this war, the revolutionary regime became consolidated as an apparatus apart from the working class, out of which the 'permanent war' dictatorship of Stalin emerged (see episode II).

Militarized Communist parties across the world learnt this perverted form of class politics from Stalin. For these new rulers, any social group was a potential threat. The ultimate conclusion of this understanding was the rule of the Khmer Rouge (see episode VII), who targeted every major category of society, from the educated intellectuals to the peasants and the ethnic minorities, in their desire to produce total power with a completely malleable population.

The link between Stalin and Pol Pot was Mao Zedong. During the long civil war that led to his rise to power in China, Mao's army killed millions of so-called rich peasants, seen as supporters of the Nationalist enemy. In power,

Mao's totalitarian rule culminated in the fateful 'Great Leap Forward' of 1959–61 (see chapter 2). Mao followed his war on the peasantry with the Cultural Revolution (1966–9) – effectively class war against the intelligentsia – which claimed several million further victims. Because this was centred on the cities, the episode is far better known in the West from books like Jung Chang's (1991) *Wild Swans*. In both cases, Mao launched violent campaigns against groups in society to further his political struggles within the party. Ironically, one of the reasons for the crisis that provoked the Cultural Revolution was the challenge to Mao's authority from leaders who recognized the enormity of the 'Great Leap Forward'.

The notion that one sex is more peaceable than another – another commonplace view – is just as problematic. It may seem obvious that war is a man's game. Feminists easily ridicule politicians and generals as 'boys with their toys'. The claim that women, as mothers, have a specific interest in preserving human life – as opposed to men who destroy it – has been a powerful pacifist idea. Certainly, although counter-examples of women soldiers and commanders (Boadicea, Joan of Arc) may be produced, men have predominated overwhelmingly in war in all its forms, for as long as it has existed.

However, the obvious fact that war is deeply gendered does not mean that one sex can be regarded as naturally warlike, and the other pacific. If war has involved societies as wholes and all social groups, it has hardly excluded women. In every social group involved in war and war preparation, women have supported men. Rulers and officers have depended on their wives, mistresses and female servants. Soldiers, too, have depended on their wives (often left at home) as well as the women who have been 'camp followers' of armies throughout history.

So the mothering–pacifism couplet does not withstand much examination. If men have been warriors, women have nurtured them throughout history. In modern times, mothers as well as fathers have placed toy swords and guns in boys' hands, while giving girls dolls and prams. The sexual division of labour has undoubtedly sustained military organization. But women have been 'in there' as much as men – as active participants in military ideology. There has been a feminist-pacifist tradition, just as there have been courageous male refusals of war. But generally, women's roles, like men's, have been defined by military ways of thinking.

In modern times, women's roles have been more actively developed. As mass armies consumed large sections of the male
working population, women were often recruited into formerly
male jobs in industry. 'Rosie the Riveter' was a feature of the
world wars in Europe and North America. Likewise, as war required mass politics to sustain it, women were recruited to pres-
surize men into 'doing their duty' to the state. The white feathers
handed out to 'cowardly' British men who had failed to volunteer
(at the outbreak of the First World War) are a notorious symbol of
this ignoble feminine contribution to modern war mobilization.

There have also been, of course, women's army corps. These
were usually excluded from combat, although there are important
historical exceptions – for example, in the Red Army's resistance to
the German invasion of the Soviet Union. In the global era, Western
states have begun to recruit women into regular branches of their
armed forces. Women make up significant minorities of military
personnel, over 10 per cent in the USA, Canada and the UK, and are
no longer excluded on principle from many 'combat' roles – a
meaningful departure from the most masculine military traditions.
Nevertheless, these changes add up to a refinement, rather than a
general overturning, of the sexual division of labour in war, and
many have been token in character so far. Thus they have troubled,
rather than overturned, the anti-militarist bias of feminism (see
box 7.3).

Box 7.3   Feminism and militarism

Historically, and especially in the present period, feminist thought and practice
have been divided over war. Precisely because this is the most sharply gendered of all areas of social life, radically different approaches are adopted by
different groups of women.

The feminist tradition has often tended towards pacifism. Early feminists'
links to the Enlightenment, liberalism and socialism have predisposed them
towards opposition to wars and armies. Feminist internationalism emerged as
a strand of anti-war thought before and during the First World War, empha-
sizing women's particular pacific leanings. The late-modern feminist movement
emerged from the radical movements of the 1960s, which were framed by
opposition to the Vietnam War. Feminist writers who have dealt most fully
with war, like Cynthia Enloe (1983), have been consistently anti-militarist.

However, the wider engagement of feminist writers with war has naturally
uncovered the more contradictory relationships of women and war, including
the major historical instances of women's military roles (Macdonald, Holden
and Ardener 1987). Practical developments have also challenged anti-militarist

feminism, as more and more women have joined Western (especially US) armed forces. Popular culture has familiarized people worldwide with the idea of women soldiers.

There are definite limits, nevertheless, to the *feminization* of armed force. Masculinist military culture has been modified, not overthrown. Women's participation in many branches of military work is at best token. The simplest method of making militaries sex-equal – extending conscription to women – is not practical politics even in liberal countries (like Germany) that maintain the draft. Elsewhere the ending of universal military service leaves military work as an increasingly specialized set of occupations, in which men will predominate for the foreseeable future. Meanwhile the uses of military power against women remain problematic enough for feminist critics fundamentally.

National and racial divisions might appear to be obvious forms of military stratification. War and genocide have been so intimately linked with nationality that the national composition of armed forces might be taken for granted. In fact, national armies had first of all to be constructed. At the beginning of the modern era, nations as we understand them were only beginning to develop in most parts of Europe, still less elsewhere. Nation-states had to mobilize men from diverse regions, often speaking mutually incomprehensible dialects. National identity was forged partly through the construction of armies, which gave soldiers from diverse backgrounds common symbols, experience and interests. In late nineteenth-century Continental Europe, many regarded conscript armies as 'schools of the nation' and scorned countries like Britain that lacked the institution.

Moreover, most nation-states were also empires. Imperial armies were the last lines of defence for complex power structures that incorporated vast diversities of society and culture. Empires often recruited local forces in their colonies, and incorporated these colonial forces more or less into their 'global' forces. 'Loyal' tribes were effective counterweights to the actually or potentially 'disloyal' – hence valuable instruments of 'divide and rule'. In each region, imperial armies relied particularly on some ethnic groups, who often developed special reputations as imperial warriors – the Nepalese Ghurkas in the British army are an example that persists into the twenty-first century, when Britain has difficulty in recruiting troops at home. Colonists were also particularly valuable to empires, and their militias and armies often played a particularly aggressive role in local wars, including genocides of indigenous peoples in North America and elsewhere. Very often empires relied on colonial or allied forces to perpetrate massacres: the role of some east Europeans in the Holocaust was only the most extreme example of this tendency. Colonial forces played supporting roles in all major inter-imperial wars.

Nevertheless, empires were based on racial and national hierarchies, and it was often difficult for imperial armies to admit even colonists, let alone 'inferior' colonized races, to equal participation. We have already noted the persistence of racial segregation in that most enlightened, 'post-colonial' centre of Western power, the United States. Until the final quarter of the twentieth century, and in many cases still today, national identities continued to rest on assumptions of racial and ethnic superiority. The multi-cultural 'cosmopolitan nation', however deeply rooted in modern history, is very much a late-modern invention. Only in very recent times have Blacks, like women, begun to rise to the higher ranks of the American military. In Western Europe, racial and national minorities of more recent provenance often have only slight toe-holds in armed forces. In the former Soviet Union and Yugoslavia, as well as in Africa, the beginning of the twenty-first century has witnessed, if anything, as I have already argued, the re-appropriation of armed forces by dominant ethnic-national groups, as armed forces have become genocidal tools.

Overlapping these class, sex and race stratifications, the difference between city and country has been very significant for war and, especially, for genocide. If fortified cities were historical centres of military power, modern industrial cities have been power-houses of military industry and, as we have seen, killing spaces of air power. Cities were also the original centres of modern revolution, but they were bypassed in its militarization – guerrilla armies built up rural bases from which to surround urban areas. Thus Chinese Communism embraced an anti-urban ideology, in which cities were seen as centres of corrupt, decadent cosmopolitanism. Anti-urban ideas played a central part in other nationalist projects, particularly those arising from the decomposition of Communism. Notoriously, the Khmer Rouge mobilized rural resentment and anti-urban sentiment in their genocide. Serbian and Croatian nationalists in former Yugoslavia organized rural and small-town hostility to cosmopolitan urban centres. In contrast, it could be argued that post-urban societies and large urban areas have been the social bases of the new pluralist humanitarianism, which has motivated Western military intervention in global-era wars.

Within this urban-rural divide, it is clear that *education* plays a crucial role. Of course, leaders on all sides are always relatively well educated. Monarchs and aristocratic officers in the European armies of the total-war era had at least the benefits of military academies, as well as private tuition or elite schools. Guerrilla leaders were often graduates of universities or party academies, although some were autodidacts. Today's Islamist terrorists are recruited not from despairing pockets of poverty, but from better-educated middle-class youth. In all these cases, however, particu-laristic national, class or religious attachments have been dominant, and elites use their intellectual formations to organize constituencies and armies along these lines. For example, ethnic-nationalist elites, although themselves often university-educated, appeal to an anti-intellectual consciousness among the less educated, especially in the countryside.

In the twenty-first century, however, education is beginning to play a different role. Cosmopolitan elites mobilize pluralist politics among relatively more educated urban populations. While nation-alists often regard mass education as suspect, cosmopolitans view it as desirable. Local cosmopolitan elites, moreover, tap into the pervasive ideology of Western and global state organizations. Through these bodies, professions uphold the universal values of liberal education: individualism and human rights. Within war-zone societies, as well as in global organizations, liberal professions such as journalism, teaching and social work are social bases for international intervention. This is a historical turn-around: throughout the last century, educated groups have been the main supports of anti-war movements. But in the global era, the old politics of war, centred on interstate and inter-bloc conflicts, is partly replaced by a new politics centred on the response to geno-cide. Not only does genocide mobilize social forces in new ways; but the anti-genocidal politics of humanitarian NGOs (non-governmental organizations) revolve around different axes from those of older peace movements.

Twenty-first-century Western society is post-military, in the sense that military participation has become very attenuated. In many countries armies are no longer conscripted, and, where they are, opportunities for young men to replace military by civilian service have expanded. Western citizens enjoy a prosperous, inter-nationalized 'consumer' life-style. The principal relationship to war of most Western people, and of non-Westerners outside war zones, is conducted through mass media. Real wars enter people's lives through television coverage: they participate as spectators. Armament culture, in which the cult of high-technology weaponry partially replaces nationalist military myths, pervades popular films and electronic games. War has become mostly a distant distraction, military organization a specialized social sector with only modest general visibility. The activist professions in the NGOs and media, alongside the armed forces themselves, are exceptional in their regular engagement with war. Mobilization, in the late Cold War and global eras, has become a matter of media manipulation and opinion polling (see box 7.4). The insulation of Western society from direct involvement in war has enabled Western states to perfect a new militarism attuned to the realities of risk-transfer war (this type of war is defined in episode X).

Box 7.4   Post-military mobilization

Unlike in total war, the majority of members of society do not participate directly, in any practical sense, in the preparation or fighting of Western states' wars today. Small professional forces fight wars on behalf of the 'nation' – or, more commonly, on behalf of a Western-led 'international community'.

Direct military and wartime participation has been replaced by 'spectator-sport militarism'. In terms of the ways in which wars become media events, Michael Mann (1988: 30) argues that they 'are not qualitatively different from the Olympic Games'. With risks transferred to 'others', who are of low visibility in the mass media, most viewers are only vaguely aware of the costs of conflicts for those directly affected. Nevertheless, wars are much more than sport: public opinion can be highly sensitive when film of harm to civilians does appear, as well as to news of loss of life among national armed forces. Since Vietnam, myths about the susceptibility of opinion to media coverage play a big part in Western governments' calculations regarding military involvement.

Governments have therefore to actively mobilize public opinion during any major use of military force. Relatively compliant media are crucial to a process that is validated through opinion polls. The Glasgow University Media Group (1985: 143) summed up the cycle as demonstrated in Britain during the Falklands / Malvinas War: 'We have here a situation in which television selectively informs people's attitudes, then selectively reports on what those attitudes are, and finally . . . uses this version of public opinion to justify its own approach to reporting.' In this kind of context, successfully achieved during the Gulf War in 1991 and the Kosovo War in 1999, Western governments are able to mobilize large majorities of passive supporters throughout relatively short, cost-free military campaigns.

Further reading

Andreski, S. (1968) *Military Organisation and Society*. London: Routledge and Kegan Paul.

Braybon, G. and Summerfield, P. (1987) *Out of the Cage: Women's Experiences in Two World Wars*. London: Pandora.

Browning, C. (1992) *Ordinary Men: Reserve Police Battalion 101 and the Final Solution in Poland*. New York: Harper Collins.

Calder, A. (1969) *The People's War: Britain 1939–45*. London: Panther.

Chang, J. (1991) *Wild Swans*. London: Harper Collins.

Creighton, C. and Shaw, M., eds (1987) *The Sociology of War and Peace*. London: Macmillan.

Doorn, J. van (1975) *The Soldier and Social Change*. London: Sage.

Elshtain, J. B. (1987) *Women and War*. Brighton: Harvester.

Enloe, C. (1983) *Does Khaki Become You? The Militarization of Women's Lives*. London: Pluto.

Glasgow University Media Group (1985) *War and Peace News*. Milton Keynes: Open University Press.

Goldhagen, D. J. (1996) *Hitler's Willing Executioners: Ordinary Germans and the Holocaust*. New York: Little, Brown.

Gross, J. T. (2001) *Neighbors: The Destruction of the Jewish Community in Jedwabne, Poland*. Princeton: Princeton University Press.

Hockey, J. (1986) *Squaddies: Portrait of a Sub-Culture*. Exeter: Exeter University Press.

Ignatieff, M. (2000) *Virtual War: Kosovo and Beyond*. London: Chatto and Windus.

Kaldor, M. (1999) *New and Old Wars*. Cambridge: Polity.

Kennedy, D. M. (1980) *Over Here: The First World War and American Society*. Oxford: Oxford University Press.

Kocka, J. (1985) *Facing Total War*. Leamington: Berg.

Koonz, C. (1988) *Mothers in the Fatherland*. London: Methuen.

Luttwak, E. N. (1995) Towards post-heroic warfare. *Foreign Affairs*, 74(3), 109–22.

Macdonald, S., Holden, P. and Ardener, S., eds (1987) *Images of Women in Peace and War: Cross-cultural and Historical Perspectives*. London: Macmillan.

Mandel, E. (1986) *The Meaning of the Second World War*. London: Verso.

Mann, M. (1988) The roots and contradictions of modern militarism. In *States, War and Capitalism*, Oxford: Blackwell, 166–87.

Marwick, A. (1974) *War and Social Change in the Twentieth Century*. London: Macmillan.

Marwick, A., ed. (1988) *Total War and Social Change*. London: Macmillan.

McNulty, M. (1999) The militarization of ethnicity and the emergence of warlordism in Rwanda, 1990–94. In P. Rich, ed., *Warlords in International Relations*, London: Macmillan, 140–63.

Middlemas, K. (1979) *Politics in an Industrial Society*. London: Deutsch.

Moser, C. and Clark, F. C., eds (2001) *Victims, Perpetrators or Actors? Gender, Armed Conflict and Political Violence.* London: Zed Books.

Moskos, C. (1970) *The American Enlisted Man.* London: Sage.

Moskos, C. and Wood, F. (1988) *The Military: More than Just a Job?* Oxford: Pergamon-Brassey.

Moskos, C., Williams, J. and Segal, D., eds (2000) *The Postmodern Military: Armed Forces after the Cold War.* New York: Oxford University Press.

Osiel, M. J. (1999) *Obeying Orders: Atrocity, Military Discipline and the Law of War.* New Brunswick, NJ: Transaction.

Pettman, J. J. (1996) *Worlding Women.* London: Routledge.

Shaw, M. (1988) *Dialectics of War.* London: Pluto.

Sheridan, D., ed. (1990) *Wartime Women.* London: Heinemann.

Twagiramariya, C. and Turshen, M., eds (1998) *What Women Do in Wartime.* London: Zed Books.

Episode VII
The Cambodian genocide

The Cambodian genocide was the most comprehensive of all modern mass killings, in the extent to which it touched *all* sections of the population within a given territory. The regime of the Khmer Rouge under Pol Pot 'probably exerted more power over its citizens than any state in world history' (Kiernan 1996: 464). Both the regime and the genocide were inextricable from war.

Pol Pot's Communist Party of Kampuchea (as it called the country) was the apotheosis of the tradition of militarized revolution that began with Mao Zedong. In China, the kind of Communist regime this movement produced was responsible for the mass death of the 'Great Leap Forward' (1958–61) and the Cultural Revolution (1966–9). In North Korea, a regime of this kind still presided over an extensive state-made famine even at the beginning of the twenty-first century.

The Khmer Rouge, a Communist Party supported by China, seized power from a pro-American regime in 1975. It had created power bases in rural Cambodia, fighting against the USA in uneasy tandem with the Vietnamese Communists. The USA under President Richard Nixon and Secretary of State Henry Kissinger invaded Cambodia after 1970, bombing relentlessly and killing up to 150,000 civilians. 'Although it was indigenous, Pol Pot's revolution would not have won power without US economic and military destabilization of Cambodia' (Kiernan, 1996: 16).

Pol Pot's regime used the political-military organization through which it came to power to reconstruct Cambodian society. It fostered extreme racism against ethnic Vietnamese and other minorities. It 'cleansed' the cities: 'We evacuated the people from the cities which is our class struggle.' It destroyed religion, land ownership and the family in the countryside. It enforced 'communal eating' and a barrack-like existence for virtually all Cambodians. In a state of total control by Angkar, the organization, peasants 'could only "curse inwardly". But their families remained uppermost in their minds. Surviving family units, physically separated, were emotionally preserved' (Kiernan 1996: 64, 215).

As Pol Pot's Centre provoked border war, it became ever more engaged in violent struggle with Vietnamese forces, with sections of its own movement, and in the slaughter of the people. This was a multi-pronged genocide: in the 'killing fields', peasants ('base people' in the regime's terminology) were increasingly slaughtered alongside city ('new people') and minorities. Through multiple ethnic and class targeting, huge numbers of Cambodians of *all* groups died: an estimated 1.6 million people, one-fifth of the population.

Pol Pot's regime ended as it began, in war. But although responsible for this most appalling genocide of modern times, its overthrow by the Vietnamese army in 1979 was welcomed neither by the West nor by China. The movement carried on guerrilla war against the new government, with active backing from China. It retained the Cambodian seat at the UN throughout the 1980s – with the support of the administrations of Ronald Reagan in the USA and Margaret Thatcher in Britain.

After the end of the Cold War, a UN intervention in Cambodia legitimized a government still led by the Vietnamese-installed Hun Sen. It was only in the late 1990s that the remnants of the Khmer Rouge were finally defeated. Pol Pot (real name Saloth Sar) died in his bed in 1999, before he could be brought to local or international justice. The outcome of proposals to bring some of his lieutenants belatedly to trial in Cambodia was still uncertain as this book was being written.

Further reading

Evans, G. and Rowley, K. (1990) *Red Brotherhood at War: Vietnam, Cambodia and Laos since 1975*. London: Verso.

Jackson, K. D. (1989) *Cambodia 1975–1978: Rendezvous with Death*. Princeton: Princeton University Press.

Kiernan, B., ed. (1993) *Genocide and Democracy in Cambodia: The Khmer Rouge, the United Nations and the International Community*. New Haven: Yale University Southeast Asia Studies.

Kiernan, B. (1996) *The Pol Pot Regime: Race, Power and Genocide in Cambodia under the Khmer Rouge, 1975–79*. New Haven: Yale University Press.

—— 8 ——

Victims

Human beings suffer in many ways, and do many terrible things that cause suffering to others. There are many forms of physical cruelty, which are often worse than instant death. Inequalities, which make poor people live more miserably and die earlier than the wealthy, claim many lives. However, as I argued in chapter 1, killing is distinctive in its use of bodily harm to destroy definitively the meaning of human lives. The core meaning of violence is the deliberate imposition of harm: the idea of poverty as 'structural violence' is derivative of this. To directly deprive others of life is the logical end-point of violence in this sense. While inequality violates lives, people often find ways to struggle with, and overcome, it. In the face of killing, by contrast, people must flee or fight. Physical violence is the point at which power becomes most unbearable and directly threatening to life. Organized mass killing is a maximum possible conclusion, in some cases viewed quite consciously, and in others hardly perceived, to large-scale inequalities of power.

These relationships between power and slaughter are of course the most sharply contested in all the discourses surrounding war and genocide. Strategic thought stresses that war is about the application of 'force' – as though coercion stopped short of killing, and destruction was mainly of things, not people. Denials of genocide minimize the extent or the intentionality of slaughter, claiming that oppression stopped short of killing, that killing was random and unplanned, or that it occurred in the context of war. In both ways, the fact that slaughter is the end-point of war is obscured. Likewise, the facts that war preparation and terror actually lead, and are designed to lead, to mass killing and other physical harm are hidden. (For more on denial, go back to chapter 4.)

Victimhood and its appropriation

To cover up realities of cruelty and slaughter is, above all, to conceal the experience of *victims*. Moreover, the prime victims are, by definition, no longer with us: by the very nature of the actions against them, their experience is hidden. But for every person killed, there are several people who are directly, often devastatingly, affected, and many more who are indirectly concerned. In societies where mass death has become common, memories of it are often central to people's understanding of the world. Victimhood is often so ubiquitous that it is inevitable that many of its cases are hidden from general view.

However, the cases that matter to an individual, family or victim community are likely to be enshrined in memory. Each has their own story of the mass killings in which they have suffered. It is right that each story should be told and remembered, so that victims' struggles to live are cherished and the particular forces that threatened them are punished, or prevented from wreaking further destruction. At the same time, it is crucial to understand that human suffering is a universal experience, and that suffering caused by war and genocide is all too common. For these reasons, we need to understand the most general factors at work. These include how experiences of slaughter unfold and what kinds of people become victims. They also include whether and how both the immediate victims and those who come after them are able to speak out and fight back.

Whether killings are widely commemorated (i.e. commonly remembered) often depends on political movements, which utilize memories so that people's deaths will inform future actions. The universality of experiences of slaughter is often hidden by the *positive appropriation* of particular experiences by certain groups, as well as the denial of other experiences. Thus, to take the highest-profile case, the Holocaust has sometimes been commemorated in an exclusive manner that limits its universal significance as an extreme instance of inhumanity (see box 8.1). This sometimes leads to the setting aside of other experiences of slaughter – even overlapping patterns of killing at the hands of the Nazis – in the Second World War. It also leads to a failure to recognize commonalities between the experience of Jewish victims in the Holocaust and others' experiences in other episodes of mass slaughter. It is essential to spell out such commonalities, for several reasons. We need to recognize the widespread danger of mass killing, the potential for which does not arise only from one kind of regime or affect only one group. We need to understand the experiences of many generations of victims, and seek for all of them the justice that some have begun to find.

Box 8.1   A Holocaust industry?

Understanding the Holocaust in part as a specifically Jewish experience is obviously legitimate, given the central role of the extermination of European Jews in Nazism's killings. However, many have noted that this terrible set of events was of much less concern, not only to the world in general, but even to Jewish people and their organizations, around 1950 than it was by 2000. Some have argued that the special place accorded the Jewish tragedy in early twenty-first-century versions of history is not just the product of greater knowledge and understanding. It is the product, critics claim, of a concerted campaign by some Jewish leaders, especially in the United States, to gain support for Israel in the Middle East conflict. And it is more widely acknowledged, notably by US politicians, because of the centrality of the Israeli alliance to US foreign policy.

Norman Finkelstein (2000), himself a Jewish American, argues that Jewish suffering under the Nazis has been exploited by a 'Holocaust industry' which arose after the 1967 Arab–Israeli war demonstrated Israel's military strength. He contends that the representation of the Holocaust as a uniquely terrible event has been exploited not only politically, but financially. Not surprisingly, this case is profoundly unpopular with many Jewish writers.

Israel's treatment of the Palestinians is thus a root cause of the controversy surrounding the commemoration of the Holocaust. Israel was created in the late 1940s by driving hundreds of thousands of Arabs from their land and homes. In a brutal case of what has more recently been called 'ethnic cleansing', thousands were killed (although, of course, Arab fighters also killed Jews). Clearly Israel has never aimed to *exterminate* the Palestinians as a people – indeed, there is a large minority of Arabs among Israel's citizens. But the establishment by force of an ethnically defined state in a multi-ethnic territory has caused a long-lasting conflict, with genocidal dimensions. Arab states and movements have sought to destroy Israel in turn. Half a century of war has created enormous reservoirs of hatred, in the context of which the Holocaust has become not only an asset exploited by Israeli supporters, but also a subject of gross denial by some Arab factions.

From battlefield to civilian death

If we are to grasp who the victims are, and how and why they suffer, we need to examine typical ways in which destroying an enemy's power produces killing and harm of human beings. Such processes are, of course, as old as war itself. Indeed, in pre-modern societies slaughter was often much more up-front. Intense cruelty towards enemies of all kinds was a hallmark of state power. Medieval war, for example, has been known in later periods for its barbarity. It has been argued that '[w]hile cruelty and violence overlap, they are not the same. Violence can be justified according to the ends that it pursues (for instance, an act of self-defence). There can be violence between equals. Cruelty, on the other hand, can never be justified because it is the intentional infliction of physical pain on individuals who are in a position of weakness. For there to be cruelty, there has to be subjugation and powerlessness in some form' (Mikaya 1993: 22).

Modern war has appeared distinctively rational in its avoidance of cruel uses of violence. Killing and harm are supposed to be restricted to what is necessary to achieve strategic goals. They have been surrounded by humanitarian conventions. The modern paradox, however, has been the combination of this 'rational' form of power with an unprecedented scale of mass killing – of civilians as well as combatants. From the point of view of the victims, moreover, this killing has often been heart-breakingly cruel. As we have seen, the most general explanations for this are the way in which society as a whole has been incorporated into the targeting of modern war, the ease with which people can be killed with modern technology and the transformations of social groups into enemies in themselves.

An index of these changes is the ratio of civilian to military casualties. As late as the First World War, military casualties predominated. At the beginning of the twenty-first century, the vast majority of casualties in wars are civilians. Yet it would be a big mistake to remove military casualties from the picture. However much soldiers are 'made to be killed', individually they are often (almost as much as civilians) in relations of 'subjugation and powerlessness'. Indeed, historically, the slaughter of soldiers has not been so separate from that of civilians. Rather, as we saw in episode 0, the enormous scale of soldiers' deaths in 1914–18 had profound ramifications, not just for the expendability of soldiers' lives in the subsequent century, but for the fate of civilians. The mass killing of the trenches was in many ways the starting-point for a generally extended scope of mass killing, not just in the First World War but throughout the twentieth century. Huge death tolls among soldiers were hardly unprecedented before 1914: most of Napoleon's million-strong army perished in the advance on, and retreat from, Moscow in 1812, and the American Civil War had shown something of the scale of death that industrialized warfare could produce. But the First World War undoubtedly opened up a new Pandora's box of killing.

At the root of this was the comprehensive application of industrial methods of killing to enemy armed forces. It was not long before they were applied to civilians as well. As the general staffs sent wave after wave of young soldiers 'over the top', they created a paradigm of 'senseless slaughter' that reverberates to this day. In the killing trenches of the Western Front, high commands sustained the old, essentially pre-democratic idea – that soldiers should die for the state – into a new era of organization, weaponry and strategy. The worker- and peasant-soldiers of Europe, paraded according to their national-imperial identities, were the primary victims of this lethal new combination.

The slaughter of the trenches was in many ways the definitive experience of modern mass killing, seminal to virtually all the mass killing activities of the twentieth century. The massacre of conscripts was a starting-point for the development of each of the other strands. As the soldier-victims were mown down in their hundreds of thousands in the Somme and elsewhere, they provided a spectacle of mass death that set the tone for a century. Simultaneously, the beginnings of aerial warfare showed the potential for extending death *en masse* to the civilian populations of the world's cities. The campaign of the Ottoman state against the Armenians signalled the beginnings of deliberately genocidal war against civilians. All the main paradigms of twentieth-century death were already visible in this first great phase of total war.

General revulsion at trench warfare and recognition of its military inefficacy served, ironically, to stimulate the demand for aerial bombing. From the Second World War to the present day, Western governments have sought to save their soldiers' lives from the attrition of the traditional battlefield. They have done this largely by transferring the cost of killing to helpless enemy populations. In the Second World War, civilians were as common among the victims as soldiers, and in a nuclear war this would be even more the case. In more recent wars like Vietnam, the indiscriminate bombing of civilians produced widespread disgust. In localized wars outside the West, the targeting of civilians has become routine, even where campaigns are not explicitly genocidal.

This *civilianization of mass death*, in defiance of the conventions nominally adhered to by states, remains shocking – however commonplace it has become. But, as the main thrust of concern, it risks distorting our perception of who the majority of current victims are. In more recent, limited interstate wars, the greater direct losses have often been among soldiers. In the Iraq–Iran war of the 1980s, for example, trench warfare once more produced a scale of killing reminiscent of 1914–18, and it was the loss of young soldiers rather than of civilians that was most striking. In the West's campaigns in the Gulf, former Yugoslavia and Afghanistan, more of the immediate victims were primarily military, although this was not the whole story, as box 8.2 explains.

Box 8.2   Direct and indirect casualties of Western war

On first examination, the pattern of victims of the West's military campaigns in the global era has swung away from the 'civilianization of death' that was a feature of warfare in the twentieth century and remains a feature of much genocidal war today. The application of computer electronics has offered the West weapons that can be targeted very precisely on a particular location, thus enabling militaries to discriminate more than before between combatants and civilians. At the same time, instant satellite communications have enabled journalists to transmit film reports more or less instantaneously from the most remote site. Hence the killing of civilians is always likely to be exposed very quickly, and governments can be pressured to avoid it.

Thus in the 1991 Gulf War, most of the West's direct victims were undoubtedly soldiers rather than civilians. But this was not always the picture delivered by the media, let alone by critics of US policy. Some incidents of civilian death – notably the shocking bombing of the Amiriya shelter in which 400 people were incinerated – were highly publicized. The mass killing of Iraqi soldiers, mostly by bombing, but also by the gruesome new technique of bulldozing them alive into desert sand, went unfilmed. The US-led coalition and the Iraqis effectively conspired to keep this off our TV screens. The truth is that tens of thousands of soldiers were killed, but only much smaller numbers of civilians.

Yet, direct, intended targets are often not the only victims of war. In the Iraqi case, more civilians died in *indirect* consequence of the bombing of the infrastructure (electricity supplies, sewage facilities, etc.) than were directly killed by bombs. Still more died as a result of the country's impoverishment, partly through UN sanctions, in the following years. The West paid less of a media price for these more lingering forms of civilian mass death than they did for dramatic incidents like Amiriya.

This example shows that the trend towards the civilianization of war death remains strong, while on the surface offset by changes in the Western way of war.

If the experience of the trenches stimulated Western aerial mass killing, however, it also had powerful repercussions for the development of genocide. Its example encouraged emergent totalitarian forces to see politics as an all-out struggle in which millions of lives could be destroyed. While liberal pacifists drew the conclusion 'Never again', Adolf Hitler – who was profoundly influenced by his personal experience of trench war – came to an opposite verdict. The loss of so many German lives in humiliating defeat only spurred him to the conclusion that more should be prepared to sacrifice themselves to restore the honour of the fatherland, while destroying its 'enemies' on an unprecedented scale.

So in our concern for the most obviously helpless victims among civilian populations – women, children, the old, etc. – we should not forget the extent to which soldiers have been victims. They have sometimes been volunteers or willing participants, but they have as often been conscripted, usually coerced and often terrorized into military service. Those who refused to serve – even more, those who refused to kill – have faced punishments that included imprisonment and death. Many soldiers (as in the paradigmatic case of the trenches) have had no more chance of escaping terror, mutilation and slaughter than have civilian victims of bombing and genocide.

In subsequent episodes of strategic mass killing, both the deliberate targeting of civilians and the relatively indiscriminate face of slaughter have meant that more civilians than soldiers have been killed. But, relative to their numbers, more soldiers have died in virtually all cases. Since war is war, combatants (together with potential or putative combatants) are always prime targets in any killing. The civilianization of enemies never eradicates the specific importance of military targets. Even in the counter-city era of nuclear war preparations, with its ideology of 'mutually assured destruction' of civilian populations, nuclear powers retained specific targeting of enemy military sites.

Military logic in genocide

In genocide, the identification, capture and killing of both real and putative combatants is often a mode of entry into more generalized killing. Since genocide is also a kind of war, the notion of combatants does not disappear. The killing of civilians generally accompanies or follows the destruction of armed elements among the enemy population. And since terror and slaughter always invoke resistance, there are nearly always some real combatants. But genocidal power usually imagines that these are far more numerous than they really are: that every young man is an actual or potential resister, that every woman and older man is aiding and abetting resistance, that every community and settlement provides support. Such beliefs are key mechanisms transforming counter-insurgency into genocide.

It is a serious mistake to overestimate the discriminating pseudo-rationality of genocide. Nevertheless, acts of slaughter, like all human actions, depend on kernels of meaning, belief and attempted relationship of means and ends. We need to explain the relationships between the perpetrators' pseudo-rational targeting and the victims' experience of senseless slaughter. Genocidal logic expands to embrace whole populations, from apparently conventional military starting-points. Quasi-military discrimination of 'combatants' and potential combatants among an enemy population leads, through circuits of ideology as well as crudities of practice, to wholesale terror and slaughter. These connections, however tenuous, are essential components of what presents as 'indiscriminate' mass murder.

Despite the indiscriminate and unpredictable side of genocide, and the uniqueness of each major episode of this kind, strong common patterns can be observed. Genocidal regimes rarely see only one major group as an enemy. Thus, although the Nazis have become notorious for their genocide of the Jews, we can identify many racial, national and ethnic groups, as well as groups defined by politics, sexual orientation and disability, against whom they pursued genocidal policies. Similar conclusions can be reached in the case of other totalitarian regimes, from Stalin's USSR to Pol Pot's Cambodia, which targeted a variety of national, class and political groups. What was total about totalitarianism was often the totalization of killing.

It is erroneous, therefore, to take at face value the identification of a single kind of enemy as the key to genocide in general, or to assume *a priori* that such an enemy will be found in a particular case. On the contrary, power centres that launch slaughter usually have more than one generalized enemy, and their enemies are identified in complex ways. On the ground, moreover, the actual killers often carry out their tasks in relatively indiscriminate ways. The results often appear random and arbitrary. The word 'sense-less' that often qualifies the slaughter of the trenches can also be applied to genocide.

Ethnic and cosmopolitan victims

The reasons for the tendency to broaden patterns of victimization are complex, but they are partly explained through pseudo-rational ideological connections. Once one social group is established as an enemy, others become targets through perceived linkages. With the Nazis, Jews were killed because they were Communists; Commun-ists because they were probably Jews; those who defended Com-munists or Jews were also likely to be murdered. With Serbian nationalists, Muslims were enemies because they were a rival na-tional group; cosmopolitan city-dwellers because they defended Muslims, defied the national principle and were linked to inter-national enemies.

In war and genocide, semi-rational ideologies often implicate both classes and occupational groups, on the one hand, and spatial communities, on the other. *Politicians, officials and teachers* are all notoriously vulnerable, and are often quickly incarcerated or killed so as to 'behead' an enemy population. The educated are singled out for their potential organizing and leadership roles within the enemy community. Extortion and looting are often practised against a wide range of people, but of course the relatively wealthy are always targets. For many genocidists, too, *intellectuals* as such are suspect. They are often picked out as carriers of universal awareness and of values that defy crude state ideologies, whether of regime or conqueror. For Nazism, intellectuals represented cosmopolitan decadence, which affronted their national-racial pro-ject. For Stalinism and Maoism, intellectuals were similarly suspect as carriers of 'bourgeois' values. Hostility to the educated and professionals was burned deeply into the Soviet purges, the so-called Chinese Cultural Revolution, and the Cambodian genocide. The irony, of course, is that these ideologies have generally been developed by the 'educated' and the 'intellectuals' of the genocidal movements. Such people have mostly shared (to some extent, at least) in the social milieus that they then seek to destroy. Dr Radovan Karadzic, Sarajevo psychiatrist, became the cosmopolitan city's chief tormentor, orchestrating the snipers who picked off its inhabitants in the war of 1992–5. Such figures are not unusual.

As we saw in chapter 5, industrial cities, political and administrative capitals, and centres of population in general become targets of bombing, so that in many wars city-dwellers are more likely than rural populations to become targets. Genocidal ideologies frequently include backward-looking myths of rural 'purity' and are lethally *anti-urban*. Urban decadence is to be destroyed by 'cleansing' the cities of cosmopolitanism. *In extremis* this may mean partially or wholly deporting educated elites, and even entire urban populations, as happened in China and Cambodia. These tendencies have been deep-rooted in both nationalism and Communism. The nation usually traces its roots to an assumed common ancestry, which invariably means a rural past – hence nationalists' ambivalence towards cosmopolitan urban life. In Communism, the absorption of these ideas stemmed from the displacement of the urban working class from its role as revolutionary agent and the move of Stalinized parties into military revolution based on peasant support. In national Communist ideology, the city was transformed from the fulcrum of social change to the bastion of the old order. In the Cultural Revolution and the emptying of Phnom Penh, 'corrupt' urbanites were directed towards peasant virtues of hard physical labour.

Anti-urbanism resurfaced at the end of the twentieth century in post-Communist ethnic nationalisms, which drew most of their support from rural and small-town areas. In Bosnia, the multi-ethnic character of the two largest cities, Sarajevo and Mostar, was as much a target of Serbian and Croatian nationalists as were the opposing nationalisms. Genocide defined twin enemies: other ethnic groups *and* plural urban populations. Sarajevo was as much a symbol of cosmopolitan as of Muslim resistance.

The deep-rooted history of anti-urbanism should not lead us into the trap of overestimating the uniqueness of urbanite victimization, however. For we can almost as easily find *anti-peasant* policies, even from the same states and movements that target urban populations. Armies that besiege cities also raze the countryside. In guerrilla war, counter-insurgency forces often target peasant households and villages, on the assumption that they harbour insurgents. In Vietnam and Afghanistan, superpower forces engaged in sweeping attacks on rural areas. Peasants are therefore (as much as urban populations) classic victims of war and genocide. Indeed, imperial and authoritarian states have often regarded peasant populations as peculiarly expendable. Throughout history, peasant rebellions have been crushed with huge loss of life; war and oppression have often led to famine. From the conquest of the Americas to the Vietnam War, Western empires have waged brutal war on rebellious peasants. From Soviet collectivization to Mao's 'Great Leap Forward', modern totalitarianisms have inflicted some of their most murderous campaigns on peasant society. Even at the beginning of the twenty-first century, non-Western states often treat peasant populations with singular disregard. From China to India and Turkey, they force the displacement of millions in the name of 'development' projects like dams.

Gendered violence

The other side of the pattern of war and genocide is that within 'enemy' populations, power targets particular kinds of people in different ways. The social structuring of victimhood, especially its gendering, tells us quite a lot about the nature of genocide (see box 8.3). As we have seen, genocidists as much as warring states assume the possibility of resistance: the educated are targeted as potential leaders; while men of fighting age, especially young men and even young boys, are often incarcerated and killed because of their warrior potential. But women are also targeted in particular ways.

Box 8.3   What gender tells us about genocide

The importance of gender has often been neglected in the understanding of genocide. The crime, it is commonly believed, involves the targeting of an ethnic or national group as such – men and women alike – not of specific genders. *Gendercide*, in which genocidists define a gender group as an enemy, like the Nazis' campaign against German homosexuals, has historically been less prominent than campaigns against other sorts of group. Nevertheless, all genocides are profoundly gendered. William Styron's novel *Sophie's Choice* highlighted the terrible moment at the start of most experiences of Auschwitz, when men and older boys were separated from women and younger children. Similar discriminations of sex and age have been part of virtually every experience of genocide.

Such discrimination can be partly instrumental. Younger adults may be kept to perform manual labour that older adults or children are not deemed useful for. Men may be valued more than women for this kind of purpose. Women may be kept as sex slaves – the Imperial Japanese army kept hundreds of thousands of enemy women as so-called comfort women for its troops. However, sex discrimination in genocide is primarily a function of power relations. Both perpetrator and victim societies are invariably highly gendered. The gendering of genocide reflects the gender assumptions of the perpetrators in general, and their perceptions of gender relations in the target groups.

Patriarchal perpetrators inevitably assume – often accurately – that men are power-holders among their enemies. Obvious authority figures are likely to be the first to be killed, but ordinary men are seen as potential resisters. Women, on the other hand, may be targeted for rape because of the humiliation that their violation will bring on the society as a whole, and especially on their menfolk. Serbian forces carried out sexual violence on Bosnian Muslim and Kosovo Albanian women partly because they understood how the humiliation involved would be experienced in these cultures.

Because gender literatures have developed out of feminist work, their main focus has been how the 'male' character of warfare victimizes women. The identification of war with certain kinds of masculinity is of course very real. The perpetrators of mass killing are overwhelmingly men. But, by the same token, traditionally men have been the overwhelming majority of those killed. Nor has this really changed with the civilianization of the targets. Where masses of people have been killed in a highly indiscriminate way, as with area bombing, men and women have died in roughly equal proportions. But where there has been more discriminate killing, including in most genocides, men have nearly always been killed in larger numbers.

Thus it was not only in the First World War that men died in their millions. In the Second World War, too, some male populations were almost wiped out: in relevant age groups of Russian men more than 90 per cent were killed in 1941–5. In the post-1945 era of more limited war, as Western military death tolls were drastically lowered, the lack of direct attacks on Western heartlands meant that those killed were almost exclusively male. In societies in zones of conflict, of course, women (and children) were much more likely to die, but the toll among men was often greater still. In genocide, too, men were more likely to be killed. Men were usually targeted first; killers did not always follow up with comprehensive slaughter of women and children. The Nazis were exceptional, not in killing women and children (all genocidists do this to some extent), but in the thoroughness with which they organized this killing in the industrial processes of the extermination camps. In the Yugoslav wars, a more common pattern was that men were incarcerated and killed, while women and children were expelled. This victimization of men needs to be stressed, because it has been surprisingly neglected. Women have been victimized, of course, but men are more likely to have been killed, in genocidal massacres as much as in battle.

Because feminist viewpoints have separated women's victimization from men's, they have also given somewhat one-sided accounts of women's experience, particularly in their almost exclusive emphasis on *rape*. Rape has long been a weapon with which male warriors have simultaneously attacked individual women and asserted their power over the conquered communities to which the victims belonged. This has been so much the norm, historically, that the violation of women by armed men has stood symbolically for that of civilian populations as a whole by their conquerors – for example, the most infamous Japanese massacre in China in 1937 is known as 'the Rape of Nanking'. But recent feminist campaigns have exposed the extent to which rape has been systematized as a weapon of genocide. The International War Crimes Tribunal for Former Yugoslavia has recognized that rape became a widespread, planned 'crime against humanity' in the Balkan wars. A similar phenomenon has been fully documented in Rwanda, where women were sexually enslaved and sometimes forcibly 'married' to murderous militiamen. The surfacing of these kinds of torment, historically hidden (for example, it has taken several decades for the fate of Korean women enslaved by the Japanese army in the Second World War to be widely exposed), is a very significant gain of feminist campaigning.

Nevertheless, rape has been only part of the victimization of women. We need to understand how closely the distinct patterns of male and female victimization are interrelated. Before women have been raped, they have typically shared with their menfolk the experience of being thrown out of their homes, communities and ways of life. Women have often suffered the loss of the male members of their families and communities – husbands, fathers, brothers and sons – through imprisonment or death. Rape, whether organized or not, has usually been part of such gross patterns of violation, and of course it has often led to killing of the raped women themselves.

The particular kinds of victimization experienced by women, like those suffered by men, are thus parts of patterns of extreme violation against families and whole communities. Even children are not spared, and witnessing the suffering of children is a most harrowing experience for mothers, fathers and other adults. Children fully experience the traumas of bombing and destruction, of injury and loss of loved ones, in even the most 'clinical' forms of modern aerial war. Children witness homes destroyed, fathers shot or taken away and mothers raped. They undergo long journeys of escape and the privations and distortions of upbringing in refugee camps. Children are sometimes kidnapped, and as young as nine or ten years old they may even be forced to participate in killing. Children are often killed, not only incidentally by bombs or mines, but, shockingly, even in individual acts of killing.

If these are the fates that children can meet, then it is hardly surprising that the old fare no better. They suffer along with every-one else, but often worse because they are less physically able to withstand brutality, homelessness, cold and hunger. Together with babies and small children, they are most likely to die from these incidental privations of war and genocide. Yet, as the paradigmatic Nazi case reminds us, the old can also be killed directly for more specific reasons: notably, the perception that they are no longer productive. In all these ways, the particular abuses of different kinds of victims add up to composite pictures of extreme victim-ization of whole groups and societies. Awareness of these differ-ences, and especially of gendering, is crucial, because it reminds us that victimization is simultaneously individual and collective. It is individuals who suffer and die, in the pursuit of military and genocidal ends against 'enemy' societies.

Irrationality of slaughter

Once one explores these kinds of pattern in war and genocide, it is difficult not to be struck by the macabre balancing of fates. In some situations, soldiers are far more likely to die than civilians, men than women, young than old. In others, these patterns may be reversed. To be a young male may be a liability in battle, or when an oppressor is searching out potential resisters; but it may be an advantage if he is looking for workers. To be old will mostly save you from battle, but may be a liability if your enemy has so little disregard for life that he destroys those without productive potential. The individual's fate depends on the chance interplay, not only of these pseudo-rational policy decisions by politicians and commanders, but also of how individual soldiers and killers behave in carrying them out. Looked at from the viewpoints of victims, war and genocide are supremely arbitrary, irrational experiences.

Victims are not only individuals, but also members of families and larger communities of many kinds. Survivors are also victims: they suffer the hideous grief of those who have lost loved ones to arbitrary death. Lifelong legacies of sorrow, guilt, anguish and vengeful hatred may mean that life offers little comfort. In this sense, although victimization affects people differently, it is a common experience, not only of people directly connected to those who are attacked, but also of everyone who belongs to attacked communities. And the experience of victimization is shared vicariously, by many who only see it on television or read of it in newspapers and books. In this sense, victimization is a common human experience. It diminishes and threatens us all.

It is natural to see the killed as the ultimate victims of war. But the processes leading to, and following from, killing are often the most profound and lasting forms of victimization. War and genocide are generally preceded by, and involve, *terror*. When an episode of slaughter is pending, threatened communities live in fear. People flee to safer regions, abandoning lives and relationships, and subject themselves to poverty and insecurity in order to escape death and persecution. Clearly, the varied characters of the threats mean that experiences of victimization differ sharply; fear and insecurity come in many gradations. Yet the experience of slaughter, when it comes to an individual, colours and is coloured by these larger patterns of suffering.

The meaning or meaninglessness of slaughter depends on the experiences of victims as well as the intentions of killers. As theorists and historians of war have long recognized, there is a tremendous fog of war, the indeterminacy and confusion that results from the clash of arms. The *fog of genocide* is no less than that of war in general. It makes a difference whether war consists of a face-to-face battlefield, the long-distance exchange of missiles, or the deliberate destruction of a civilian population. But each war develops its own fog, in which arbitrariness in the protagonists' general intentions is compounded by the chance interplay of individual actions and motives.

In the end, individual people carry out mass killing. High-altitude bombing is less discriminating, but it is also less messy for the perpetrators: it enables them to preserve more of their 'rationality' in the implementation of death. Close-up slaughter, especially of civilians, exposes killers to direct interaction with their victims. In order to carry out killing, people must overcome deep inhibitions. Conversely, once they have committed themselves to killing, people find it easier to kill again. Once perpetrators have relinquished the absolute value of life, particular lives do not seem so important again.

Slaughter contains its own dynamics. Killing is about more than realizing pre-set values or policy objectives. It is the outcome of a clash of arms. This is true whether it involves the clash between two relatively equal armed forces or the clash of killing power with the flesh of unarmed civilians. The moment of slaughter contains both the triumph/sickness of the perpetrator and the horror/pain of the victim. In the end, its outcomes depend on the balance of such experiences. No wonder that so many victories are pyrrhic.

Dynamics of slaughter, as much as pre-ordained objectives and ideologies of combatants, contain (in a double sense) the logic of escalation. As Clausewitz argued, escalation is a law of war. We may say that it is a law of slaughter in general, including genocide. Once inhibitions on violence are broken, there is no logical limit: only what is dictated by its outcomes. This means that, on the one hand, once killing has begun, perpetrators will often continue until they have reached their objectives (which the process of killing may enlarge) or, more likely, until they are checked.

On the other hand, it means that the response of the victims has a profound influence on the outcome. This is most obvious when they resist in an open manner, with counter-violence or with passive resistance. But it is also true when the victims can show the killers only indirectly the poverty of their actions, by oblique acts of defiance. Theoretically, it is even true when the victims' fate is so completely sealed that there appears nothing they can do. So long as the crimes against them can become known, and their experience can be described or imagined, their deaths are not entirely devoid of meaning. If victims' suffering is understood, even only in retrospect, then it can enter the historical process. Others – maybe even unborn at the time of the crimes – may be able, if only partially, to avenge or put right the wrongs that have been committed. If only in this sense, the experience of the victims is always part of the process, with a chance to affect outcomes.

The experience of victims would only have no bearing if all members of the victim groups were killed, if no knowledge of their treatment survived, or if their fate had no influence on anyone else. In reality this situation never holds, as the (so far) limiting case of European Jews shows. Extermination has left whole swathes of eastern and central Europe, formerly heavily populated by Jews, with virtually no Jewish population. Yet this success of Nazism is offset, not only by the slow renewal of the Jewish population in Germany and elsewhere, but by the profound influence that the knowledge of Nazi crimes has had on subsequent world politics. Not only was this all-powerful killing regime defeated in 1945; its failure helped engender a deep shift that fundamentally delegitimized the ideas associated with its project.

In the short term, it may appear that victims do nothing but suffer. Indeed, for very many individuals, this *is* the end of their experience. In a larger picture, however, the experience of victimization is as much a part of the balance of violent contests as the intentions of the perpetrators. Victims have often had very limited possibilities for making their voices heard in larger world arenas. Soldiers in First World War trenches could write (censored) letters home; but mostly they couldn't air their grievances directly to war correspondents at the time. Polish Jews were herded into ghettos, and from there into cattle trucks and extermination camps, mostly away from the gaze of mass media. Iraqi Shi'ites were massacred by Saddam Hussein's troops in 1991, with international journalists and their cameras kept out of the killing zones.

In all these cases, however, individuals fleeing carnage gave contemporary accounts. These were compounded later when testimonies could be collated and investigated. It is sadly true that victims' voices made little difference to their fates at the time. Yet the knowledge of suffering, to which individual voices contributed, had some bearing on the overall outcomes of the struggles in which these individuals were involved. They had even more influence on how these struggles came to be perceived in retrospect, and on how people came to think subsequently about war, genocide and human rights in general.

Killers very often try to hide their killing. It is quite normal for them to add insult to injury by silencing their surviving victims and those who speak on their behalf. In this they are helped by propagandists of all kinds, who place their loyalty to the historical interests represented by the killers over the demands of truth. As we saw in chapter 4, outright denial of the facts of atrocity and suffering is only one form of such arguments, most notorious in the case of 'Holocaust deniers', who argue that gas chambers never existed in Nazi camps. But more subtle forms of denial are more widespread, and are not confined to obvious 'extremist' groups. Virtually every episode of mass killing brings forth apologists who minimize its extent and character. Thus it is a common experience of victims and those who speak for them to have to re-establish the depths of killing and terror and the experiences they have undergone (see box 8.4).

Box 8.4   Truth, justice and denial in the Yugoslav wars

The Yugoslav wars (1991–2001) are paradigmatic cases of wars in which some victims' experiences have been widely publicized. These wars, within modern Europe, shocked a complacent Western world that thought, even after the Gulf War, that war was something that happened in other regions of the world. Because of this, the wars commanded unprecedented attention. From the start, Western journalists covered the conflict extensively and had great freedom, which some used, to expose the violence that was being committed. Later, the International Criminal Tribunal for Former Yugoslavia carried out unprecedented judicial investigations, which meant that the worst atrocities committed by all sides to the conflict were subjected to international law. Major perpetrators, including the former Serbian and Yugoslav president Slobodan Milosevic, were indicted, and many from all sides were committed to trial and condemned.

But despite this extensive opening up of the horrors of the wars, many victims gained neither truth nor justice, in either a moral or a legal sense. More than a quarter million civilians were killed, and several million people made homeless. Most of their individual stories were never told, most of the specific incidents of their victimization never described and most of the individuals responsible never brought before a court. There were hundreds of thousands of perpetrators, members of parties, armies, paramilitaries, local governments and police, as well as civilians. The cases that were exposed or brought to justice were at best representative. Those who were condemned, while mostly richly deserving of their punishments, were only a few of those responsible for the crimes of genocidal war.

Not only this, but the wars were extensively misrepresented. In the conflict zones, the perpetrators' media propagated national myths and fictional accounts of events. In the West, political angles often distorted the wars. Mainstream journalists in Britain, for example, frequently equalized the 'warring ethnic groups', making little distinction between perpetrators and victims or between the extents to which different groups were involved in perpetration and victimhood. Some 'left-wing' journalists – on the principle of 'my enemy's friend is my enemy' – denied or minimized the massacres of groups like the Kosovo Albanians whose cause had been taken up by NATO. At the same time, they attacked the International Tribunal as a Western tool, attempting to de-legitimize the limited justice that it managed to achieve. In all these ways and more, the victims' struggles for recognition and justice remained fraught, even in this relatively high-profile region. It was even more so in regions that received less international attention than Yugoslavia.

The historical trend, however, is towards greater transparency of slaughter. Modern society involves comprehensive, multi-centred, mutual *surveillance* – not just of rulers by ruled, but of the powerful by the relatively powerless, indeed (almost) of everyone by all. There are great inequalities of gaze, and certain kinds of media, as well as state, organizations have major advantages. But in a world with global media, opportunities for any state organization to gain total control of knowledge, even within relatively small territories, are narrowing. Because episodes of political mass killing have been largely eliminated within the Western world, when they occur elsewhere they are especially shocking and are always likely to be exposed.

Surviving victims of slaughter often suffer almost as much in the aftermath as in the course of killing. Trauma and loss are often combined with displacement, harsh treatment and poverty as refugees and asylum-seekers. To people in these conditions, belated exposure of the terror to which they have been subjected is often small consolation. Yet recognition is essential to retrieving some meaning from appalling victimization. Victims' voices are not always heard directly, or straightforwardly. Of course, victims of the most drastic abuse are often unavoidably silent: the dead cannot speak. But there are often ways in which surviving victims' stories, and even the stories of victimized groups, are appropriated by intermediaries. Paradoxically, the assignment of victim status is one of the means of silencing. Victims are assumed to be passive – 'pure' victims who lack their own cause or the means to speak for it. Media representation is a form of acknowledgement, but it often allows people to be recognized *only* as victims, not as actors or participants (see box 8.5).

Box 8.5   Cult of the pure victim

One of the most insidious results of the categorical separation of genocide and war is the separation of victimhood, as an experience, from other aspects of victims' lives, especially their roles as agents. The shock of being brought face to face with abuse often makes it difficult for us to see that the abused, in political situations, are often also actors. Thus, when we think about the Holocaust, we often think of Jews going passively into the gas chambers, not of Jews who resisted in the ghettos and the forests of eastern Europe, or who joined the Allied and Soviet armies that defeated Nazism.

It may be true of some individuals that, in a particular situation, they are pure victims. But this is never true of a collectivity. Groups are always to some extent actors, participants in conflict, as well as victims of it. In the global era, Western ways of viewing non-Western groups are particularly prone to concealing this reality. Liberal humanitarianism often finds it easiest to represent victim groups as pure victims – innocent civilian populations attacked by state or paramilitary power. Thus the West sees Iraqi Kurds and Kosovo Albanians only as helpless civilians, not as groups that have supported political movements or guerrilla struggle.

Although attacks on civilians should always be distinguished from conflicts between armed actors, in practice they are often closely linked. Civilians are often attacked because the armed groups with which they are identified, or which they actually support, are engaged in a struggle with the attacker. Genocide is an outcome of war, as well as a form of it. Armed groups may even carry out mutually genocidal war, against each others' populations. In these situations, we need to recognize the complex patterns that make groups – and often individuals – both participants and victims, at different times.

Recognizing these relationships is partly about acknowledging the causes of victimized groups as well as their suffering. But it is also important because of the dishonest way in which political organizations trade on the victimhood of 'their' group. It is all too easy for combatants to distort the genuine suffering of their civilians, to present them as pure victims – and hence to legitimate the acts of reciprocal victimization that they are themselves perpetrating.

Victimhood is a necessary product of any kind of violence: people generally suffer as they are killed, or injured, or oppressed, and people suffer when these things happen to those for whom they care. It is a truism to say that there are victims on every side in every war, even if the extent and character of victimhood vary enormously. The general recognition of victimizing processes is of great importance in getting people to think critically about what is involved in war. The particular recognition of experiences of victimization is crucial to survivors and their wider communities. Even if this recognition is often highly mediated – for example, through journalists and international organizations – it helps victims' experiences to be known, and their grievances vindicated. Moreover, while media representation creates its own problems, it is not intrinsically bad: even the best justice is mediated by the rationalizing complexities of law and judicial process.

These are all ways in which victims redress the powerlessness of the moment of victimization, and achieve – indirectly, even posthumously – some form of power. Slaughter is above all a moral, and indeed a political, battle. It is one that it is difficult for the most determined killers to win in the long term. Even the most 'helpless' victims can, in the end, redress the terror and killing to which they have been exposed.

Further reading

Browning, C. (1992) *Ordinary Men: Reserve Police Battalion 101 and the Final Solution in Poland*. New York: HarperCollins.

Buruma, I. (1994) *The Wages of Guilt: Memories of War in Germany and Japan*. London: Cape.

Chang, J. (1991) *Wild Swans: Three Daughters of China*. London: HarperCollins.

Finkelstein, N. (2000) *The Holocaust Industry*. London: Verso.

Guttman, R. and Rieff, D., eds (1999) *Crimes of War*. New York: Norton.

Hayner, P. B. (2001) *Unspeakable Truths: Confronting State Terror and Atrocity*. London: Routledge.

Honig, J. W. and Both, N. (1996) *Srebrenica: Record of a War Crime*. Harmondsworth: Penguin.

Lentin, R., ed. (1997) *Gender and Catastrophe*. London: Zed Books.

Mikaya, K. (1993) *Cruelty and Silence: War, Tyranny, Uprising and the Arab World*. London: Cape.

Minow, M. (1998) *Between Vengeance and Forgiveness: Facing History after Genocide and Mass Violence*. Boston: Beacon Press.

Moser, C. and Clark, F., eds (2001) *Victims, Perpetrators or Actors?* London: Zed Books.

Omaar, R. and de Waal, A. (1994) *Rwanda: Death, Despair and Defiance*. London: Africa Rights.

Ryan, M. D., ed. (1981) *Human Responses to the Holocaust: Perpetrators and Victims, Bystanders and Resisters*. New York: Edwin Mellen.

Skjelsbaek, I. (2001) Sexual violence and war: mapping out a complex relationship. *European Journal of International Relations*, 7(2).

Stiglmayer, A., ed. (1994) *Mass Rape: The War against Women in Bosnia-Herzegovina*. Lincoln: University of Nebraska Press.

Twagiramariya, C. and Turshen, M. (1998) 'Favours' to give and 'consenting' victims: the sexual politics of survival in Rwanda. In Twagiramariya and Turshen, eds, *What Women Do in Wartime*, London: Zed Books, 101–17.

Veer, G. van der (1992) *Counselling and Therapy with Refugees: Psychological Problems of Victims of War, Torture and Repression*. Chichester: Wiley.

Wilson, R. (2001) *The Politics of Truth and Reconciliation in South Africa: Legitimizing the Post-Apartheid State*. Cambridge: Cambridge University Press.

Episode VIII
Genocidal war in
Yugoslavia

The post-Yugoslav wars of the 1990s were genocidal wars, in the sense that they were wars of organized states against civilian populations as such, as well as wars between state centres. Their causes lay in conflicts between political elites in the republics of the Yugoslav federation, who jostled for power and resources and sought to manage the democratic transition in their own interests. For the leaders of all the republics, ethnic-nationalist politics, unifying ethnic populations across republican boundaries, was the new basis for consolidating power. In particular, Serbian and Croatian leaders sought to create 'greater Serbian' and 'greater Croatian' states. In pursuing these goals, they sought to break up the non-Serbian and non-Croatian populations in the areas they controlled or aimed to control.

Slobodan Milosevic, president of the largest republic in the Yugoslav federation, Serbia, tore up the constitutional autonomy of the province of Kosovo, where 90 per cent of the population was Albanian, and instituted a repressive apartheid-like regime. Milosevic forced Albanians out of all public institutions, including schools; they set up parallel, unofficial bodies, creating an uneasy situation of dual power in Kosova (as the Albanians called it). Milosevic's control of Kosovo helped Serbia gain control of the federal presidency and the federal (but increasingly Serbianized) Yugoslav army (JNA), which had bases in all the republics. When Slovenia and Croatia (the wealthiest and most Westernized republics) rebelled against Milosevic's attempt to assert Serbian dominance in Yugoslavia, and moved towards independence, their authorities came into conflict with the JNA. In Slovenia, the ten days' war of 1991 involved few deaths and led to a JNA withdrawal. In Croatia, where 600,000 Serbs lived and local Serb leaders were poised to create the Krajina statelet linked to Serbia, the JNA unleashed the first serious interstate war in Europe since 1945.

The Serbian war drive was directed both at the fledgling Croatian state and at the Croat population. Nationalist Croatia, under its first elected president, Franjo Tudjman, had frozen Serbs out of state jobs; it also celebrated the Croatian fascists who had killed large numbers of Serbs in the Second World War. But from the start the Serbian campaign was genocidal: in its ruthless destruction of the cities of Vukovar and Osijek, where many civilians were slaughtered by the JNA and paramilitary gangs (which Milosevic used as the cutting edge of his campaign); and in the dispersal of Croat populations and Croat-dominated communities. The Croatian war came to an uneasy halt in 1992, when UN troops were despatched (ironically, in view of later developments, to Sarajevo in Bosnia) to police a cease-fire.

The logic of this violent unravelling of Yugoslavia posed especially extreme problems in the most 'Yugoslav' of republics, multi-ethnic Bosnia-Herzegovina, where Bosnian-Muslim, Serbian and Croatian nation-alist parties vied for control. The Muslim and Croatian parties supported an independent Bosnia; Serbians (with the JNA in Bosnia transformed into a Bosnian-Serbian army, BSA) opposed this. When the Muslim-Croat majority voted for independence, the Serbians used their superior military strength to assert total control over Serbian-majority areas and to extend Serbian power over a large part of the republic (seeking to link this to Serbia proper).

The Serbian campaign, combining the BSA, local militia and the notori-ous Arkan and Seselj murder gangs from Serbia proper, used extreme force to terrorize non-Serbs and expel them from Serbian-controlled territory. Non-Serb leaders, officials and educated people were killed in many places. Many non-Serb males were killed or incarcerated in camps, some of which were places of torture and mass killing. Women were often raped, many of them in places established by Serbian leaders as part of a strategy to humiliate the Muslim population. Mosques and the homes of non-Serbs were burnt down. Ninety per cent of the three-quarters of a million non-Serbs who lived in Serbian-controlled territory were killed or expelled. These expulsions became widely known by their Serbian eu-phemism: the perpetrator term 'ethnic cleansing' entered general dis-course.

Croatian forces were initially allied to Bosnian government forces in defending non-Serbs against the Serbian campaign. But they established their own statelet in western Bosnia and Herzegovina, closely linked to the Croatian state (Tudjman aimed at integrating these areas with Croatia). Here they carried out their own 'cleansing', and in early 1993 turned against the Bosnians, carrying out genocidal massacres in central Bosnia and an equally genocidal siege of Bosnian-Muslim East Mostar, with the aim of taking Bosnia's second city for Croatia. Even Bosnian forces, although generally defending multi-ethnic communities such as Sarajevo and Tuzla, expelled non-Muslim populations in places. Moreover, genocide in Bosnia was not just of Muslims and Croats by Serbians, or of Muslims by Croatians, but by ethnic-nationalist forces against multi-ethnic centres of population. Plural urban Sarajevo was a standing reproach to nationalism, and Serbian forces terrorized the besieged city for four years before it was finally relieved.

War in Bosnia, as in Croatia, was simultaneously interstate and genocidal. Owing to the military structure of Yugoslavia, designed for guerrilla
war against a Soviet invader, all republics had a militia structure and some
weapons, and most men had undergone military training. Croatian and
Bosnian government forces were hurriedly improvised from 1991, and they
lacked the heavy fire-power of the Serbians. But with some support from
the USA and in Bosnia's case Muslim states, they were able to develop
armies which prevented all-out Serbian victory in 1992, and by 1995 were
able to turn the tables.

Genocidal war claimed over a quarter of a million deaths in Bosnia, the
overwhelming majority of them civilian, and made two million people
refugees. The worst massacre took place at Srebrenica, in eastern
Bosnia, in 1995, when Dutch UN troops handed over 7,000 male Muslim
refugees to the BSA under Ratko Mladic, who proceeded to have most of
them slaughtered. Serbian genocide was ended only by the (re-allied)
Croatian and Bosnian armies, supported by NATO air strikes, advancing
across Serbian-controlled Croatia and Bosnia later in 1995. After this,
Milosevic was forced into the Dayton settlement, which nevertheless
ratified a separate Serbian entity – the spoils of genocide – in much
of Bosnia. Croatian forces, in retaking the Serbian 'Krajina', killed thousands of Serb civilians and forced hundreds of thousands into exile.
Just after Tudjman's death in 2000, it emerged that his name was included
in the International War Crimes Tribunal's indictment relating to this
operation.

However, Dayton was a 'settlement' only for Bosnia and Croatia.
In Kosovo, the stalemate between the Serbian regime and the pacifist
Albanian leadership, which had saved Kosovans the horrors of war for
most of the 1990s, broke down in its aftermath. Following mass protests
against his regime in Belgrade, Milosevic stepped up repression in Kosovo.
Albanians, who had seen the successes of Croatians and Bosnians against
Serbian power, began to move towards violent resistance, through the
emergent Kosova Liberation Army (KLA). In early 1998 this crisis erupted
into war, with fighting between the KLA and Serbian forces, and the
burning of Albanian villages. By early 1999, 2,000 were dead, a quarter
of a million homeless and genocidal massacres of Albanians escalated
under the noses of international monitors.

Having failed to get agreement to install international forces on
the ground, NATO finally intervened militarily with the air campaign
launched against Serbian power in March 1999. This inadequately
prepared intervention gave Milosevic the pretext to begin a full-scale
genocidal clearance of Kosovo, while provoking Serbian forces and
civilians in the province against the Albanians. In a short period, Serbians
slaughtered probably 10,000 people in over 100 massacres. The terror

drove or frightened up to a million Albanians into flight out of Kosovo, and tens of thousands more from their homes into wooded mountain areas.

Only escalation of the bombing campaign (increasingly tipping over into destruction of the civilian infrastructure of Serbia), combined with the uncertain threat of NATO ground intervention, the reality of increased KLA activity and withdrawal of Russian political support, eventually forced Milosevic to a settlement. NATO forces took over Kosovo, ended Serbian military-police terror and allowed most of the Albanians to return. They were unable, however, to prevent extensive revenge attacks from KLA elements and other gangs, which drove most of the remaining Serb population, innocent as well as guilty, from the province in a short period after the Serbian withdrawal. The cycle of genocidal war had not ended with NATO's victory.

Further reading

Booth, K., ed. (2001) *The Kosovo Tragedy: The Human Rights Dimensions.* London: Frank Cass.

Clark, H. (2000) *Civil Resistance in Kosovo.* London: Pluto.

Cohen, L. J. (1995) *Broken Bonds: Yugoslavia's Distintegration and Balkan Politics in Transition.* Boulder, CO: Westview Press.

Honig, W. and Both, N. (1996) *Srebrenica: Record of a War Crime.* Marmondsworth: Penguin.

International Independent Commission on Kosovo (2000) *The Kosovo Report: Conflict, International Response, Lessons Learned.* Oxford: Oxford University Press.

Judah, T. (2000) *Kosovo: War and Revenge.* New Haven: Yale University Press.

Rogel, C. (1998) *The Breakup of Yugoslavia and the War in Bosnia.* Westport, CT: Greenwood Press.

Simms, B. (2001) *Unfinest Hour: Britain and the Destruction of Bosnia,* London: Allen Lane.

Thompson, M. (1994) *Forging War: The Media in Serbia, Croatia and Bosnia-Hercegovina.* London: Article 19.

Weller, M. (1999) *The Crisis in Kosovo, 1989–1999.* Cambridge: Documents and Analysis Publishing.

Woodward, S. (1996) *Balkan Tragedy.* Washington, DC: Brookings Institution.

─ 9 ─

Movements

We have seen that very large sections of modern society may be participants in, or victims of, war and genocide. Frequently, individuals and groups are both. People have recognized and tried to respond to this reality, and the situations that it involves, in many ways. Some have upheld the absolute rejections of killing prescribed by Christianity and other world religions. Others have proclaimed secular versions of this general pacifism. But mostly only marginal sects, and relatively small numbers of individuals, have sustained such positions. Practices and ideas of slaughter are so embedded in our culture and society that, rather than working for a wholesale rejection of war, most opponents of violence have campaigned for more limited peaceful goals. We have seen that this tendency has been labelled 'pacificism', as distinct from straightforward pacifism; it has been manifested in a wide range of ideas and movements throughout modern times. For example, 'nuclear pacifism' has rejected the possibility that nuclear and other weapons of mass destruction can ever be legitimate.

Although war has long been recognized as a fundamental moral and political issue, it is during the last two centuries that it has most exercised thinkers and actors. Most concern has been in response to the singular modern forms of mass killing. Yet there is something deeply paradoxical about ever more extensive slaughter, surrounded by broader ideas and campaigning for peace. War has been 'rationalized' and, since the slaughter of the trenches, stripped of much of its traditional mystique. International conventions defining the protection of non-combatants have been elaborated with apparently universal support. Genocide has been excoriated as the ultimate international crime. Yet practices of mass killing have been as widespread as ever, brutal manifestations of power's priority over morality and law.

Individual and collective responses to slaughter reflect these contradictions. Preparation of mass killing is so regular a component of the apparatuses of power, the industrial infrastructure and the ideological world of modern society that it goes mostly unremarked. Generally, people respond most actively when directly affected by the practice, preparation or organization of slaughter. But in Western society since 1945, mass killing has become mostly either an abstract possibility (as with nuclear war) or something that happens far way (in non-Western societies). Yet many also respond when distant slaughter or its threat impinges seriously on their mental world.

Resistance

The majority of people are only indirect participants in war and genocide. Most people who make weapons and military equipment, vote for parties that support armies and war, or give opinion pollsters their approval for military action, do not see bodies pile up. Ideology and culture shield them from confrontation with the consequences of chains of action in which they are implicated. However, sometimes the insulation is broken: people face the realities of killing and make active responses.

Most obviously, this happens when people actually become victims. The transformation of victims into agents is not as automatic a process as we might imagine. Potential victims often deny the fact or the extent of the danger in which they exist. Few Polish Jews in early 1941, despite having been herded by the Nazis into ghettos for over a year, in ever-worsening conditions, imagined the extensive mass killing – indeed, systematic extermination – to which they would be subjected within a short space of time. Connections that seem obvious in retrospect are less so in prospect. The Sarajevo resident who remarked that, until 1992, war was something that he watched on television, spoke for many people in today's war zones.

Nevertheless, victimhood is certainly a condition for resistance. Populations that are bombed, besieged, conquered and imprisoned can hardly avoid daily engagement with the realities of violence. Their moral and physical resources, as well as the varying threats they face, explain shifting balances between accommodation and fighting back. The literature of the camps has demonstrated that people continue to resist in the most apparently hopeless conditions. Even where resistance can have little immediate effect on people's fates, many do not give up. Vindication may be posthumous and historic, but it is often the stronger for that.

In contrast, where conditions for active, especially armed, resistance are better, victims risk themselves becoming perpetrators of relatively arbitrary violence. There are too many cases where the oppressed, victorious, become new oppressors. This is the risk of resistance and the dilemma of armed struggle. It is not one that can be easily legislated out of existence by pacifist principles. Nevertheless, it is a question that has been addressed by far-sighted resisters in modern times, from Mahatma Gandhi onwards. Non-violence has not always been sufficient answer for those facing extreme violence; fighting has often seemed the only way out. Among those seeking political change, however, there has been an increasing tendency to recognize the merits of non-violent resistance (see box 9.1).

Box 9.1   Non-violence

In a violent world, non-violence often appears 'unrealistic'. Although there have been important shifts in twenty-first-century world politics towards peaceful models of change, there are always counter-examples of how violence can trump non-violent resistance and change. Since violence is not only the most radical coercion, but also the most dramatic form of action (an important consideration in the age of global media), it is often a relatively simple way of gaining political leverage. The case for non-violence needs to be made repeatedly.

This case must always be partially negative. The enormous costs of violence to individual people and to human society over the last century should give anyone pause, before indulging in even the most limited violent action. Just because a community has itself suffered a violent wrong, it cannot be assumed that violence is necessary. For the truth is that even 'just' violence involves perpetrating new harm: it taints those who commit it, as well as those on the receiving end. War, it has been shown in this book, always transcends its justifications and, in modern times, has systematically degenerated into violence against innocents on a large scale. On the basis of this experience, there should be a *presumption* that war is increasingly an evil that should be avoided, rather than a possible just means.

The case for non-violence, however, is also that peaceful protest can work – indeed, can work where violence will not. It gains in moral stature what it loses in direct coercion. It has the capacity to unite, whereas violence always antagonizes those who identify with the other party. It gives highly armed states less excuse to resort to violent repression and massacres. Instead, it undermines them where it ultimately matters most, especially in today's conditions of surveillance: namely, their legitimacy and authority, potentially both with their 'own' people and with a global audience. Non-violent action can break, instead of reinforcing, the cycles of violence – the constant reproduction of military and even genocidal modes of thought and practice – which are so deep-rooted.

Movement

Victimhood, we saw in the last chapter, should not be seen as an absolute condition. Victims of violence are not necessarily passive. Indeed, they almost always resist, to a greater or lesser extent, by one means or another. Upheaval and movement are characteristic of the social conditions of war and genocide. These violent relations occur where old political relations cannot be maintained unchanged. They involve rapid changes in people's social existence. They stir people out of passivity, forcing them to examine anew their lives and their ideas.

It is not only when people become direct victims of violence that they are affected in these ways. The historical literature on modern war is full of accounts of the *radicalizing effects* of war mobilization and participation on social relations. From sexual liberation to increased women's roles in industry and politics, from emancipation of racial minorities to increased trade union membership, from state economic management to the consolidation of social democracy, great changes have been ascribed to war. 'The locomotive of history', as Trotsky called it, has created circumstances in which people have made radical alterations to their lives and societies. But history is not just speeded up by wars. People do things differently, and new tracks are laid that shape subsequent periods of peace. Much social upheaval in war is therefore not *about* war – in the sense of concerning the contest of force. Wars generate mass movements for economic and social change that often have only indirect bearings on the clash of arms. They lead to revolutionary movements that challenge power – and lead in turn to new civil and interstate wars.

Wars also lead, however, to a range of social movements more directly concerned with war as such. Participants become *agents*, transforming the process of a war. This is true even of soldiers.

Forced both to inflict and to endure hideous violence, it is no wonder that individuals who find the pressure traumatic go mad, or that those who find it intolerable desert. Sometimes soldiers have found covert means of protection against the violence of war, avoiding firing their weapons and concentrating on self-protection (see box 9.2). But in many circumstances, such inventive approaches have not been available to troops. The only way to respond to intolerable circumstances has been to revolt collectively. The absolute nature of military discipline has meant that rebellion has been a highly dangerous business, not embarked upon lightly. Deserting and mutinous soldiers have been lucky to be incarcerated; most commonly they have been executed. Sensing the dangers of rebellion, mutineers have often made only limited demands; but any rebellion has usually been momentous. A successful revolt with small beginnings could frequently lead to larger change.

Box 9.2   Soldiers avoiding slaughter

The most famous example of soldiers' war avoidance was the 'live and let live' system of the First World War trenches. This has been represented in popular culture by the Christmas truces of 1914, when some of the opposing soldiers left their trenches and even played each other at football. But it was actually a much more comprehensive system of largely tacit understandings, through which soldiers on wide sections of the Western Front avoided killing for weeks or months on end.

In stalemated conditions, with relatively stable positions, soldiers on opposing sides engaged in mutual avoidance of slaughter – and parallel conflict with their own generals. Direct fraternization was rare, and generally impossible. Simple inaction, so as not to attract enemy fire, was more common, but this would inevitably attract the attention of commanders. In order to break up quiet spells, they would order troops to fire certain quantities of ammunition each day. Soldiers adapted to this, however, by ritualizing their bombardments, firing at the same 'safe' points at the same time of day, day after day, so that each side knew that the other meant it no harm. In these ways deaths were minimized on both sides.

In 'live and let live', the direct solidarity of soldiers on the same side was complemented by the reciprocal understandings between the opposing sides (Ashworth 1981). Junior officers within the trenches were often complicit, but elite regiments with strong patriotic traditions were less prone. The conflict between soldiers' attempts at self-preservation and high commands' attempts to prosecute the war led, moreover, to more drastic tactics being ordered, like raiding the enemy trench, which almost invariably led to people being killed, and often broke up the understandings that had been established.

Defeated and failed armies have been particularly prone to rebellious eruptions. But soldiers in successful armies have also felt empowered – they become impatient when their own situations fail to improve in the aftermath of victory. In extreme cases, soldiers' revolts have been catalysts for general revolutionary movements. Thus the implosion of the Tsar's massive peasant army led directly to the revolution of 1917 – and Russia's withdrawal from the First World War. Everywhere, soldiers' rebellions have signalled that states' very abilities to wage war were under threat. Nevertheless, military discipline has always remained a powerful deterrent; the number of wars halted or undermined by such movements is quite small (see box 9.3).

Box 9.3   A fulcrum of revolution?

Friedrich Engels saw militarism as carrying 'in itself the seeds of its own destruction'. Universal military service, he argued, was 'making the whole people familiar with the use of arms'. When the people found their independent will, 'at this point the armies of princes become transformed into armies of the people; the machine refuses to work, and militarism collapses of its own contradictions' (extract in Semmel 1981: 57).

Wars were actually more favourable conditions for revolt than the economic crises that Marxists have more generally stressed. In wars, state machines did sometimes begin to disintegrate: from the Paris Commune of 1871 (after the defeat of France in the Franco-Prussian War), through the Russian Revolution of 1905 (Russian–Japanese War), to the revolutions in Russia, Germany, Hungary and Italy in 1917–19, at the conclusion of the world war. State power could not withstand the desertion of large numbers of soldiers to the revolution.

However, this was not as widespread as Engels might have hoped, and the end of the First World War was the high point of this trend. War became more ideological, and states became better at integrating their soldiers. War also became more total, and in 1945 the defeated armies were mostly too comprehensively demoralized to rebel. At the same time, revolution became militarized. Communists like Mao in China and Tito in Yugoslavia organized their own armies and used the conditions of general war to seize power.

Depressingly, the major recent example of a nation schooled in warfare using its military expertise in the opposite way to how it was planned is former Yugoslavia in the 1990s. The Yugoslav system of locally based territorial defence, designed to beat off a Soviet invasion, lent itself not to revolution, but to the development of local armies and militias on all sides during the recent wars.

Of more importance in recent times have been *anti-draft movements*. At the time they are drafted, conscripts face a loss of personal freedom, perhaps of their lives. Where this personal threat combines with moral rejection of the cause for which they are called to fight, there are powerful incentives to resist. Before being inducted, potential conscripts still have the freedom and resources of civilian society. When a sizeable proportion of draftees refuses to kill or be killed for a cause, this undermines its general legitimacy. In cases like the American campaign in Vietnam and the Soviet campaign in Afghanistan, draft resistance, evasion and desertion have been the sharp ends of general anti-war movements. Even in popular wars, individual conscientious objectors are significant voices. States initially resisted granting them rights, but many have gradually relented. A century ago, conscientious objection was seen as legitimate only, if at all, on religious grounds. As Western states have struggled to retain the legitimacy of armed force within democratic societies, they have increasingly accommodated objectors of all kinds (see box 9.4).

Box 9.4   Conscientious objection

Armed forces have always coerced men into military service, and men have always resisted. Since the modern development of universal military service systems, conscientious objection has been an increasingly important response. As these systems declined in the West at the end of the twentieth century, objection became both common and fully recognized by states. This was not always so: in earlier periods, and still today in more authoritarian states, conscientious objection has been a courageous stance, often carrying with it severe punishment.

Conscientious objectors (COs), propose Moskos and Chambers (1993), can be either *religious* or *secular* in motivation. They may be *universalistic*, opposed to all wars (this kind of objector is most readily recognized by states); *selective*, opposed to a particular conflict; or *discretionary*, rejecting the use of particular methods, such as weapons of mass destruction. They also vary in the degree of co-operation that they are prepared to give to the state: *absolutist* COs refuse to co-operate with the conscription system in any way; *alternativists* are prepared to undertake alternative, non-military service; while *non-combatants* are prepared to undertake non-military roles within military organizations.

There has been a secularization of conscience, argue Moskos and Chambers. In pre-modern society, objectors were in limbo, not consistently recognized by states. In early modern society, members of 'historic peace faiths', of which one of the best known is Quakerism, gained some recognition. In later modernity, states recognized a wider range of religious reasons for objection. Today, many are finally prepared to accept secular objection. The state with the most liberal provisions is Germany, where by 2000 around half of all young men regularly opted out of military service and into the *Zivildienst*, or civilian service, which propped up the country's social work system.

In the global era, mass armies and conscription are in decline in the West. Even states that keep conscripts rarely deploy them within internationalized forces in crisis situations. Better-paid, more motivated professional soldiers, whose lives are more highly valued, do not revolt in the classic manner. Performing politically sensitive peacekeeping tasks, with a more proactive concept of the soldier's role, they sometimes generate open disagreement on policy and operational matters that was unimaginable among military personnel in earlier periods. This in turn means that military dissatisfactions are fed more directly into public debate and policy making.

Soldiers' revolts have often given the clearest signs of a war's unpopularity. But in the end, civilian anti-war movements have tended to be more powerful. Even in authoritarian states, civilians typically have much greater freedom than soldiers to criticize and organize. While military revolts have signalled sharp crises for states, civilian dissatisfactions have undercut political legitimacy and power on a broader scale. Wars have often created strong labour demand, which has increased workers' bargaining power; they have drawn new masses of workers into urban industrial areas, often in harsh living conditions. Together, these factors have made war-workers liable to revolt. Correspondingly, the depletion of rural labour through conscription and industrial recruitment has increased the pressure in rural areas.

In unpopular wars, these social pressures – combined with sufferings of soldiers – have led to widespread anti-war movements. States' abilities to wage war have been brought into question. In the First World War, open revolts spread across many states in the war's later stages. In the Second World War, generally more popular in combatant states, these pressures were more effectively controlled than in the First. In the limited wars that Western states have fought since 1945, they have also generally been contained – often because war's effects on the economy and society have been much reduced. The big exceptions to this pattern were lengthy wars of decolonization, as in Algeria and Vietnam, which became unwinnable in terms of the resources and values of Western states.

The US war in Vietnam symbolizes, far more than any other, war's changed significance in Western society. In that war, casualties among both American troops and Vietnamese civilians exceeded the increasingly thin moral and political construction of the war. The resulting illegitimacy was blamed on the messenger, television, which made this a 'living room war', with images of violence in American homes. Although this was a largely mistaken explanation, given that media coverage turned unfavourable to US policy only *after* it had begun to fail, it fed myths that have constrained the Western way of war ever since. Western policy-makers have believed that they must avoid casualties at all costs; the West's enemies that they have only to inflict them for Western states to withdraw.

The protracted American failure in Vietnam stimulated a large anti-war movement, itself fanned by media attention (see box 9.5). This was the last major movement against a particular war in the West, largely because Western governments drew from this experience the conclusion that they must not risk long drawn-out campaigns. Although each subsequent Western war has produced anti-war protest, this has rarely had wide popular resonance. State leaders simply don't allow wars to drag on, to cause large casualties to their own forces, or to inflict massive slaughter on enemy civilians. Fighting wars within the parameters created by media coverage, opinion polls and electoral cycles, Western governments avoid the conditions that classically have produced significant anti-war movements.

Box 9.5 The anti-Vietnam War movement

The movement against the Vietnam War in the late 1960s was the definitive anti-war movement of modern times. Like the French movement of the late 1950s and early 1960s against the Algerian War, it was a major national movement, but it also had huge international repercussions. It coincided with a loss of nerve among the US elite as the long period of unchallenged US hegemony after 1945 came to an end. As the USA faltered in its war with the Vietcong, the anti-war movement helped provoke a more general crisis in US and Western politics.

The anti-war movement was the peak of a decade of protest on American campuses that began with the Civil Rights movement. Drawing on the confidence of the post-war youth generation, which had grown up in the security of the long boom, demonstrations snowballed into gatherings of millions by 1967. The anti-war movement was the political sharp end of a more general youth rebellion, underpinned by the 'counter-culture' and focused on college power structures. Outside the USA, it was the spark that lit a worldwide student revolt – fuelling the May Events in France, the 'Prague Spring' and new protests against apartheid in South Africa and dictatorship in Pakistan at its high point in 1968.

In the USA, the anti-war movement saw a new wave of protest at Richard Nixon's bombing of Cambodia, marked by the killings of student protesters by Members of the National Guard at Kent State University, Ohio, in 1970. Nixon's legitimacy took a blow from which it never recovered, and this event was part of the trail leading to his eventual resignation and the unprecedented weakness of US power in the mid-1970s – the 'Vietnam syndrome', which US leaders sought to expunge during the following decades.

Non-Western states have continued to wage longer, more murderous wars. Soviet intervention in Afghanistan and Russian wars in Chechnya have both led to anti-war feeling, somewhat comparable to American sentiment over Vietnam. States like Iran and Iraq, Serbia and Croatia, have fought long and bloody wars, but these states been able to limit opposition, by using mass media as instruments of nationalist propaganda, as well as through repression. Citizens have protested more at the economic and political consequences of war for themselves than against the slaughters that their governments have perpetrated on others.

After Vietnam, Western anti-war movements focused mostly on the threat, rather than the actuality, of war. In the early 1980s, as at the end of the 1950s, mass movements developed against nuclear weapons. In both cases, new developments in weapons technology coincided with heightened political tensions between the Cold War superpowers. These changes turned the abstract danger of the arms race into a concrete threat to society. They activated otherwise limited popular awareness of military developments. Nuclear disarmament movements, like many other 'peace movements', were expressions of fear as well as concern about the immorality of mass killing. In a situation in which the threat of slaughter had become completely general and mutual, self-concern and concern for others coincided.

These new peace movements, like social movements in general, were more effective in mobilizing social concern than in translating it into political results. Peace movements were internationalized across Europe and the rest of the Western world on an unprecedented scale. They were largely defeated, however, on immediate decisions about weapons deployment: cruise and Pershing II missiles had been installed in Western European countries by 1985. But they had a major impact on the cultural and political climate. When Mikhail Gorbachev, who came to power in that year, recognized the Soviet Union's need to back out of the nuclear arms race, the pro-disarmament momentum in the West gave him reason to expect a more favourable reception. In this way, peace movements triumphed not over, but through, interstate dynamics. The major contribution of the 'peace' movements to peace was not, therefore, to remove weapons, but to help undermine the political conditions for nuclear conflict (see box 9.6).

Box 9.6   From the Western peace movements to 1989

The 1980s began with mass peace demonstrations on the streets of West Berlin, London, Amsterdam and other Western European cities. They ended with mass democracy movements on the streets of Leipzig, East Berlin, Prague and Bucharest. Between these two phenomena, the Cold War unravelled. What was the connection?

In the Western peace movements of the early 1980s, there were several main strands. The main British organization, the Campaign for Nuclear Disarmament, worked, as in the 1960s, to remove all nuclear weapons from the UK. The US movement sought a 'nuclear freeze'. The main European movements, however, sought to prevent the new cruise and Pershing systems being installed on the Continent. Within them, European Nuclear Disarmament (END) aimed to subvert the Cold War by linking citizens' movements in East and West. As part of this strategy, activists from the Netherlands, West Germany and Britain supported small independent peace groups in East Germany, Hungary, Czechoslovakia and elsewhere, and entered into dialogue with human rights activists, e.g. in the Czech Charter 77 and Polish Solidarity.

Ironically, Solidarity, the only mass oppositional movement in the 1980s Soviet bloc, was relatively impervious to Western peace activism. But elsewhere the peace groups were among the first independent political groups in Eastern Europe. Western activists, moreover, supported the human rights and democratic campaigning of the oppositionists. When Gorbachev's reforms undermined the position of Communist regimes outside the Soviet Union, peace activists were among those who helped develop the mass movements on the streets of Eastern European capitals. Although these movements developed beyond the influence of the activists, it could truly be said that their initiatives had helped begin the change, and that it was their ideas of people power undermining the bloc system that were vindicated by the events of 1989.

Change

The positive contributions of social movements to the end of the Cold War were quite novel. Historically, although there has been much anti-war resistance, popular politics was as likely to aggravate conflict as to create peace. It has not just been conservative thinkers, following Clausewitz, who have seen the revolutionary involvement of the people as responsible for the intensified violence of modern war. Lenin and other Marxists also saw class conflict as inherently likely to lead to violence and civil war. True, 'class war' often meant irreconcilable social antagonism rather than organized violence, so that revolutionaries frequently used the term 'civil war' in a political rather than a military sense. But in the twentieth century change was often seen as inevitably violent. Revolutionaries often embraced war and military organization as their principal means.

War has never been entirely legitimate as an instrument of radical politics. Revolutionaries have usually blamed the old order for the violence of political upheavals. Counter-revolutionaries have usually obliged with repression of radical movements – and counter-revolts against successful revolutions. However, the dominance (outside the democratic West) of military insurrection as the dominant model of change is not an automatic result of the conditions in which change has been sought. It has been a strategic choice of radical elites, who have preferred to rely on centralized means of violence rather than democratic social movements. This choice has often been hidden behind a more general critique of the structural 'violence' of established power. Yet physical violence, as we have seen, is a particular kind of abuse. Poverty and misery cannot provide a simple justification for the resort to arms by the oppressed. The extremity of social conditions against which people struggle does not exempt radical politics from the same moral scrutiny which its exponents rightly apply to the violence of established power.

In fact, the historic experience of revolutionary violence has been little short of disastrous. Counter-revolutionary repression is a foreseeable consequence, so military struggle often brings terrible consequences for populations that support it. To the extent that this result is foreseeable, revolutionaries cannot avoid their share of the responsibility for provoking it. Moreover, armed struggle has harmful political consequences for emancipatory projects. The centralization usually considered essential to armed struggle leads to unaccountability of power within movements. The violence of the struggle is usually turned, to a lesser or greater degree, against dissidents within radical movements and the populations they control – as well as against the ostensible main enemy, established power. Violence becomes a habitual mode of power. Regimes established through armed struggle often resort to it as their method of rule.

There is no simple inevitability to these consequences of armed struggle. Leaders – and others who become aware of them – may combat such tendencies. But they were very widely prevalent within armed movements in the twentieth century. There were important differences of degree between authoritarian repressive movements, on the one hand, and totalitarian, openly geno-cidal movements on the other. But we cannot overlook the gener-ally destructive effects of militarization on the century's revolutionary movements. This was not an unfortunate product of particular circumstances or ideologies, whatever parts these may have played. It was a common phenomenon of revolution, and especially of armed struggle.

Linkages of militarization with authoritarian, totalitarian and genocidal outcomes were apparent in revolutions that began as social and political struggles and were subsequently militarized, like the Russian Revolution. They were even more obvious in revolutions that were organized from their beginnings on a military basis – as most were in the later twentieth century. The Communist trail of slaughter, from the Soviet countryside in the early 1930s through the Gulag to the Cultural Revolution and the Khmer Rouge, is too consistent to be viewed as an aberration. This history also makes it difficult to distinguish revolution and counter-revolution. The affinities between Stalinism and Fascism, the non-identical totalitarian twins, are well known. The latter was from the start counter-revolutionary, externally opposed to proletarian revo-lution. The former was a kind of counter-revolution within the revolution. Fascism borrowed some of the methods of revolution; Stalinism those of Fascism. Militarized revolutions, from Mao on-wards, combined revolutionary struggles for national liberation with many of these counter-revolutionary modes of power.

Two developments have challenged this link of war and political transformation. First, revolutionary regimes, established by armed struggle, have themselves been opposed by a new wave of peaceful democratic movements at the end of the twentieth century. These movements have erupted, across Asia, Latin America and Africa, against all kinds of authoritarianisms, pro-Western as well as pro-Soviet. But there was a particular poignancy in their challenges to regimes that claimed to be 'revolutionary'. As the People's Liber-ation Army mowed down the demonstrators in Tiananmen Square in 1989, the bankruptcy of the militarized 'revolutionary' state was obvious. Democratic movements, from Berlin and Prague to Soweto and Seoul, were the new political revolution of the late twentieth century. They sought both fundamental changes in local political structures and new linkages to global structures of power. They represented, however, a radical departure from earlier revo-lutionary traditions: no centralized, let alone militarized, revolu-tionary party seized power; and they sought not the overthrow of the dominant world order but integration into it.

Second, some existing revolutionary movements, engaged in armed struggle against local regimes, began to recognize the limits of this method. This happened for several principal reasons: difficulties in overthrowing relatively sophisticated states, the need to avoid being sidelined by democratic mass movements and the decline in the support provided by the Cold War blocs. Armed struggle often did not work; it could cut across political mobilization, and it generated less international support. Hence many movements, following the paradigm case of the African National Congress in South Africa (see box 9.7), sought political change by non-violent means.

Box 9.7   The transformation of armed struggle

The African National Congress (ANC) was founded in 1912 as a political movement of the oppressed black majority in South Africa. After the National Party, the party of the Afrikaaner section of the White population, took power in 1948 and began to construct a regime of apartheid (separate development of the different racial groups), the ANC became the focus of resistance. The suppression of peaceful protest, with the banning of the organization in 1960, the Sharpeville massacre of 1961 and the treason trials of ANC leaders like the lawyer Nelson Mandela, imprisoned in 1964, pushed the movement increasingly underground and towards violent resistance.

Between the 1960s and the early 1990s, the ANC organized a military wing, Umkonto we Sizwe ('Spear of the Nation') that organized guerrilla struggle and terrorist actions inside South Africa. Based mainly in independent African states, and with support from the Soviet Union as well as liberal anti-apartheid movements in Western countries, the ANC remained the principal focus of opposition for South Africans. However, the ANC's military campaigns did not seriously challenge the regime. After the development of the Black Consciousness movement (led by Steve Biko, who was murdered by the regime) in South Africa's townships in 1976, internal movements posed a more serious threat to apartheid.

By the late 1980s, with the Cold War that had sustained the National Party regime breaking down, elements of the government were looking for a reformist compromise with Black politicians. The ANC, on the other hand, was not confident of its ability to win a destructive civil war with the heavily armed state – it was already becoming involved in a localized civil war with the Zulu nationalist Inkatha movement. The ANC also feared that so long as it remained illegal, newer movements could upstage it. It therefore pushed the government towards a historic compromise that legalized the ANC and organized free elections based on universal suffrage, while protecting minority rights. When elections were finally held in 1994, the ANC won two-thirds of the votes and was able to establish itself legally and relatively peacefully as the new ruling party, with Mandela as its first president.

The ANC's new model of change was a major inspiration to other armed movements, like the IRA in Northern Ireland. But it was not easily transferred to other settings. The failure of the Palestinian Liberation Organization to consolidate its 'peace process' with Israel in the 1990s showed an alternative path, leading back to armed insurrection and terrorism. The failure of the pacifist Ibrahim Rugova to achieve independence for Kosovo Albanians through non-violent resistance led to the formation of the Kosovo Liberation Army. Its armed struggle, which provoked Serbia into genocidal repression, which in turn led NATO into war against Serbia, could be said to have helped produce the 'liberation' of Kosovo after 1999. However, it was at the price of 10,000 Albanian deaths and the wrecking of homes, villages and towns, not to mention the KLA's counter-violence against Serb civilians.

So, at the beginning of the twenty-first century, just as major interstate relations became unprecedentedly peaceful, so did models of political transformation. In 1989, Czechoslovakia's 'velvet revolution' could easily have been violent if the old regime had resorted to force. It wasn't, partly because, like other local elites from South Africa to Indonesia, the old rulers recognized their historic need to change before the stage of all-out confrontation with democratic forces was reached. In this sense, the Eastern European revolutions consolidated a new paradigm of change that has since spread across the continents.

By the beginning of the new century, progressive politics was beginning to be disentangled from armed struggle. In contrast, war was becoming embedded ever more deeply in the strategies of authoritarian states and parties that resisted the new democratic wave. In the face of democratization, authoritarian elites found militarist nationalism the most viable strategy for holding or gaining power. Neo-democratic regimes mobilized ethno-national electorates against other ethnic groups – and against cosmopolitans and international power – to legitimate their rule. As we have seen, their wars typically involved genocides. Thus reactionary violence challenged the emergent pacifism of cosmopolitan politics. War was declining generally, both as a means of interstate politics *and* as a normal method of political transformation. But the new wave of genocidal wars demanded answers from the internationalized and globalized structures of state power. Could they defeat violence without more violence?

Two new cases presented sharp challenges to the idea of peaceful transformation. In Kosovo, where peaceful Albanian political movements had been ignored by both the Serbian regime and the West, the Kosovo Liberation Army succeeded in provoking Western intervention to free the province from Serbian rule. (Albanian militants then partially repeated this success in Macedonia.) In the USA, the terrorist attacks of 11 September 2001 led to the declaration of a 'war' on terrorism. Although policing and legal action were the obvious ways of tracking down covert terrorist networks, nothing less than war appeared to satisfy the American need to avenge a terrible wrong and humiliation. So at the beginning of the twenty-first century, the central question in the politics of war was whether a new form of 'good war' was being renewed as a means of controlling new forms of reactionary violence.

Further reading

Ashworth, T. (1981) *The Live and Let Live System*. London: Macmillan.

Cohen, E. A. (1984) *Human Behavior in the Concentration Camp*. Westport, CT: Greenwood Press.

Crome, L. (1988) *Unbroken: Resistance and Survival in the Concentration Camps*. London: Lawrence and Wishart.

Dallas, G. (1985) *The Unknown Army: Mutinies in the British Army in World War I*. London: Verso.

DeBenedetti, C. (1990) *An American Ordeal: The Antiwar Movement of the Vietnam Era*. Syracuse, NY: Syracuse University Press.

Garfinkle, A. (1995) *Telltale Hearts: The Origins and Impact of the Vietnam Antiwar Movement*. Basingstoke: Macmillan.

Glaessner, G.-J. and Wallace, I. (1992) *The German Revolution of 1989: Causes and Consequences*. Oxford: Berg.

Goossen, R. W. (1997) *Women against the Good War: Conscientious Objection and Gender on the American Home Front, 1941–1947*. Chapel Hill: University of North Carolina Press.

Haimson, L. and Tilly, C., eds (1989) *Strikers, Wars and Revolutions in International Perspective*. Cambridge: Cambridge University Press.

Heineman, K. J. (1993) *Campus Wars: The Peace Movement at American State Universities in the Vietnam Era*. New York: New York University Press.

Hinton, J. (1989) *Protests and Visions: Peace Politics in Twentieth-Century Britain*. London: Hutchinson Radius.

Joppke, C. (1995) *East German Dissidents and the Revolution of 1989*. Basingstoke: Macmillan.

Kaldor, M. (1990) *Europe from Below: An East-West Dialogue*. London: Verso.

Kaltefleiter, W. and Pfaltzgraff, R. L. (1985) *The Peace Movements in Europe and the United States.* London: Croom Helm.

Langbein, H. (1994) *Against All Hope: Resistance in the Nazi Concentration Camps, 1938–1945.* London: Constable.

Liebknecht, K. (1972) *Militarism and Anti-Militarism.* London: Writers and Readers.

Moskos, C. and Chambers, J. (1993) *The New Conscientious Objection.* New York: Oxford University Press.

Oldfield, S. (1989) *Women against the Iron Fist: Alternatives to Militarism, 1900–1989.* Oxford: Blackwell.

Rochon, T. R. (1988) *Mobilizing for Peace: The Antinuclear Movements in Western Europe.* London: Adamantine Press.

Ryan, M. D., ed. (1981) *Human Responses to the Holocaust: Perpetrators and Victims, Bystanders and Resisters.* New York: Edwin Mellen.

Semmel, B., ed. (1981) *Marxism and the Science of War.* Oxford: Oxford University Press.

Shaw, M. (1988) *Dialectics of War: An Essay on the Social Theory of War and Peace.* London: Pluto.

Small, M. (1994) *Covering Dissent: The Media and the Anti-Vietnam War Movement.* New Brunswick, NJ: Rutgers University Press.

Taylor, R. (1988) *Against the Bomb: The British Peace Movement, 1958–1965.* Oxford: Clarendon Press.

Taylor, R. and Young, N., eds (1987) *Campaigns for Peace: British Peace Movements in the Twentieth Century.* Manchester: Manchester University Press.

Tismaneanu, V., ed. (1999) *The Revolutions of 1989.* London: Routledge.

Todorov, T. (1996) *Facing the Extreme: Moral Life in the Concentration Camps.* New York: Henry Holt.

Useem, M. (1973) *Conscription, Protest, and Social Conflict: The Life and Death of a Draft Resistance Movement.* New York: Wiley.

Episode IX
War and genocide in Rwanda

The most terrible genocide of the late twentieth century, in Rwanda in April–May 1994, has also been one of the most misunderstood. Too often it is seen as the product of tribal savagery. In reality it was the outcome of war and political conflict, in which ethnicity was manufactured and exploited by the powerful. The genocide also contributed to new wars that bedevilled central Africa into the twenty-first century.

President Juvénal Habyarimana's one-party regime had ruled Rwanda since a *coup d'état* and pogrom of the minority Tutsi population in 1973. This followed genocidal massacres in 1959, which first brought Hutu nationalist parties to power, and in 1963 and 1967. Large numbers of people fled from these killings to neighbouring countries; Habyarimana prevented their return. Many Rwandan exiles fought in Yoweri Moseveni's National Resistance Army, which overthrew the Ugandan dictatorship of Milton Obote in 1986. With this experience, some subsequently formed a military-revolutionary force, the Rwandan Patriotic Front (RPF), to fight for change in their country of origin.

In 1990, the RPF launched a war to topple the Rwandan regime, in which hundreds of thousands of people were displaced. Regime supporters carried out increasing numbers of massacres and other human rights abuses; but the government was forced to allow multi-party politics and faced demands for democracy. By 1993 the RPF was moving towards the capital, Kigali; only French troops enabled the regime to halt their advance. International pressure forced the regime to negotiate with the RPF, and the Arusha Accords were signed. These provided for the rule of law, power sharing, repatriation of refugees and integration of the RPF and the Rwandese Armed Forces.

Habyarimana blocked implementation of the Accords and his supporters in the state machine planned mass killing in order to maintain their hold on power and prevent peace. They established the *Interahamwe* militia that would be its main organizer on the ground. On 6 April 1994 the president was flying back from an international meeting in Tanzania, where he had faced pressure to stop his prevarication, when his plane was shot down (probably by elements of the regime). This was the signal for the planned genocide to begin. The first targets were opposition politicians, Hutu as well as Tutsi, then journalists and other potential dissidents, local officials and other educated people. From here, the campaign spread rapidly, fanned by the notorious Radio Télévision Libre des Milles Collines, into comprehensive massacres of the Tutsi population.

The genocide was well planned and organized by politicians, army officers and local officials, with extensive complicity of the Church, and claimed up to a million lives. Army, police and 'professional' *Interahamwe* used guns; unofficial militia and the large numbers of Hutu civilians who joined (or were pressed into) the campaign often slaughtered with machetes and clubs. Among the majority of the Tutsi people who were killed, young men were particular targets, while women were raped and enslaved by militia. Huge numbers of people of all ages were hacked to death or mown down, in their homes, on the streets and in churches where they had taken shelter. Hundreds of thousands fled to Tanzania and other neighbouring states, where international agencies supplied makeshift camps.

The small UN forces that were stationed in Kigali were withdrawn after they were attacked, but only after they had rescued most of the resident European population. UN troops abandoned Rwandans to their fate, even handing over thousands of men, women and children who had taken refuge with them to the *génocidaires*. In New York, the Security Council debated and resolved, and the Secretariat prevaricated; the Western powers failed to provide the forces which might have halted the genocide; neighbouring African states did not manage to put their concern into practice. Only France intervened, its *Opération Turquoise* in south-west Rwanda protecting perpetrators as well as saving some victims.

The genocide was ended, and the genocidal regime dispatched, by the Rwandan Patriotic Front, which renewed its war and took over the country. In the face of the RPF's advance, more than a million Hutus – including most of those implicated in the genocide – fled to Zaire (the name given to Congo-Kinshasa by the corrupt Mobutu regime which had ruled since the early 1960s). This second wave of 'refugees' was also supported by international agencies, but the camps (mainly around Goma in western Congo) became bases for the regrouped *Interahamwe*. The latter allied themselves with the army and local administration of the disintegrating Zairean regime, terrorizing local Banyumalenge (people linked ethnically to Rwanda's Tutsis) in a new, potentially genocidal campaign.

In 1996, as this new war in the Congo escalated, the West once again began to discuss a 'humanitarian' intervention (to be led by Canada). Again, however, they were pre-empted by local military actors. Rwandan forces, with support from Uganda, allied with the Congolese opposition led by Laurent Kabila. They first dispersed the Goma camps, forcing the majority of Hutu exiles to return to Rwanda, while sending the militia fleeing further into the Congo. Kabila's forces then advanced across the vast, shambolic territory of Congo to overthrow Mobutu and take power.

Kabila (once linked to the oft-romanticized guerrilla leader Ché Guevara) rapidly disappointed the hopes placed on him both within and beyond the Congo. His forces were responsible for numerous atrocities, and, once installed in Kinshasa, his regime rapidly became almost as autocratic as Mobutu's. By 1999, a new war was raging in the renamed Democratic Republic of the Congo. The Rwandan and Ugandan governments now supported the anti-Kabila opposition. Zimbabwe, Angola and other states backed Kabila. This could be described as an internationalized civil war: it reflected the general breakdown of state power across a wide region of central Africa, comparable to that in west Africa and Somalia. At the beginning of the new century, the war in the Congo had degenerated into local tribal conflict in the north-west of the territory.

In Rwanda, the aftermath of the genocide is appalling. Those who were mutilated and raped, and who lost children, husbands, wives and parents continue to suffer; they coexist uneasily with the returnees, including many suspected killers; and prisons are full of tens of thousands of alleged killers that the judicial system cannot cope with.

Further reading

Barnett, M. (2002) *Eyewitness to a Genocide: The United Nations and Rwanda.* Ithaca, NY: Cornell University Press.

Gourevich, P. (1999) *We Wish to Inform you that Tomorrow we will be Killed with our Families: Stories from Rwanda.* London: Picador.

Human Rights Watch (1996) *Shattered Lives: Sexual Violence during the Rwandan Genocide and its Aftermath.* New York: Human Rights Watch.

Mamdani, M. (2001) *When Victims become Killers: Colonialism, Nativism and the Genocide in Rwanda.* Princeton: Princeton University Press.

Melvern, L. R. (2000) *A People Betrayed: The Role of the West in Rwanda's Genocide.* London: Zed Books.

Omaar, R. and de Waal, A. (1994) *Rwanda: Death, Despair and Defiance.* London: Africa Rights.

—10—

Just Peace

Organized killing is a supreme evil of modern society. In its twin forms of degenerate war and deliberate genocide, it is comprehensively produced, I have argued throughout this book, in modern social relations. As we saw in the last chapter, it has been difficult even for progressive social movements to disentangle themselves from the politics of killing. Likewise, each episode of slaughter has far-reaching impacts not just on the immediate survivors, but on whole communities and indeed all who become aware of it. These effects do not lead to a simple desire to halt killing. They also raise powerful questions of justice – which can provoke new conflict.

There is widespread recognition, therefore, that the demands of justice must be addressed in peaceful ways if new rounds of killing are to be avoided. So the answer to the problem of war is not merely peace, but *just* peace. As we have seen, progressive political thinkers have recognized, for more than two centuries, that lasting peace between states depends on durable and equitable international arrangements. For much of that time, as rival national empires have marched across the world, this idea has seemed fanciful. In the twenty-first century, however, interstate conflicts have begun to be curbed. Lasting peaceful relations between the largest centres of power are more conceivable than ever before in the modern era, even if they are far from guaranteed.

At the same time, it has become apparent that in other power relations, violence remains intractable. Organized killing is widely seen to be more than a problem of conventional war. Correspondingly, it is understood that agreements between states are only part of the answer. It is increasingly recognized that mass killing is produced by all kinds of political conflicts. The divisions between 'international' war, 'internal' revolt and genocide are blurred. Thus it is acknowledged that justice is not simply a condition to be established *between* states or political communities. Once we see individuals, families and many kinds of social group as victims of organized violence, then we see that justice belongs to all of them. In the emergent global society, the problems of just peace and of justice within society are ultimately the same.

These kinds of understanding are developing around the political conflicts of the early twenty-first century. The Cold War reinforced the legitimacy of traditional state centres; it shored up authoritarian regimes and inhibited democratic movements. As this old set of power relations has dissolved, so new visions of global justice have developed. Local democratic movements in many non-Western regions, Western non-governmental organizations and Western and global interstate organizations have all helped to evolve these alternative ideas. Horrific new experiences of mass killing have stimulated the linkages of peace and justice – in campaigns and in international practice. New understandings of past episodes have reinforced this new climate.

In this chapter, I explore these issues in both short-term and long-term contexts. I look first at how war and genocide have increasingly been seen as problems to be managed through internationalized political institutions; second, at how war and genocide have raised demands for just peace. Finally, I examine how experiences at the turn of the century may reshape fundamental ways of thinking about these issues, laying the basis for new solutions in global society over the coming decades.

Old thinking about war

Internationalization has proceeded far in the advanced West, and represents a major historic shift that has profound implications for peace. The main states of today's West (the USA, the major European powers and Japan) were imperial rivals in the world wars in the first half of the last century. Now they are increasingly integrated into a single internationalized power conglomerate, closely linked to the legitimate global institutions of the United Nations. Likewise, Russia and the West were in armed confrontation for forty years: now the West is drawing its Cold War rival into its sphere. Yet the full impact of these remarkable transitions, which have abolished war between most of yesterday's greatest enemies, has not yet fully registered. Old ways of thinking about war still retain great power in our time.

Across the advanced world, politicians and people cling to the ideas of the earlier epoch. At the turn of the new century, America's power is embedded within complex international alliances and institutions. But its leaders and people still think of themselves chiefly as members of a powerful nation: a tendency that was powerfully reinforced in the reaction to the terror massacres of 11 September 2001. Britain and France are subordinated to the USA, as well as enmeshed in European institutions; but their governments sometimes talk as though they still had independent imperial capabilities. Japan has been dependent on the American alliance for half a century, a dependence reinforced today by the challenge of Chinese power; but some Japanese still nurture illusions of national military revival. It is chiefly in smaller or weaker states, like Canada, the Benelux and Scandinavian countries, and those of east-central Europe, that internationalization is positively embraced. With deepening integration, however, elites throughout the European Union are beginning to think in more internationalized ways.

Leaders of the large and medium-sized non-Western powers have mostly changed their ways of thinking even less than Western leaders. Governments and elites in semi-democratic Russia, still authoritarian China, would-be regional superpower India and its rival Pakistan, not to mention most Middle Eastern states (and many others), still behave as though they can use their undoubtedly considerable military power in serious interstate war. The West's regional allies, like Israel, Saudi Arabia, Taiwan and South Korea, also envisage such wars and spend heavily on weapons supplied by the USA, Britain and France. On the other hand, these same states are all caught up in strong globalizing processes that cut across old-style conceptions of armed rivalry. Rapid growth in world and regional markets means that trade and investment mesh non-Western states more thoroughly into Western-dominated world institutions. Even still Communist China is joining Western-led global organizations like the World Trade Organization: when Russia's application is also completed, all major states will belong. Remaining outside Western-led global networks is no longer a serious option, and engaging in interstate war always has costs for governments. The examples of bankrupt, sanctions-stricken Iraq and Serbia, whose rulers chose military confrontation with the West and lost, undoubtedly act as a partial deterrent to other elites tempted along this path.

Thus there are stronger disincentives than in earlier periods for states – outside as well as within the West – to engage in major interstate war. Nevertheless, localized war remains a viable option for many states – and even more for unrecognized, parastatal elites. The contradictions of state power still open up possibilities of several kinds of war (see box 10.1).

Box 10.1   A future for interstate conflict?

It is widely believed that old-style interstate war is on the way out. Certainly most of the faultlines that produced war – and Cold War – in the twentieth century are unlikely to activate military conflict in the coming decades. But this is not an end to the issue. New lines of division are still producing conflict. Three types are likely to cause most trouble:

1   Conflicts between state centres formed from the breakup of existing states. After all, the Yugoslav wars were not simply 'civil wars', but wars between the rump Serbian-Yugoslav state and the emergent new states of Croatia, Bosnia and Kosovo.
2   Conflicts between local powers. For example, the Congo civil war that began in the late 1990s was also a regional war between states like Zimbabwe and Angola, on one side, and Rwanda and Uganda, on the other.
3   Conflicts between local states and the West. In little more than a decade of the global era, the West has fought wars against Iraq, Serbia and Taliban-run Afghanistan, so-called rogue states.

All these examples show the enmeshing of interstate war with civil war, on the one hand, and Western-global power, often legitimated by the UN, on the other. But less than fifteen years since the end of the terrible Iran–Iraq war, it would be rash indeed to rule out classical clashes between two established states. In future, such conflicts will always raise huge questions of global order, and we will probably see much more developed efforts to contain them. But such efforts may not always succeed.

War management

The West, with its political, military, financial and ideological power, dominates world-level organizations. Yet it puts very limited resources into the development of genuine global political and legal institutions. The USA, in particular, prefers the direct exercise of its own and its allies' power, intermittently legitimated by the UN, to any substantial development of global bodies. The USA has attempted to manage major interstate rivalries, such as India–Pakistan, China–Taiwan, Israel–Palestine–Syria, through its own diplomatic and financial interventions. Less central conflicts are often managed politically through *ad hoc* mechanisms like 'contact groups', comprised of major Western and non-Western states, rather than under direct UN auspices. Even within the West, the full activation of alliance organizations is the exception rather than the rule; so, while NATO fought over Kosovo, the USA has preferred *ad hoc* arrangements with individual allies for its other campaigns in the Gulf and Afghanistan. The West, which provides the real drive and muscle for major UN-legitimated interventions, has little political will to prevent or halt the majority of local wars.

The UN itself lacks independent military forces; its active role is confined mostly to those local conflicts which, while murderous for civilian populations, are of less political and strategic importance to the West. UN intervention forces have proliferated, but they are frequently under-resourced and under-trained, with weak political mandates and military command systems. A dismal pattern of failure in crises can be traced to the point that the UN has repeatedly handed over the civilians they were supposed to protect to genocidal killers (in Rwanda, Bosnia and East Timor in the 1990s). Thus the worst instances of slaughter have not been halted through UN intervention. They have sometimes been stopped through more decisive action by local states or armed movements (such as Vietnam's invasion of Cambodia, Tanzania's of Uganda and the Rwandan Patriotic Front's of Rwanda). Likewise, they have also been halted by Western state organizations (the USA, Britain and France in Iraqi Kurdistan; NATO in Bosnia and Kosovo; Australia in East Timor). The UN has generally legitimated Western actions – although in Kurdistan, legitimation was indirect, and in Kosovo, retrospective. The pattern of interventions has grown since the end of the Cold War, and the doctrine of 'humanitarian intervention' has been developed (see box 10.2).

Box 10.2   Humanitarian intervention

Third parties have always 'intervened' in local wars, whether interstate or civil, despite the international norm that states do not interfere in the internal affairs of other states. Historically the principal interveners have been the great powers, and during the Cold War the superpowers. Intervention   has also taken diplomatic, political and economic forms – but military intervention is generally seen as the most important, and is what 'intervention' usually means.

Such intervention has become more common in the global era, and has increasingly been described as humanitarian. Of course, humanitarian aid for the victims of conflict – providing food, shelter, medical assistance, etc. – does not need to be undertaken by military organizations. But such non-military humanitarian activities may need military protection, or military action to create access for aid. This is the most basic meaning of 'humanitarian intervention', but usually it means more than this. It describes *a military campaign motivated at least in part by concern to protect civilian lives, or to create political conditions in which people may live in relative freedom and security.*

In these senses, humanitarian interventions are often contrasted with those motivated by the national interests of the interveners. When Cold War strategic rivalries declined, it appeared that interventions were becoming more altruistic. Interventions have increasingly been legitimated, as Wheeler (2000) shows, by new international norms that gave human rights priority over respect for state sovereignty. Critics argue that this kind of humanitarianism is the ideology of a 'new imperialism'. Certainly, interventions are never solely altruistic: states always have their own economic, political and other interests in taking military action. However, this combination of motives does not mean that humanitarianism has no content. Humanitarianism may sometimes be a cover for other interests, but often it does provide real protection for threatened people.

The continuing paradox of Western and global military power at the beginning of the new century was especially apparent in the 'war to prevent slaughter' in Kosovo in 1999. The West's preference for air power meant that it could only indirectly affect events on the ground – where Serbian forces were massacring and expelling Albanian civilians. The West's leverage depended on precision bombing of Serbian targets; but the bombing campaign was widened to the point where it caused several hundred civilian deaths. The United Nations was unable to take a unified stand, because Russia and China, permanent members of its Security Council, would not back action against Serbia. Yet this was a case of relatively strong intervention. Western–UN management of war was usually more ineffectual, and did little to address the proliferation of mass killing across many regions.

Furthermore, neither the West's three nuclear-armed states (the USA, the UK and France) nor the major non-Western states (Russia and China) had made any deep moves towards nuclear disarmament by the end of the twentieth century, despite their commitments to do so under the Non-Proliferation Treaty. More states are scrambling for nuclear status; even more, probably, are investing in simpler biological weapon capabilities. It is not a promising basis for comprehensive war management, let alone war prevention. While there are powerful pacifying tendencies between larger states, no one can guarantee that these states will not use the enormous arsenals that they are accumulating. In that case, the level of slaughter would dwarf the horrific instances to be found in the new wars of the post-Cold War period.

Demands for justice

Law and war may be opposed at the most general level. Historically, however, attempts to apply ideas of justice to war have been unsuccessful. The 'just war' tradition has done as much to justify war as to constrain or prevent it, as I pointed out in chapter 5. The tradition's fundamental acceptance of the legitimacy of organized state killing has meant that its standards have been easily interpreted in the light of states' interests. The priority of *ius ad bellum* has meant that *ius in bellum* has rarely been addressed comprehensively in practice. Once ends have been legitimated, means have been challenged only in the most shocking cases.

Certainly, the general rationalization of modern society has been reflected in codified rules for the conduct of war. But in the twentieth century, the ferocity of the world wars and the enormity of modern weaponry often reduced these norms to little more than window-dressing. At the margins, certainly, they made a difference to some people's lives. Even the Nazis treated many British and American prisoners of war more or less in terms of the Hague Conventions – even as they massacred Soviet prisoners together with vast numbers of civilians. But breaches of the central prohibition on the slaughter of non-combatants have been central to the practice of modern war. Indeed, these gross violations are deeply embedded in the social organization of warfare.

Despite their own deep complicity in these violations, the victorious Allies did mark the specific character of the defeated empires' crimes. Between 1945 and 1948, there were new international responses to the specific types of terrible crime perpetrated by the losers. The Genocide Convention (see chapter 2 for details) defined the supreme crime against civilian populations, while the Universal Declaration of Human Rights provided a positive statement of new international norms. The 1907 Hague Conventions on the laws of war were updated in the Geneva Conventions of 1949. Equally important as a precedent were the means of enforcing universal norms represented by first International Military Tribunals, at which German and Japanese leaders were tried. Together these developments have framed moral, political and legal discourse ever since (see box 10.3).

Box 10.3   The laws of war after 1945

The trials of the main German, and later Japanese, war leaders before international tribunals represented two major changes in the history of the laws of war. At Nuremberg (1945–6) and Tokyo (1946–8), for the first time, the principle of individual political and command responsibility was firmly established. Leaders who had been responsible for terrible episodes of violence were brought to account for violations of the laws of war. Moreover, they were tried not only for 'crimes against peace', the waging of aggressive war, and 'war crimes', violations of the laws and customs of war. They were also tried on new charges of 'crimes against humanity', defined in the Nuremberg Judgment as including 'murder, extermination, enslavement, deportation, and other inhumane acts committed against any civilian population, before or during the war'.

Crimes against humanity, Geoffrey Best notes, 'were a canny, cautious halfway house to human rights. They were ... invented ... in order to make possible the prosecution of Axis leaders for the dreadful things they had done distant from battle-fronts and in time of peace as well as war; crimes which the traditional law of war could by no means be stretched to cover.' But the Allies were concerned not 'to set a precedent that could immediately be used to their own disadvantage'. The category was therefore qualified so that crimes against humanity 'could be viewed less as harbingers of new-style crimes against human rights than as extensions of old-style war crimes' (Best 1994: 67–8).

In the discussions leading to the Geneva Conventions, 'the same tightrope was walked, increasingly crystallizing as the tension between the *sovereignty of states* and the *universal enforcement of human rights*'. The 1945 UN Charter enshrined state sovereignty, but alongside it 'ran a parallel legislative stream of humanitarian and human rights rules and standards which States undertook at least to take note of and which, if words mean anything, they should in some last resort be required to observe' (Best 1994: 79). The Geneva Conventions added a number of detailed articles extending the protection of civilians in war. Meanwhile the Genocide Convention committed the contracting parties to regarding genocide as a crime 'which they undertake to prevent and to punish'.

In framing the Geneva Conventions, the Western powers protected their own interests, especially in excluding specific provisions against their favoured method of aerial bombing. But Best is probably right to conclude: 'Enough of the human rights programme was nevertheless achieved in the immediate post-war years to mark a revolution in international law and organization' (Best 1994: 79). These achievements were to be picked up in the 1990s, when new genocidal wars, in new world conditions, created new challenges for global justice.

The lines that were drawn after 1945, excluding the crimes of the victors from the understanding of genocide and from specific pro-hibitions under the laws of war, were deeply problematic. Throughout the Cold War, the blocs' preparation of nuclear exter-mination further compromised the tainted moral strength of the positions that the United Nations had adopted. The effectiveness of universal norms was simultaneously undermined by the blocs' cynical denials of many new episodes of slaughter, often commit-ted by their allies; by the lack of any attempts to bring even the worst mass killers to justice; and by the easy recourse to 'politics as usual' with genocidists. The case of the Khmer Rouge, a Commun-ist Party supported by China but also covertly backed by the USA and Britain, can stand for the general corruption of Cold War politics in this respect (see episode VII).

Further, although some of the vilest episodes of the Second World War were dealt with judicially at Nuremberg and Tokyo, many others were hardly exposed any more fully in the early post-war decades. After the rough reckoning of the late 1940s, with Cold War rivalries in place, there was little appetite for further uncover-ing the enormities of the gigantic conflicts that had been brought to a close in 1945. Hollywood and Ealing cemented 'heroic' national myths of the war in the USA and Britain. French elites were reluctant to confront the extent of collaboration. Soviet myth-makers celebrated a heroic struggle against fascism, the Great Patriotic War, but covered over Stalin's own huge crimes during the war. Similar stories were repeated in most countries across the world.

Only gradually did the extermination of the Jews assume its now central role in narratives of Second World War victimization. This was a tremendously important development, even if it had its down side. The gain was the recognition of the deliberate slaughter of civilians, for reasons of their ascribed identity, as a uniquely evil facet of modernity. The horrendous Nazi crimes against European Jews were rightly regarded as the nadir of the worldwide slaughter. Their exposure underlined the terrible depths of human cruelty to other humans. Jewish suffering stood for all the suffering of a whole epoch, and commemorating the Holocaust powerfully re-inforced the human rights institutions and culture that had been so compromised by the Cold War. Here was a paradigm of evil, and an apparently indisputable lesson for the future. As the Cold War finally faded, the meaning of the Holocaust became stronger, not weaker. There were, however, several problems with this centrality of the Jewish story, as we saw in chapter 9. In some hands the story of the Holocaust was abused to justify new persecution; the suffering of non-Jews at the hands of the Nazis was neglected; anti-Semitism was taken out of the larger mixture of Nazi hatreds; the connections between war and genocide were lost to understanding. Perhaps most important, as I have emphasized before, the links between the Nazis' slaughter of the Jews and the larger problems of killing in the war were increasingly erased in popular conscious-ness – and even in academic understanding.

This appropriation of the Holocaust exacerbated the difficulties of understanding new genocides. The Holocaust was a paradigm; but it was often considered 'uniquely' horrific in very important respects. This meant that all other major episodes of slaughter in which killers failed to match, for example, the clinical extermin-ation methods of the gas chambers, could be represented as not quite as bad. From this it was an easy step, for those who had political axes to grind, to minimizing the relevance of genocide law and discourse to the new cases. The equation of genocide with gas chambers ignored the Nazis' forest and roadside massacres, which were faithfully reproduced in many new cases. It also neg-lected the genocidal potential in persecution, terror and expulsion: in this sense, Nazi policies before 1939 were a relevant model, mirrored across the late twentieth-century world.

The unique sensitivity of the issue of slaughter meant that it was always ideologically and politically contested. The Nazis were the original 'Holocaust deniers': in carrying out the extermination of the Jews, they utilized secrecy and euphemism to the maximum. They were followed by generations of racists, nationalists and fascists: as the Holocaust grew in symbolic importance, so it was more fervently denied. Political, legal and academic battles over the meaning of the genocide were still taking place as the new century began. But denial is a general feature of a genocidal world. Western leaders denied the genocidal aspect of atomic bombing and stra-tegic nuclear war preparations. Soviet fellow-travellers denied the Gulag. Western apologists minimized massacres carried out by anti-Communist Third World regimes in states like Indonesia and

Chile. And, as genocide has become both more widespread and more recognized in the post-Cold War years, the political, ideological and legal conflict over it has intensified.

The end of the Cold War was not a simple defeat of an inefficient, backward and authoritarian Soviet bloc by a more advanced, integrated and democratic West. It was marked by two kinds of momentous political struggles across the non-Western world:

1 *Democratic movements* and human rights activists challenged authoritarian regimes – not only the Communist states of the Soviet bloc, China, Yugoslavia and Ethiopia, but also anti-Communist dictatorships from the Philippines to Chile, South Africa to South Korea and Indonesia.
2 *Nationalist movements* across eastern Europe, Asia, Africa and the Middle East demanded secession from quasi-imperial states, where rulers dependent on central national groups denied the rights and aspirations of subordinate peoples.

Democracy and nationalism went hand in hand to the extent that the opening up of closed regimes allowed suppressed nationalities to express their aspirations, and gave secessionists space to organize. On the other hand, they were contradictory, as both central and secessionist elites invoked national causes as a reason for restricting human rights. The demand for democracy for one national group was often linked to expelling other groups from a given territory; while the breakup of multinational states sometimes led to central rule becoming more imperial in character. Genocide was often 'the dark side of democracy', as the sociologist Michael Mann (2001) has observed. Ethnically exclusive national 'democracies' were means by which more or less authoritarian elites achieved or maintained power.

In this new political situation, wars have increasingly centred on the ethnic character of the political community (and indeed society) in a given territory. Both established regimes and their opponents have committed extensive violations of the human rights of 'enemy' national groups, and genocidal wars have been directed against these populations (see episodes VIII and IX for examples). Violations have been vigorously contested, not only by organizations of the oppressed nationalities, but by Western-based human rights movements. In partially open conditions, local journalists have often been able to report injustice. Western-led international media – less tightly bound by national interests than in wars where their states are protagonists – have sometimes broadcast news of repression and atrocities to Western and world publics. Non-governmental organizations have expanded their campaigning, using the Internet to achieve instantaneous publicity about abuses. Thus human rights have come to the fore in the surveillance of war by Western and global organizations.

This development has been reinforced by – although it does not simply originate in – state-level changes in the West and by world order. The West, especially the USA, has abandoned its Cold War ideological defence of authoritarian regimes. Although *realpolitik* is far from dead, and Western policy-makers have not shrunk from dealing with repressive local regimes – especially powerful ones like Communist China – there has been a new policy presumption in favour of democratization. In Europe this has centred on the democratic conditions for European Union and even NATO membership. Elsewhere it is more variably enforced by a welter of national and international practices, from political and economic sanctions to the incorporation of global human rights regimes into national law.

Justice thus acquired a new salience in world politics during the 1990s. When genocidal war returned to Europe, the United Nations established the first international criminal tribunal since 1945, for former Yugoslavia. After the genocide occurred in Rwanda, a tribunal was established for that country, too. In both cases, of course, these judicial institutions were most effective in punishing some perpetrators *after* the event, when the West and the UN had failed to prevent slaughter; but they were important developments all the same. Finally, agreement was reached to establish an International Criminal Court, which was coming into existence in 2002 as this book went to press – although the USA and China both fought to restrict its jurisdiction and independence to a minimum. These developments are far from consolidated, but it is clear that they have enormous new potential (see box 10.4).

Box 10.4 The new global justice

In the 1990s and 2000s, for the first time since the 1940s, international justice has brought war criminals to account. By far the most important instrument of the new rise of justice has been the International Criminal Tribunal for the former Yugoslavia. From modest beginnings, with the trials of important local criminals from the Bosnian wars, by the early 2000s it had convicted both Serbian and Croatian generals. Most crucially, it was trying (as this book went to press) the chief architect of the Serbian war campaigns, Slobodan Milosevic, as well as important political figures from Republika Srpska, the Serbian entity in Bosnia. Other major indictees remained at liberty after a number of years, but the net appeared to be closing on them.

The real achievement of the Tribunal is that it has re-established the principle of detailed responsibility, at all levels of armies and parties on all sides in the Yugoslav wars. It has established a reputation for judicial impartiality among the Balkan parties, trying responsible officials, not only among Serbian and Croatian aggressors, but also in the Bosnian army and administration (investigations are under way too against Kosovo Liberation Army leaders). It has also responded to charges against NATO over its bombing of Serbia, although a special committee concluded that there was no case to answer for war crimes. The International Tribunal for Rwanda has also made some headway, although with fewer resources and less publicity; a much larger number of those accused of genocide are in Rwanda's own gaols.

The principle of judicial accountability, extending to heads of state and government, has been reinforced by extensions of human rights law in national jurisdictions. Chile's Cold War dictator, Augusto Pinochet, found that European courts could bring him to account for his murderous and torturing regime, that international enthusiasm for justice could affect the courts at home and that his old American and British political allies could do little to help. In 2001, Israel's serving prime minister, Ariel Sharon, faced charges in a Belgian court over the massacres at Sabra and Chatila in Beirut in 1981, for which he bore an important responsibility.

International justice has clearly advanced in a political context. The tribunals were partly compensation for the failures of the UN and the West to prevent genocide and widespread human rights abuses in Bosnia and Rwanda. The Yugoslav Tribunal gained its greatest momentum, and fuller Western support, only after NATO decided to confront Serbia militarily in 1999. It captured Milosevic only after the 2000 revolution overthrew him, and through Western pressure on the new regime. The political context also limited the worldwide scope of international justice at the beginning of the new century. After the World Trade Centre massacre in 2001, the USA sought to kill its perpetrators through military action, rather than capture them and put them on trial. The dilemma summed up the continuing tension between law and war.

At the beginning of the twenty-first century, the demand for international justice was thus growing rapidly, but it remained small and uneven in its effects. As an approach to war and even to genocide, it competed in Western capitals with older conceptions of power politics – losing out particularly badly when President George W. Bush reached for a mainly military, rather than judicial, response to the 2001 terror massacre. In many other states it was only beginning to take hold, although in democracy movements, among oppressed peoples and in the global human rights movement it had a great deal of momentum. It was also contested by some people who might have been expected to support it: new left-wing contrarians denied the genocidal character, if not the very occurrence, of some of the crimes investigated by the Yugoslav Tribunal and attacked the Tribunal itself as a tool of Western power. Because it was very difficult to defend Milosevic, this new 'denial' more commonly took the relatively subtle form of minimizing the extent of Serbian slaughter.

The claims of justice were not, however, a simple agenda for peace. The legal pursuit of even the worst war criminals could provoke new resentment in the communities to which they belonged. There was often a partial conflict between the demands of justice and the processes of managing, scaling down and eventually ending conflicts that produced slaughter. Most 'peace processes' offered a high level of amnesty, so that many victims correctly believed that their wrongs were ignored. Thus in Northern Ireland, the perpetrators of terrorist crimes were released in order to facilitate agreement between the political groups in the conflict. In order to reconcile the needs of victims for justice and of de-escalating conflict, 'truth and reconciliation', pioneered in post-apartheid South Africa, was sometimes seen as a partial alternative to legal process. Here the demand for truth was separated from punishment of killers and abusers. Victims settled for the perpetrators' public acknowledgement of the wrongs they had committed. Truth and reconciliation procedures were, however, as fraught with difficulties as formal justice and amnesty (see box 10.5). On any sober assessment, these various developments of global and national justice have had only modest effects: few warmongers and genocidists have yet been convicted, let alone deterred. Yet for some victims, in some places, they have offered a belated sense that even the most horrific wrongs can begin to be righted. The sign that this offers for the future is indeed powerful.

Box 10.5   Truth, reconciliation and justice

The powerful trend towards applying criminal justice to acts of war is of enormous significance in showing that perpetrators of organized killing, torture and violence can be made accountable. In this way it breaks down the conventional distinction between the law-bound sphere of national society and the essentially lawless sphere of war between states – where international law is weak and unenforceable, if not irrelevant to what powerful organizations do to innocent civilians.

However, formal mechanisms of criminal law have severe limitations as ways of establishing truth and justice for victims. In many cases, national as well as international jurisdictions cannot even begin to bring the major perpetrators of violence to account. International tribunals apply only to certain regions, while the International Criminal Court began work only in late 2002 and does not have retrospective jurisdiction. In many national contexts, the supporters of those who committed violence still hold too much power, or the political will and other resources to sustain a complex prosecution are not available. In other cases, even if these obstacles could be overcome, the evidence necessary to secure a criminal conviction may not be easily produced, despite general knowledge of who is responsible. Even where trials take place, most criminals are not prosecuted, and even a successful prosecution does not necessarily produce the truth of the victims' experience, let alone justice.

Truth commissions have been advocated partly as an alternative to criminal justice. The most prominent case, the South African Truth and Reconciliation Commission, clearly reflected a political imperative to avoid extensive punitive action against the apartheid regime and the White population that supported it. It was seen as a means of providing a forum which would encourage voluntary admissions of crimes in return for amnesty, so giving something to both victims and perpetrators (and their wider communities), and promoting a new political dispensation. While it had many positive aspects, and exposed some cases that could not have been brought to law, it also blocked the possibility of criminal action against many perpetrators of violence and killing. Critical debate on the experience led many to recognize that 'truth and reconciliation' was not an overall alternative to justice. Both take place in a political context that helps shape their varying strengths and limitations.

From slaughter to safety

The twin agendas of global war management and global justice reflect two major changes in the world. First, more stable relations among major centres of state power give new meaning to the idea of a regulated world order, and therefore to legitimate global institutions. Second, there is a growing determination, more clearly in democratic and human rights movements than in governments, that the often murderous politics of many regions should be brought, first, under international control and, second, within the scope of a law-bound world.

Ideas of global order, world peace and universal justice were powerfully outlined by Enlightenment thinkers at the beginning of the modern age. Throughout the nineteenth and especially the twentieth centuries, they could be little more than dreams. War-ridden rivalries of empires, which dominated world politics until 1945, were succeeded by nuclear-armed conflicts of Cold War blocs. Only the very recent changes of the period since 1989 have opened up greater possibilities of realizing these previously utopian ideas. So much of what is happening in the world at the beginning of the twenty-first century could lead us to believe, moreover, that order, peace and justice are still utopian. The gap between ideals and reality has narrowed, but it is still large. There are realistic grounds for believing that the new century *could* be different from the century of total war and genocide that has ended. But the cause of peace and justice implies much more than an agenda of institutional and legal change, or even the educational and cultural policies that might accompany them. The tensions between ideals and historical reality still concern big structures of power. In the remaining pages of this book, I shall try to define, for contemporary purposes, what the ideals entail. I shall also look at how the contradiction between ideals and reality might be overcome.

As Enlightenment thinkers grappled with the problem of political community, the most perceptive saw that reason required that war should be abolished not only within, but also between, communities. A rational order could not be created within a particular state, but only by linking states in a world context. Just as philosophers and practical thinkers proposed republican constitutions for nations, so they argued for constitutional arrangements between nations that would prevent war and secure perpetual peace. At the dawn of the modern era, the demands of the modern republic appeared very different, however, from those we expect today. Only a radical few advocated a democracy in which all adult members of society, regardless of property, sex or race, possessed full rights of citizenship. And, as socialists pointed out, even such a democracy would not lead to full emancipation for most members of society; a purely political democracy based on legal equality would leave intact deep inequalities of social and economic power. Nineteenth-century socialist thinkers barely elaborated on these ideas, even though they contended that a world commonwealth of socialist republics would produce this kind of peace, while competing capitalist empires could not.

So the twin ideas of democratic republic and international federation remain seminal to projects for a just and peaceful world today. Following Immanuel Kant, we cannot confine democracy and justice to national contexts and hope to establish peace between separated sovereign states. The 'democratic peace' theory of some US social scientists, according to which establishing national democracies will lead more or less mechanically to peaceful international relations, takes one half of the story for a causal relation. On the contrary, establishing democracy and justice on a world scale is a necessary condition of contemporary world order, including a stable framework for national democracies.

In this sense, the radical ideas developed in the early years of the modern age are more relevant in the twenty-first century than they have been for most of the last 200 years. These ideas are important to how we think about our relationships with other human beings worldwide. But if these early projects are seminal, the context has changed greatly. Two centuries ago, most people's social networks were intensely local, with relatively thin layers of national and international relations. The state of travel and communications meant that, while it was more possible than ever to project power over long distances, local centres were still radically separated in time and space. The most radical proposals for world order, such as those of Kant and Paine, involved relatively loose federations or confederations of national and local republics. But, as a result of successive industrial revolutions and the ways in which powerful institutions have deployed them, much thicker worldwide networks have developed than these early thinkers ever envisaged. True, society has not become global in a simple sense. There remain huge differences across local and national economies, polities and cultures. But the importance of international, transnational and world-regional connections of all kinds has increased enormously. At the maximum, this leads to an increasing sense of the globe as the largest, most inclusive context of social life. The global aspect of early twenty-first-century society is often seen as a matter of more rapid, intense connections that obliterate differences of time and space. These are clearly important, but what is even more so is that they are linked to a growing sense of commonality, in which the old cosmopolitan universalism has gained new life. It is in this context that the new ideas of peace and justice have developed. (The significance of 'global' change is examined in box 10.6.)

Box 10.6   Globalization, war and peace

Debates about 'globalization' pervaded politics at the end of the twentieth century. Business, financial and communications firms embraced the idea. So did some political leaders – notably 'Third Way' liberal and social democrats (like US president Bill Clinton and UK prime minister Tony Blair), who were influenced by the ideas of global thinkers like Anthony Giddens (1990). Early global debates centred, however, on economics: thus, critics of the idea, like Paul Hirst and Grahame Thompson (1995), emphasized how much of economic life remained nationally framed. A sterile debate over whether global change 'undermined' the economic power of the state was overcome only by writers like David Held et al. (1999) who argued that 'global transformation' was a multi-dimensional process, including political and military, as well as economic and cultural, dimensions. Global political change included the development of universal human rights regimes and global institutions, emphasized in this chapter. Military globalization included the development of worldwide small arms markets, as well as UN authorization of 'humanitarian' and other military actions. Although globalization was rarely understood as centred on military changes, I have argued (Shaw 2000) that the outcomes of the Second World War and the Cold War, in internationalizing Western state power, were crucial to the emergence of the kind of global order that emerged at the end of the twentieth century.

A new 'anti-globalization' movement also emerged, primarily among educated young people in Western countries. At its heart were dilemmas over whether it sought a more progressive global order or a rejection of all globalism, and whether it regarded democratic change and human rights as partial gains or as forms of Western domination. The movement thus contained several groups, including *global reformists*, who wanted global institutions that were more accountable and more responsive to the needs of the world's poor; *anti-capitalists*, who saw global inequalities as pernicious new forms of capitalism; and some *anarchists*, who embraced violence as a means of dramatizing these evils. Although all opposed the main forms of Western power, they generally regarded corporate, rather than state, power as their primary enemy. They were therefore caught off guard by the dominance of the military agenda after the 2001 terror massacre, and they divided over issues to do with justice for the victims of wars and genocides perpetrated by anti-Western forces. For example, many 'anti-globalizers' failed to recognize the advances in global justice represented by international tribunals and the new International Criminal Court. Some even saw accused tyrants like Slobodan Milosevic as unfairly victimized. Few had confronted fundamental issues concerning violence, war and genocide, and some were sympathetic to anti-Western violence, even where it was targeted primarily against civilians.

Peace and cosmopolitan democracy

Peace has often been understood as the simple absence of war. Certainly, any respite from slaughter is always welcome to victims. But it is obvious that new rounds of warfare are often prepared during such respites. While victims lick their wounds and rebuild their lives, armies regroup, re-arm and lay plans for new campaigns. Peace can be seen as an *inter-war*, rather than *post-war*, condition so long as it lacks deep foundations in a pacific social and political order. Eighteenth- and nineteenth-century thinkers rightly sought the basis of lasting peace in new kinds of world relations.

War results from, and presumes, a lack of common authority. International thinkers have long argued that this is what is missing from the world, as opposed to the 'domestic' arena. Indeed, for this reason, would-be international 'realists' believe that the kind of peace that exists in stable national societies cannot be established on a world scale. The only international orders that they believe possible are where one state achieves hegemony, or a balance of power is established between powerful states. Certainly it is true that peace depends on power. In a world where many organizations, not only established states, can carry out immense killing, only powerful bodies can control them. Such means as exist for preventing and limiting war, and punishing genocide, have been creations of powerful states. To the extent that they are effective, it is largely because such states support them. Where they are not, it is often because of a lack of political will on the part of these state leaders. While major states can project power on a world scale, they do not themselves have sufficient authority to make their actions more or less universally acceptable. Authoritative power projection depends also on international legitimacy. This is formally conferred through world institutions, but its substance depends on real acceptance among the world population. As NATO found when it intervened in Kosovo without formal UN authorization, its legitimacy was weakened. (This was true even though it did so not out of a lack of concern for UN backing, but because of the threatened vetoes of Russia and China.)

We live in a world in which world political authority is organized through complex sets of institutions, regional as well as global. The old idea of federating nations in an international federation leading to world government is behind, as well as ahead of, reality. It lags behind, to the extent that layers of international institutions already mesh states together in an often deep, but highly uneven, integration of worldwide state power. There is already a dominant centre of power in the interlocking conglomerate of Western state institutions. This comprises many national entities linked through innumerable bilateral and international mechanisms. Despite continuing partial conflicts, the West recognizes common economic, military and political interests. In one region of the West, in Europe, deep and wide formal institutions (political, economic and legal) are being created. To a large extent the institutions of the dominant West are also global in reach. Western-led institutions dominate the regulation of the world economy, communications, etc. The reality is that all centres of state power are enmeshed, to variable extents, in these common frameworks of decision making. Nevertheless, internationalized Western dominance cannot fully legitimate itself worldwide. It still needs valid, genuinely global institutions, and needs to mobilize the extensive layer of global bodies that has developed.

In three important ways, however, global institutions fall far short of a credible framework for world order at the beginning of the new century:

1   They are based on states that in many cases lack democratic legitimacy, or even internally peaceful relations. In dealing with war and genocide, the United Nations often finds that its own 'sovereign' members are among the chief perpetrators. These include even some with permanent seats in the Security Council and the capacity to block any attempts to reconcile, prevent, halt or punish violations of peace and justice.
2   Just as many member states lack democratic legitimacy, so does the UN itself. UN institutions contain no direct mechanisms for representing opinion in world society.
3   The UN lacks real autonomous resources of any size. It is almost entirely dependent on states' contributions, and can act in any major crisis only with the votes of, and resources supplied by, major states. The effects of these weaknesses can be seen in many of the UN's failures that we have discussed earlier.

It is widely recognized that the UN needs reform; but many proposals by states are limited and self-interested – for example, to create more permanent members of the Security Council rather than transforming the way the organization represents world society. More radical proposals have been developed, however, centring on the idea of 'cosmopolitan democracy' (see box 10.7).

Box 10.7   From the UN to cosmopolitan democracy

Cosmopolitanism is the belief that society should be based on treating people as of equal worth, and subject to the same moral criteria, whatever their background, beliefs or nationality. In the state-divided world of modern history, the practical possibilities for applying the same values and norms worldwide have been small. In today's still highly unequal world, there are still huge obstacles. But cosmopolitans argue that this is still what needs to be done; and many believe that it is more possible in today's 'global' world than in earlier periods.

The UN system is based on a compromise, within its founding Charter as well as between the Charter and the Universal Declaration of Human Rights, between universal values and state power. At its heart, in the Security Council, five nuclear-armed states (USA, UK, France, Russia, China) are permanent, veto-carrying members. The UN system is not democratic, either in the sense of representing the peoples of the world or in the sense of putting universal human rights before state interests. Many proposals for UN reform would simply modify the system of state domination: new powerful states, like Japan, India or Brazil, might be added to the permanent membership of the Security Council, for example. But the most radical ideas for reform would move away from this basis towards more genuine democracy.

Writers like David Held (1995) have argued that democracy today, in its classic twin senses of representation and rights, can no longer be restricted to a national framework. Instead, the challenge of 'cosmopolitan democracy' is to genuinely embed democracy in world-regional and global institutions and practices. Democratic freedoms and elections would be developed in regional and world contexts, including a reformed UN General Assembly, elected by the people of the world. Clearly, political and legal justice need to be complemented by global economic and social justice. At a time when many parts of the world do not even have a stable state, let alone a functioning national democracy, this is a long-term programme for reform that could be realized only through extensive political struggles. Yet global democracy, as a historical possibility, actually informs many campaigns by the oppressed as well as actions of solidarity. It offers a concrete embodiment of a 'humane' model of global governance, in opposition to the 'inhumane' governance of powerful states and corporations (Falk 1995).

Transformations of world political institutions can make an important contribution to a more permanent, just peace. But global transformation also depends on changes within national and local contexts. Problems of world order are inseparable from problems of equality, democracy and acceptance of global responsibility within, as well as between, states. The new period of extensive democratic change across the world has created a situation in which, for the first time, the majority of states are formally democratic, and the majority of the world's people live in these states. But China, one of the most important states, remains largely unreformed, and many states have undergone only partial democratic changes. Democratization is incomplete: across Asia, Africa and Latin America, and even in parts of Europe, oligarchic and authoritarian regimes cloak themselves in crudely manipulated electoral legitimation. Fundamental human rights are still blocked. In many regions political change is unaccompanied by social protection: large sections of society are exposed to the worst effects of open markets. In Russia and parts of Africa, employment and living standards had crumbled, and life expectancy was actually falling, at the turn of the century. Even major Western nation-states suffer crucial democratic and human rights deficits. In the USA, judicial execution is rampant, while money and patronage dominate elections – the outcome of the cliff-hanging 2000 presidential election was blatantly fixed in the Supreme Court. In Italy at the beginning of the new century, a media-mogul premier controlled 90 per cent of television coverage through a mixture of ownership and political power.

Economic crises are rarely a direct cause of wars, but economic insecurity and unstable rule often reinforce each other in vicious circles. Elites with little ability to deliver – or interest in delivering – popular welfare are unable to use economic satisfaction as a basis for political loyalty. Political interests are built, instead, along ethnic-national identity lines, reinforced by political conflict up to and including war and genocide. War provides new opportunities for elite interests to profit, as well as pretexts for repressing and controlling the majority of society. In many cases, war has become central to the mode of rule, difficult to break through either internal revolt or external defeat. Longer-term responses to this cycle can lie only in creating durable political institutions, linking local to international organizations, in which sufficiently wide constituencies have incentives to support normal politics and eschew violence. These incentives clearly need to be socio-economic in a broad sense. Large sections of society need to perceive a stake in peaceful politics linked to wider networks of power. For some states of the former Soviet bloc, participation in a prosperous, democratic European Union is seen as a way in which economic viability and stable democratic politics can be linked as an alternative to insecurity and war. On a world scale, especially in many regions of Africa, no such alternatives are yet available in any developed form. But this is a useful model.

The challenge of perpetual peace at the beginning of the new century is thus far bigger than existing international institutions recognize in practice. The promise of a new era, tantalizingly offered by the end of the Cold War, has been almost lost to view in new waves of slaughter that global action has done little to stem. There are some beginnings of a reorganization of world politics to create a framework that could inhibit mass killing. But, given the depths of the problems, only far-reaching socio-economic, as well as political, reforms, of kinds that Western elites and publics can hardly imagine, are likely to provide a basis for change. There is the challenge of global imagination, which the readers as well as the author of this book must try to meet. There is also the sobering likelihood that more major killing crises will have to happen before leaders grasp the nettle of reforming world politics and abolishing war.

Further reading

Barnett, M. (2001) *Eyewitness to a Genocide: The United Nations and Rwanda.* Ithaca, NY: Cornell University Press.

Best, G. (1994) *War and Law.* Oxford: Oxford University Press.

Bloxham, D. (2001) *Genocide on Trial: War Crimes Trials and the Formation of Holocaust History and Memory.* Oxford: Oxford University Press.

Brackman, A. C. (1989) *The Other Nuremberg: The Untold Story of the Tokyo War Crimes Trials.* London: Collins.

Chesterman, S. (2001) *Just War or Just Peace?: Humanitarian Intervention and International Law.* Oxford: Oxford University Press.

Douglas, L. (2001) *The Memory of Judgment: Making Law and History in the Trials of the Holocaust.* New Haven: Yale University Press.

Falk, R. (1995) *On Humane Governance.* Cambridge: Polity.

Giddens, A. (1990) *The Consequences of Modernity.* Cambridge: Polity.

Goldstone, R. J. (2000) *For Humanity: Reflections of a War Crimes Investigator.* New Haven: Yale University Press.

Held, D. (1995) *Democracy and the Global Order: From the Modern State to Cosmopolitan Governance.* Cambridge: Polity.

Held, D., McGrew, A., Goldblatt, D. and Perraton, J. (1999) *Global Transformations.* Cambridge: Polity.

Hirst, P. and Thompson, G. (1995) *Globalization in Question.* Cambridge: Polity.

Jones, J. R. W. D. (2000) *The Practice of the International Criminal Tribunals for the Former Yugoslavia and Rwanda.* Ardsley, NY: Transnational Publishers.

Kuperman, A. J. (2001) *The Limits of Humanitarian Intervention: Genocide in Rwanda.* Washington: Brookings Institution.

Magnarella, P. J. (2000) *Justice in Africa: Rwanda's Genocide, its Courts, and the UN Criminal Tribunal.* Aldershot: Ashgate.

Mann, M. (2001) The colonial darkside of democracy. www.theglobalsite. ac.uk/press103mann.htm.

Marrus, M. R. (1997) *The Nuremberg War Crimes Trial 1945–46: A Documentary History.* Boston: Bedford.

Minow, M. (1998) *Between Vengeance and Forgiveness: Facing History after Genocide and Mass Violence.* Boston: Beacon Press.

Ramsbotham, O. and Woodhouse, T. (1996) *Humanitarian Intervention in Contemporary Conflict: A Reconceptualization.* Cambridge: Polity.

Roberts, A. and Guelff, R., eds (1999) *Documents on the Laws of War.* Oxford: Oxford University Press.

Rotberg, R. I. and Thompson, D., eds (2000) *Truth v. Justice: The Morality of Truth Commissions.* Princeton: Princeton University Press.

Sadat, L. N. (2001) *The International Criminal Court and the Transformation of International Law.* Ardsley, NY: Transnational Publishers.

Scharf, M. P. (1997) *Balkan Justice: The Story behind the First International War Crimes Trial since Nuremberg.* Durham, NC: Carolina Academic Press.

Shaw, M. (2000) *Theory of the Global State: Globality as Unfinished Revolution.* Cambridge: Cambridge University Press.

Toffler, A. and Toffler, H. (1994) *War and Anti-war: Survival at the Dawn of the 21st Century.* London: Little, Brown.

Weiss, T. G. (1996) *Humanitarian Challenges and Intervention: World Politics and the Dilemmas of Help.* Boulder, CO: Westview Press.

Wheeler, N. (2000) *Saving Strangers.* Oxford: Oxford University Press.

Episode X
The new Western
way of war

At the beginning of the twenty-first century, the West, led by the USA, has fought wars with new vigour and determination, against Iraq (1991), Serbia (1999) and the Taliban regime in Afghanistan (2001–2). It has been able to do so despite the overwhelming constraints on risking its own soldiers' lives that resulted from the American experience in the Vietnam War, which are still perceived in Western capitals. In prosecuting (successfully for the most part) new, limited wars, the West has partially reversed the anti-war feeling that predominated from the 1960s to the 1980s mainly because of the fear of nuclear war. It has done so by *reinventing* war in a way that not only avoids the political penalties of Vietnam, but also appears to have bypassed the historical trend towards degeneracy that I have discussed in this book. Because of how the new Western way of war is articulated, with its new way of mobilizing mass media and public opinion, we can describe it as a new form of militarism.

At the centre of this way of war is a new form of the reliance on air power that has been central to Anglo-American military thought and practice since the 1920s. Western aerial warfare has entered a distinctive new phase since 1990. The new mode relies on bombing even more than before – by both manned bombers and cruise missiles. It uses the enhanced precision that computer electronics brings to targeting to avoid the large-scale, widespread massacres of enemy civilians that occurred in the Second World War and Vietnam. But small massacres of civilians are key features of this kind of war, and the ways in which their political effects are neutralized are central to risk-transfer militarism.

These, then, are the main elements of what I call *risk-transfer* war and militarism:

1   *A transfer of the major share of death from enemy civilians to enemy armed forces*, thus reversing the twentieth-century trend towards overwhelmingly civilian casualties. This is important, because it goes some way towards bringing war back within the limits of the 'just war' tradition, prioritizing killing the enemy, rather than killing innocents.
2   *A transfer of the risks of ground combat from Western forces to their local allies, wherever possible.* The increasing interdependence between

Western air power and local armies on the ground enables the West to transfer a greater share of the risk of battle casualties to local armed forces. For the most part, only Western special forces are active in combat on the ground.

3   *A transfer of risks in bombing from Western air forces to both 'enemy' and 'friendly' civilians on the ground.* Repeated 'small massacres' of civilians are understood to be a feature of the new Western way of war. These are 'accidental' in the sense that, like all 'collateral damage', they are not specifically intended. Indeed, efforts are made to avoid them.

4   *However, the transfer of risk to civilians is deliberate and systematic,* since the risks to civilians (from errors in targeting and delivery) are known to be much greater than the risks of Western planes being shot down or crashing accidentally. They are simultaneously programmed into the risk analysis of war. Civilians are still exposed to far greater risk than the West's own military personnel.

5   *The avoidance of direct civilian killing on a scale that could threaten the media-formed legitimacy of the war is a key element in the new militarism.* Western governments want no more TV pictures of direct victims than are absolutely unavoidable; and they want no threateningly large direct casualty numbers. Media coverage and surveillance have become intrinsic to this refined mode of post-total war, but they make it particularly problematic.

6   *The corollary of this is that indirect, less visible casualties are more acceptable.* Where there are other possible causes of death – enemy policies, civil war, drought, etc. – responsibility is less easy to pin down, and therefore the West finds the risks more acceptable. This undoubtedly compounds the degeneracy of the new mode.

7   *Even relatively small massacres may be magnified by the media, so having unprecedentedly large consequences for Western powers.* Thus a fundamental contradiction of the new Western way of war is the unpredictability of intensive exposure through television and other mass media.

8   *The failure of any of the transfers of risk could expose the West to risk rebound.* If air power is insufficient to break the enemy, if the local forces are incapable of carrying out ground operations – or if they commit too many atrocities – the risks of the new mode of war could return to the West.

The legacy of degenerate war is clear, in this new mode, in the way in which civilians are exposed to greater risks than military personnel. Even within the just war tradition, this is open to fundamental criticism: 'Simply not to intend the death of civilians is too easy. . . . What we look for in such cases is some sign of a positive commitment to save civilian lives. Civilians have a right to something more. And if saving civilian lives means risking soldiers' lives, that risk must be accepted' (Walzer 1992: 153–4). The key thing about risk transfer is that it reverses this demand, by risking civilians' lives in order to save those of soldiers.

However, in the widespread concern for the innocent victims of Western bombing, even though they are many fewer than in earlier campaigns, we may be employing new standards. If we question *any* actions that knowingly kill innocents, we may be arguing on grounds of human rights more than of just war (I develop this argument further in Shaw 2002). We may be starting to apply to war moral standards from which, as we saw in chapter 1, it has historically been exempted.

There is another reason for questioning the assumption that the historical degeneration and illegitimacy of Western warfare has been overcome. We should note that if the West found itself in a major war with other states, the limits of 'risk-transfer militarism' would be breached. The capacities for large-scale conventional war and nuclear war both remain, and could still return Western warfare to classic degeneracy. These linkages must always be taken seriously; the new Western way is a refinement of degeneracy, not its transcendence.

Further reading

Freedman, L. (1998–9) The changing forms of military conflict. *Survival*, 40 (4) 39–56.

Latham, A. (1999) Reimagining warfare: the 'Revolution in Military Affairs'. In C. A. Snyder, ed., *Contemporary Security and Strategy*, London: Macmillan, 210–37.

Mandelbaum, M. (1998–9) Is major war obsolete? *Survival*, 40 (4), 20–38.

Shaw, M. (2002) Risk-transfer war, the militarism of small massacres and the historic legitimacy of war. *International Relations*, 17 (3), 343–60.

Walzer, M. (1992) *Just and Unjust Wars*. New York: Basic Books.

Conclusion

War is an almost universal feature of human life. Whether we like it or not, our world has been, and continues to be, shaped by organized killing. Although the majority of the world's people have never been involved at all directly in war – and may have reasonable hope of avoiding this during their lives – none of us can escape the effects of war and genocide in our minds. When any human beings suffer these kinds of violence, we are all affected. Nor can we shut out entirely the awareness that, however safe most of the prosperous world appears to be from open warfare, some of the conditions that produce war in other places are present everywhere, even in the West.

In the Cold War period, it was often pointed out that nuclear weapons could not be 'uninvented'. This meant, it was argued, that – even if all states carried out nuclear disarmament – we are condemned for ever to live with the threat that some state or group would use known nuclear technology to make new weapons. But, as social anthropologists have argued, war itself is a social 'invention', which has been heavily institutionalized and deeply embedded in social relations. Obviously, war cannot be uninvented. Millennia of continuous warfare provide states and state-like organizations with a rich repertoire of military possibilities and modes of violence. Genocide is, in this perspective, only the latest modern way in which the killing power of war has been directed at civilians. Clearly it would be naive, after all that we have seen in the last hundred years, to expect war and genocide to fade away in a matter of decades.

But, if war cannot be uninvented, we can *learn* not to use it, and to prevent others from using it too. Governments and organized movements have choices over whether, when and how they use military force. People, especially citizens of democracies, have choices over what kinds of state policies they support. We can try to extend the powerful existing models of peaceful international- ization, so that they are increasingly applied in all relations be- tween organized states and state-like organizations. We can learn from the positive examples of peaceful political and social change. We can correspondingly reduce the priority that governments assign to military spending and challenge warlike mentalities that affect even oppositional social movements.

The argument of this book has led away from the old assumption that war is a legitimate method of political action, towards a new presumption of the illegitimacy of war. I have called this new pos- ition 'historical pacifism'. This means neither an absolute rejection of all uses of physical force under all circumstances, nor the too limited rejection of only particular kinds of violence (such as weapons of mass destruction). It means instead that we start from the position that organized killing is a supreme problem, and that the use of military force – which inevitably entails the possibility of killing – should be avoided. We may recognize that there are circumstances in which force is necessary – for example, when innocent lives may be saved only by military action against the perpetrators of geno- cide. But it is for the protagonists of force to justify this, as an *exception* to a rule of no-war, rather than starting (as in traditional just-war thinking) from the possibility of legitimate force.

As we go further into the global era, we seem to be leaving behind the optimism (about the possibility of marginalizing violence) that many felt in the first decade after the Cold War. US politicians believe that new threats such as terrorism call, above all, for military responses. Arms budgets are rising again after the cutbacks of the 1990s, and new technologies seem to offer prospects of quick and relatively cost-free military success. There are conflicts over new institutions, like the International Criminal Court, that might rein in the use of force by subjecting all users to a more rigid enforcement of international law. We are entering a period in which the deep anti-war feeling, which arose in response to the horrors and dangers of twentieth-century war, is being challenged by a new confidence in the possibility of achieving goals by means of armed force.

This book has not offered an easy answer to these assertions, but it has shown that anti-war consciousness is grounded in the real- ities of modern war and genocide. It is for you, the readers of this book, to decide how this understanding should form the basis of your own responses to organized killing and war.

Index